W9-ATN-634

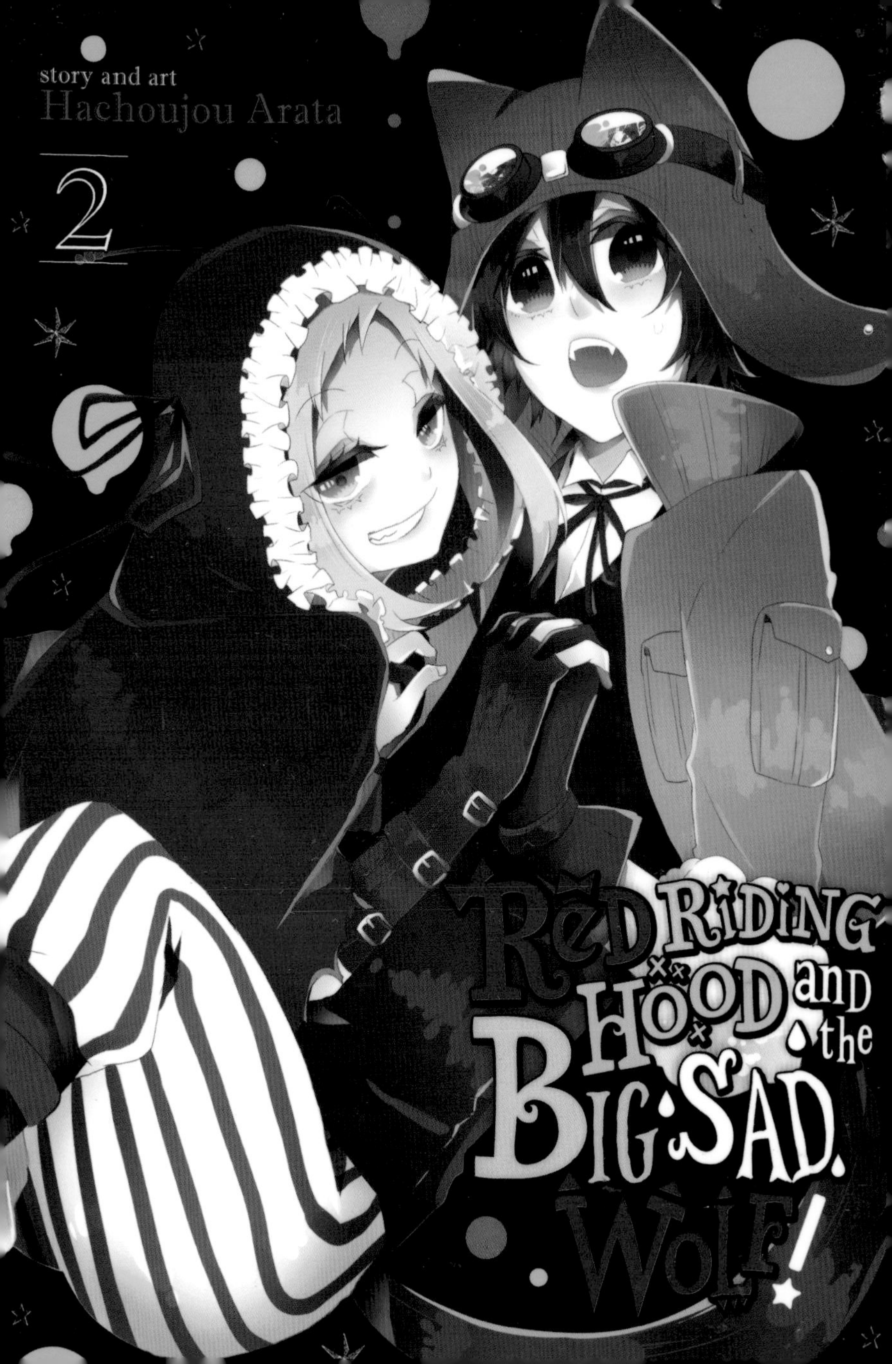
story and art
Hachoujou Arata
2
Red Riding Hood and the Big Sad Wolf!

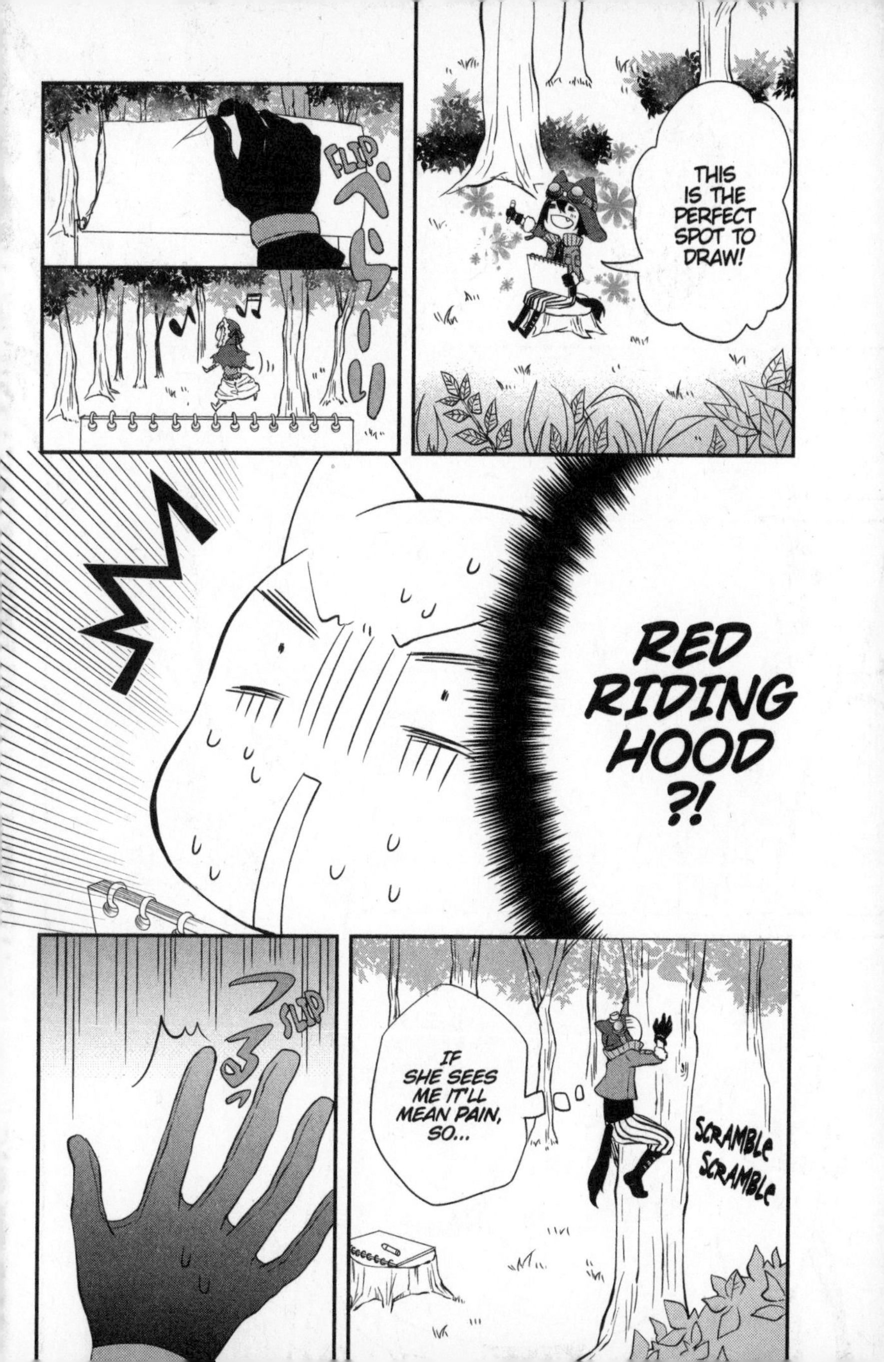
THIS IS THE PERFECT SPOT TO DRAW!
FLIP
RED RIDING HOOD ?!
IF SHE SEES ME IT'LL MEAN PAIN, SO...
SCRAMBLE SCRAMBLE
SLIP

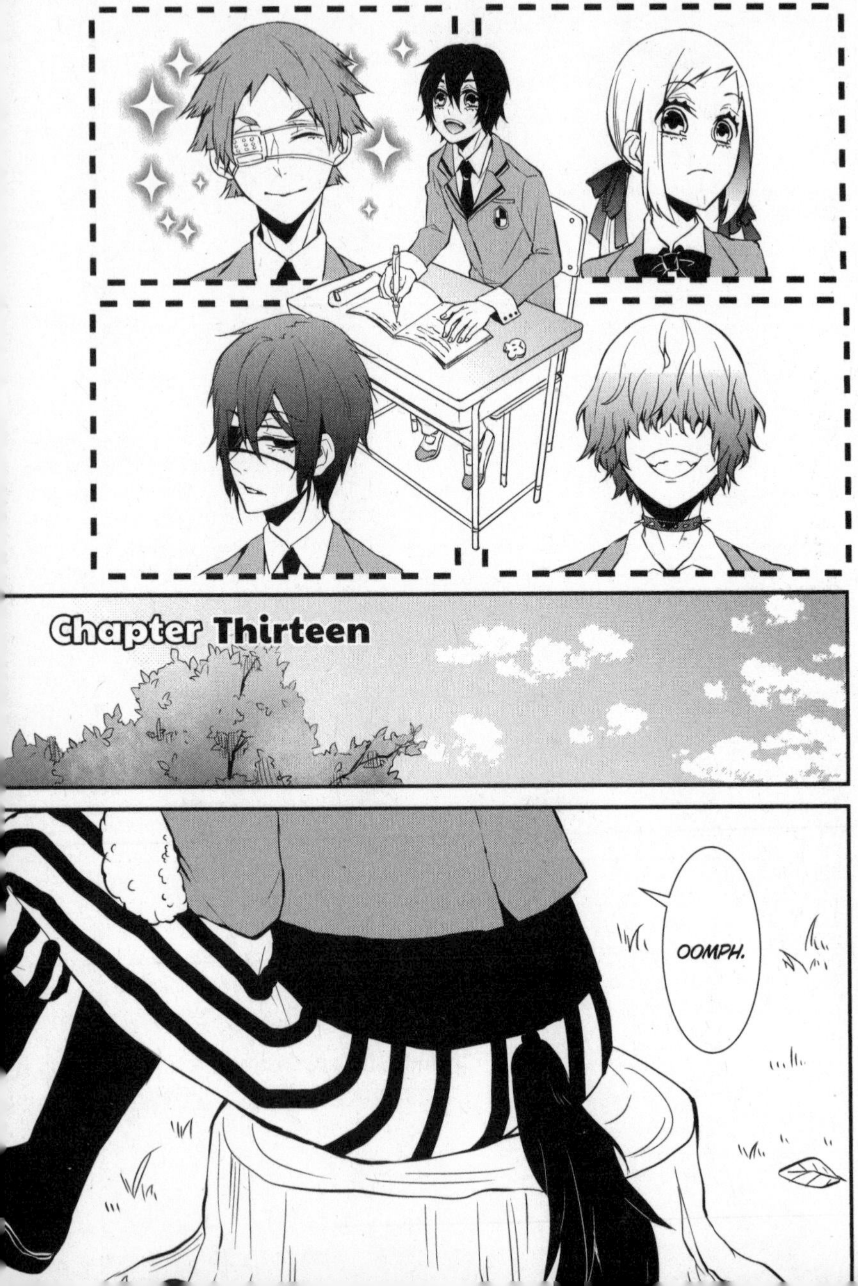
Chapter Thirteen
OOMPH.

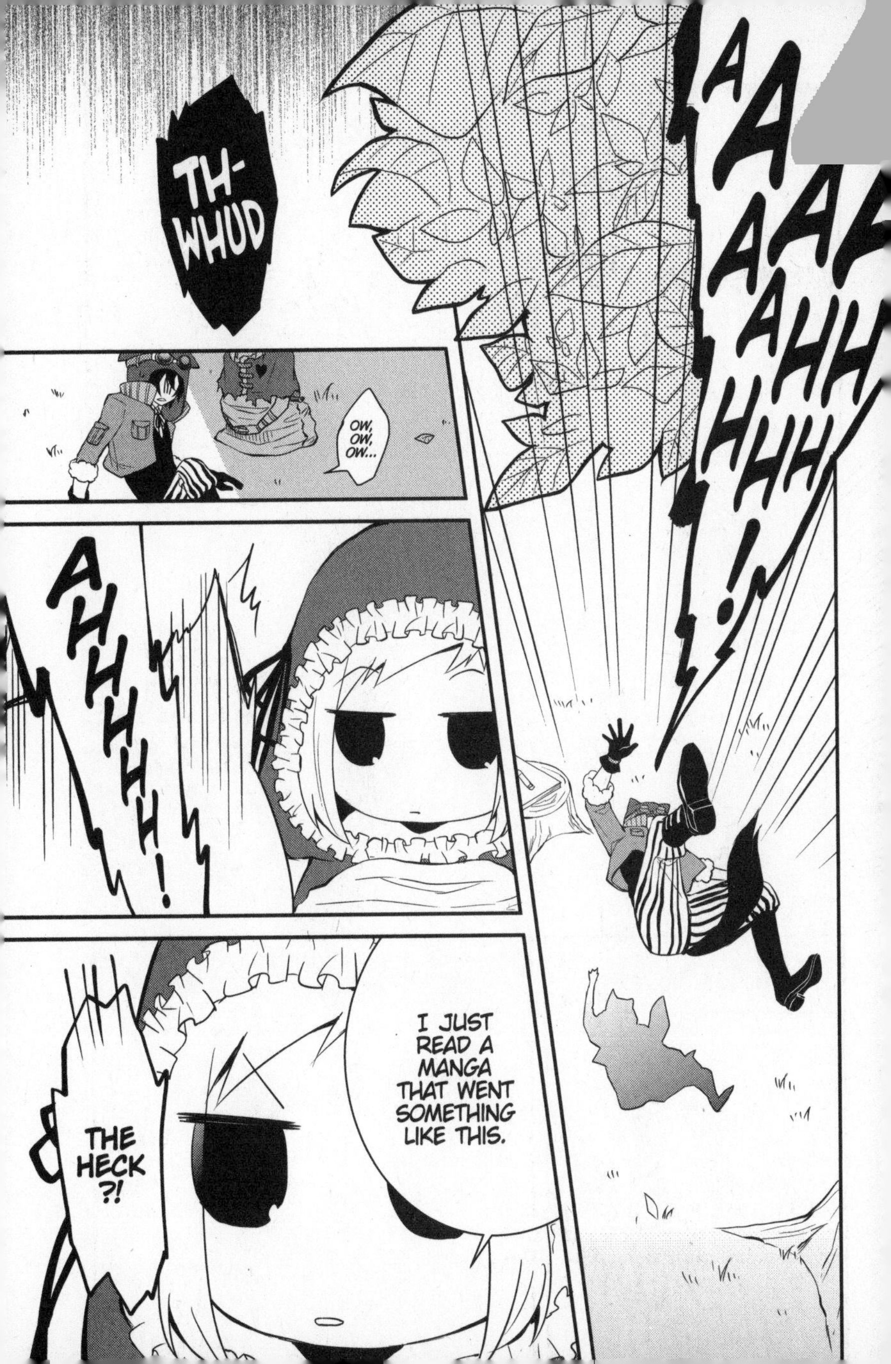

AAAAAHHHHH!!
TH-WHUD
OW, OW, OW...
AHHHHHH!
I JUST READ A MANGA THAT WENT SOMETHING LIKE THIS.
THE HECK?!

EVERYONE FEELS THINGS IN THEIR OWN WAY

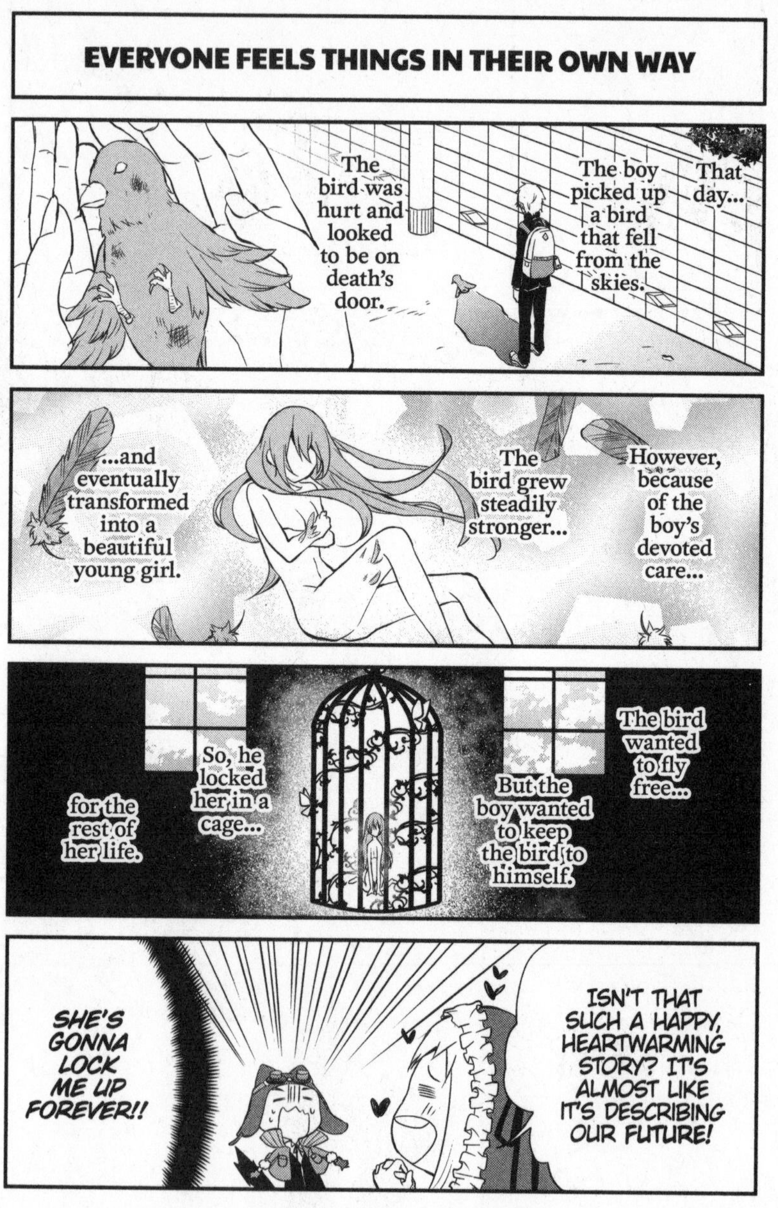
That day...
The boy picked up a bird that fell from the skies.
The bird was hurt and looked to be on death's door.
However, because of the boy's devoted care...
The bird grew steadily stronger...
...and eventually transformed into a beautiful young girl.
The bird wanted to fly free...
But the boy wanted to keep the bird to himself.
So, he locked her in a cage...
for the rest of her life.
ISN'T THAT SUCH A HAPPY, HEARTWARMING STORY? IT'S ALMOST LIKE IT'S DESCRIBING OUR FUTURE!
SHE'S GONNA LOCK ME UP FOREVER!!

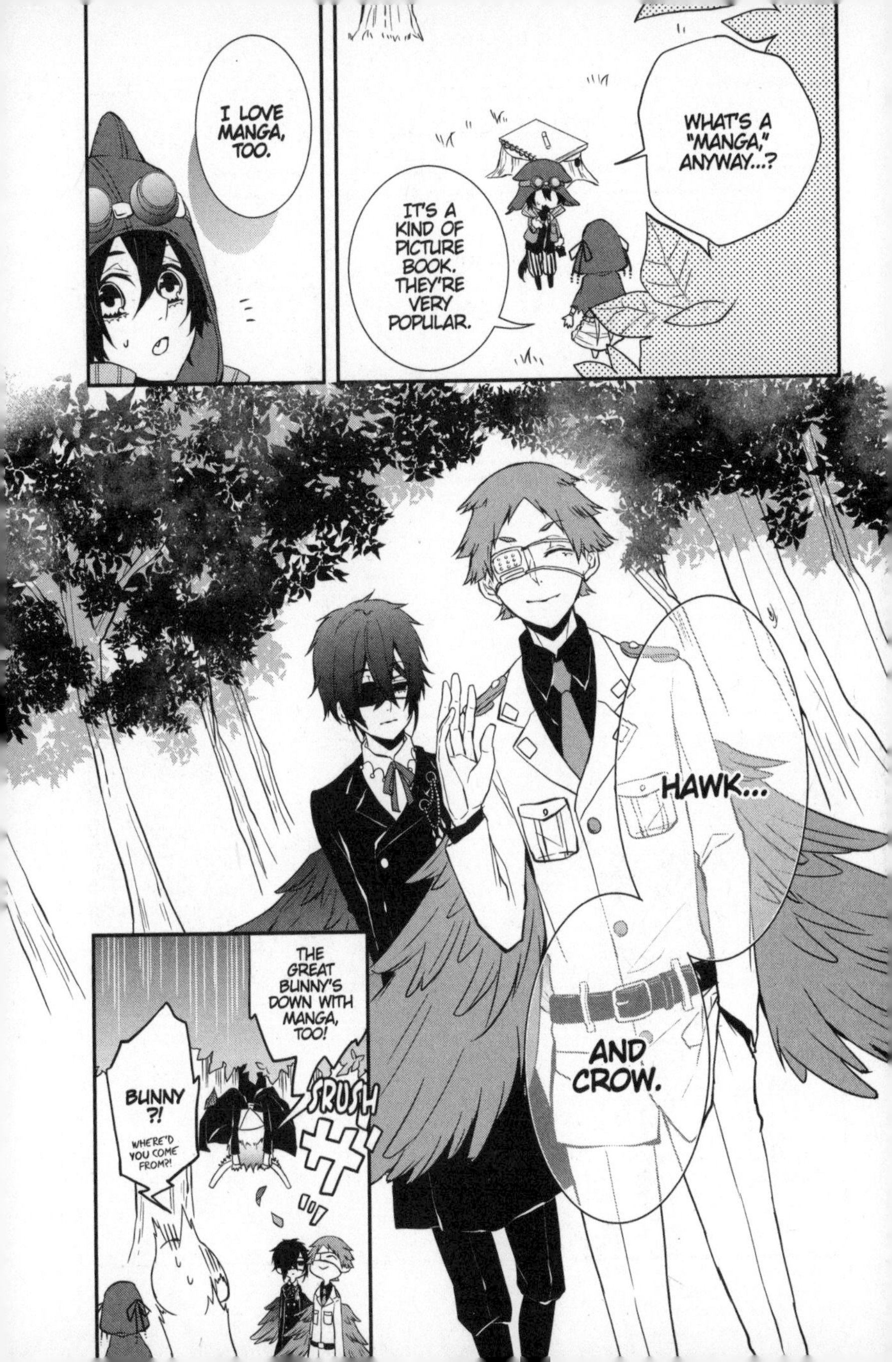
WHAT'S A "MANGA," ANYWAY...?
IT'S A KIND OF PICTURE BOOK. THEY'RE VERY POPULAR.
I LOVE MANGA, TOO.
HAWK...
AND CROW.
THE GREAT BUNNY'S DOWN WITH MANGA, TOO!
SRUSH
BUNNY?!
WHERE'D YOU COME FROM?!

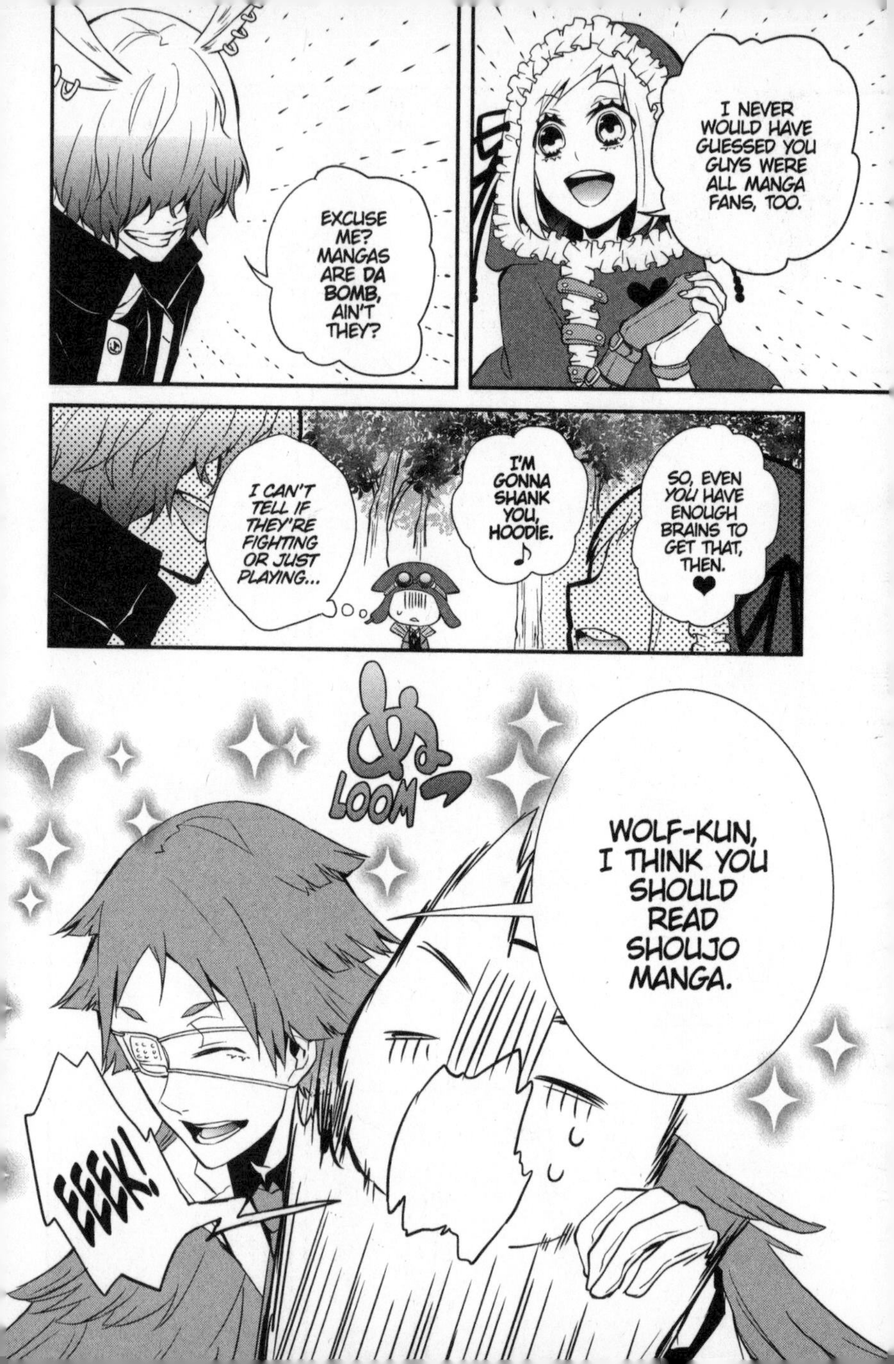
I NEVER WOULD HAVE GUESSED YOU GUYS WERE ALL MANGA FANS, TOO.
EXCUSE ME? MANGAS ARE DA BOMB, AIN'T THEY?
SO, EVEN YOU HAVE ENOUGH BRAINS TO GET THAT, THEN. ♥
I'M GONNA SHANK YOU, HOODIE. ♪
I CAN'T TELL IF THEY'RE FIGHTING OR JUST PLAYING...
WOLF-KUN, I THINK YOU SHOULD READ SHOUJO MANGA.
ぬ LOOM
EEEK!

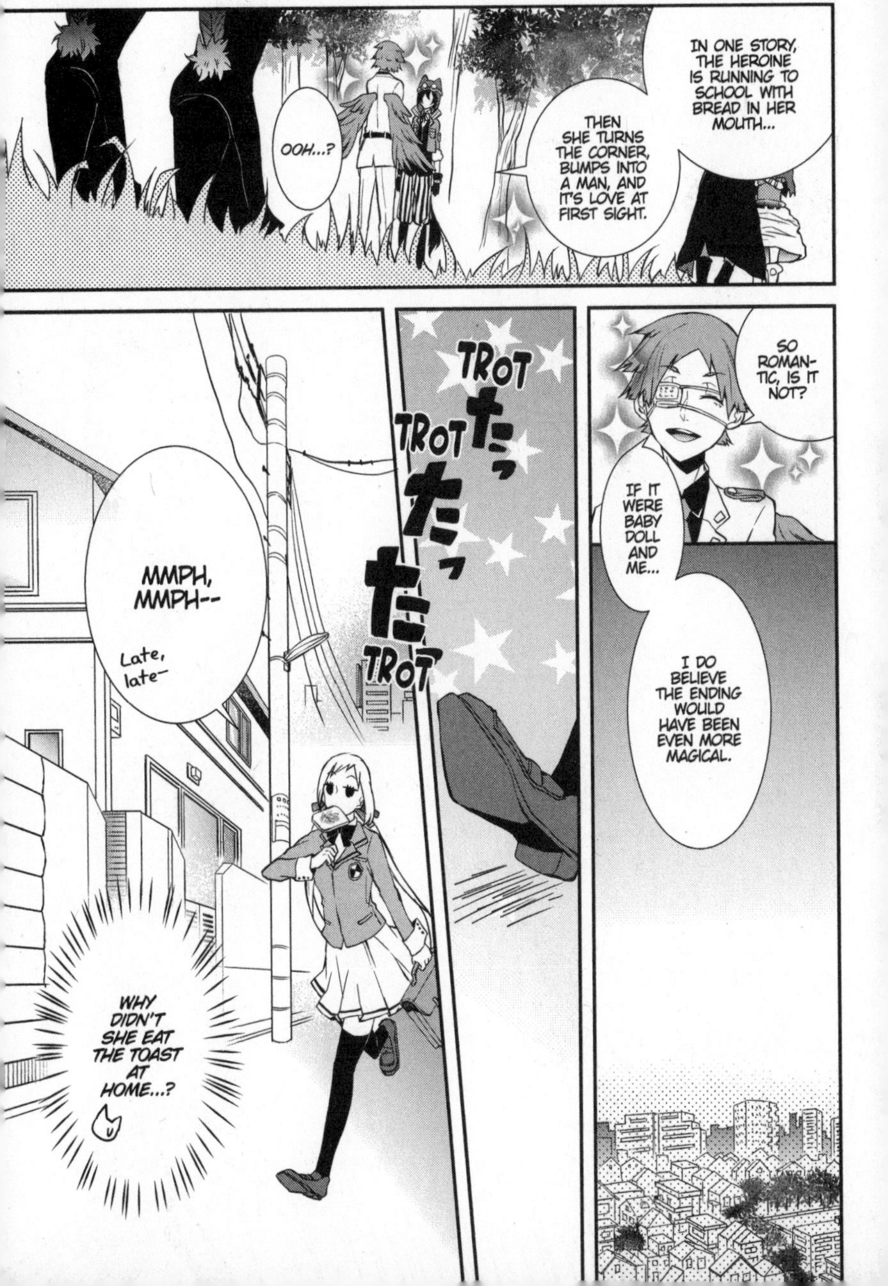

IN ONE STORY, THE HEROINE IS RUNNING TO SCHOOL WITH BREAD IN HER MOUTH...
THEN SHE TURNS THE CORNER, BUMPS INTO A MAN, AND IT'S LOVE AT FIRST SIGHT.
OOH...?
SO ROMAN-TIC, IS IT NOT?
IF IT WERE BABY DOLL AND ME...
I DO BELIEVE THE ENDING WOULD HAVE BEEN EVEN MORE MAGICAL.
TROT たっ
TROT たっ
たっ TROT
MMPH, MMPH--
Late, late~
WHY DIDN'T SHE EAT THE TOAST AT HOME...?

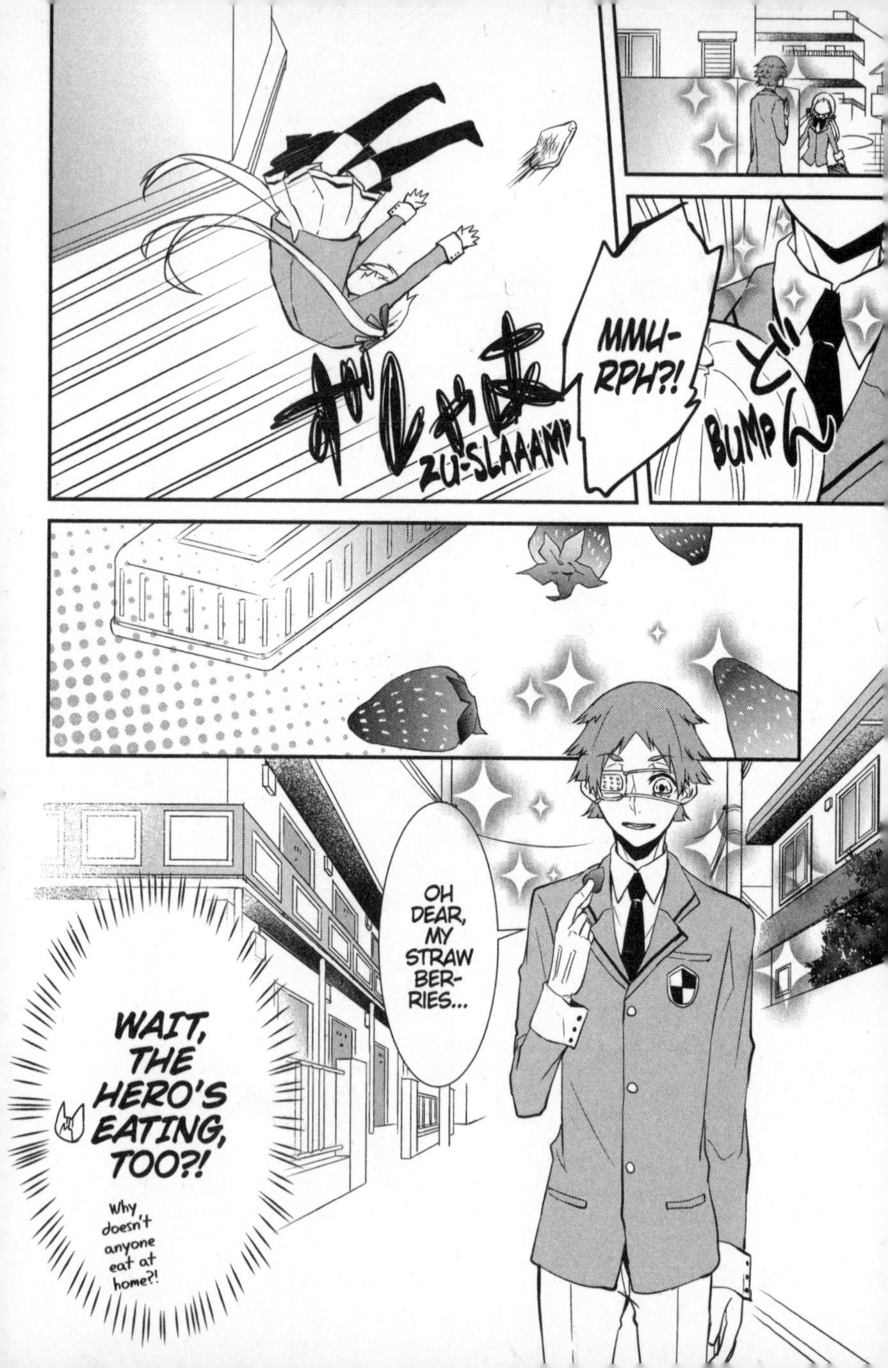
MMU-RPH?!
どん
BUMP
ZU-SLAAAMP
OH DEAR, MY STRAWBERRIES...
WAIT, THE HERO'S EATING, TOO?!
Why doesn't anyone eat at home?!

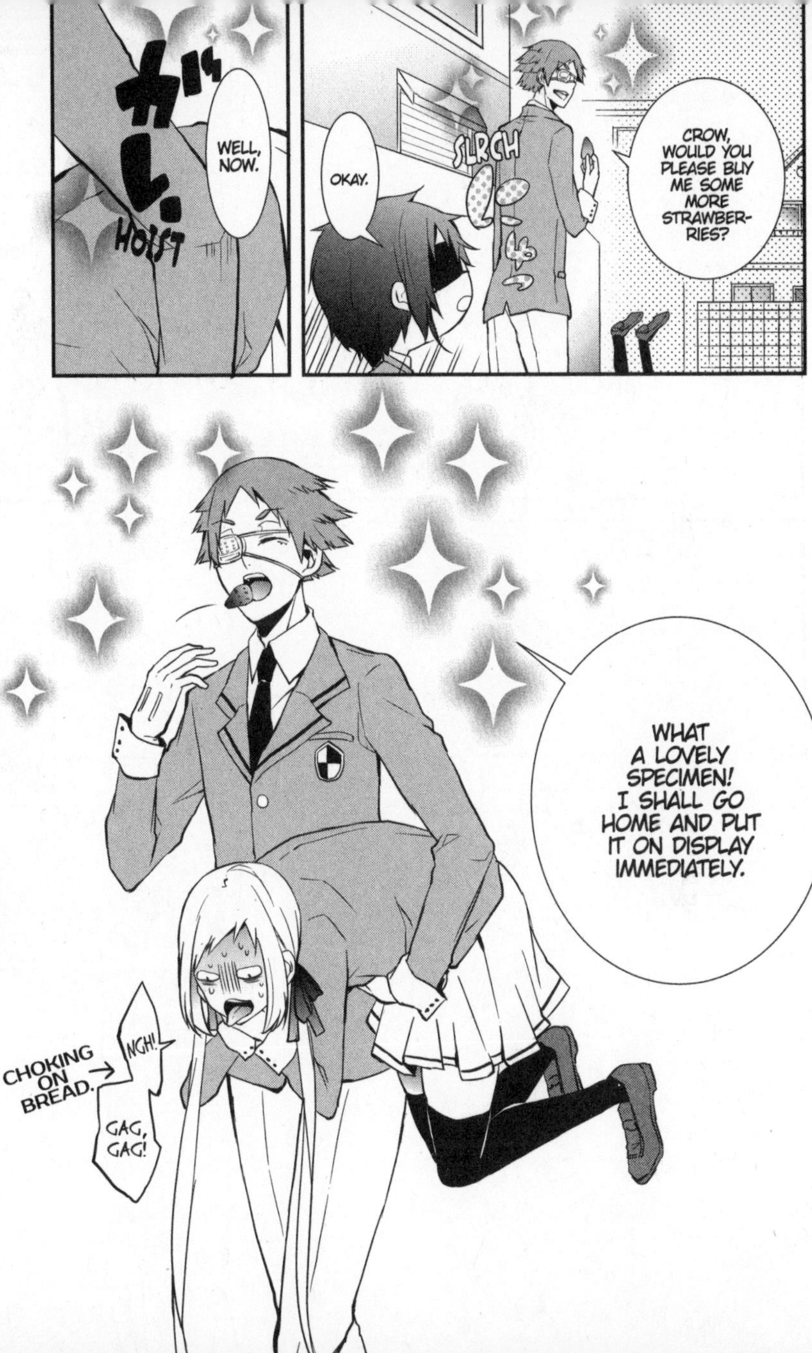
CROW, WOULD YOU PLEASE BUY ME SOME MORE STRAWBERRIES?
SLRCH
OKAY.
WELL, NOW.
HOIST
WHAT A LOVELY SPECIMEN! I SHALL GO HOME AND PUT IT ON DISPLAY IMMEDIATELY.
NGH!
GAG, GAG!
CHOKING ON BREAD.

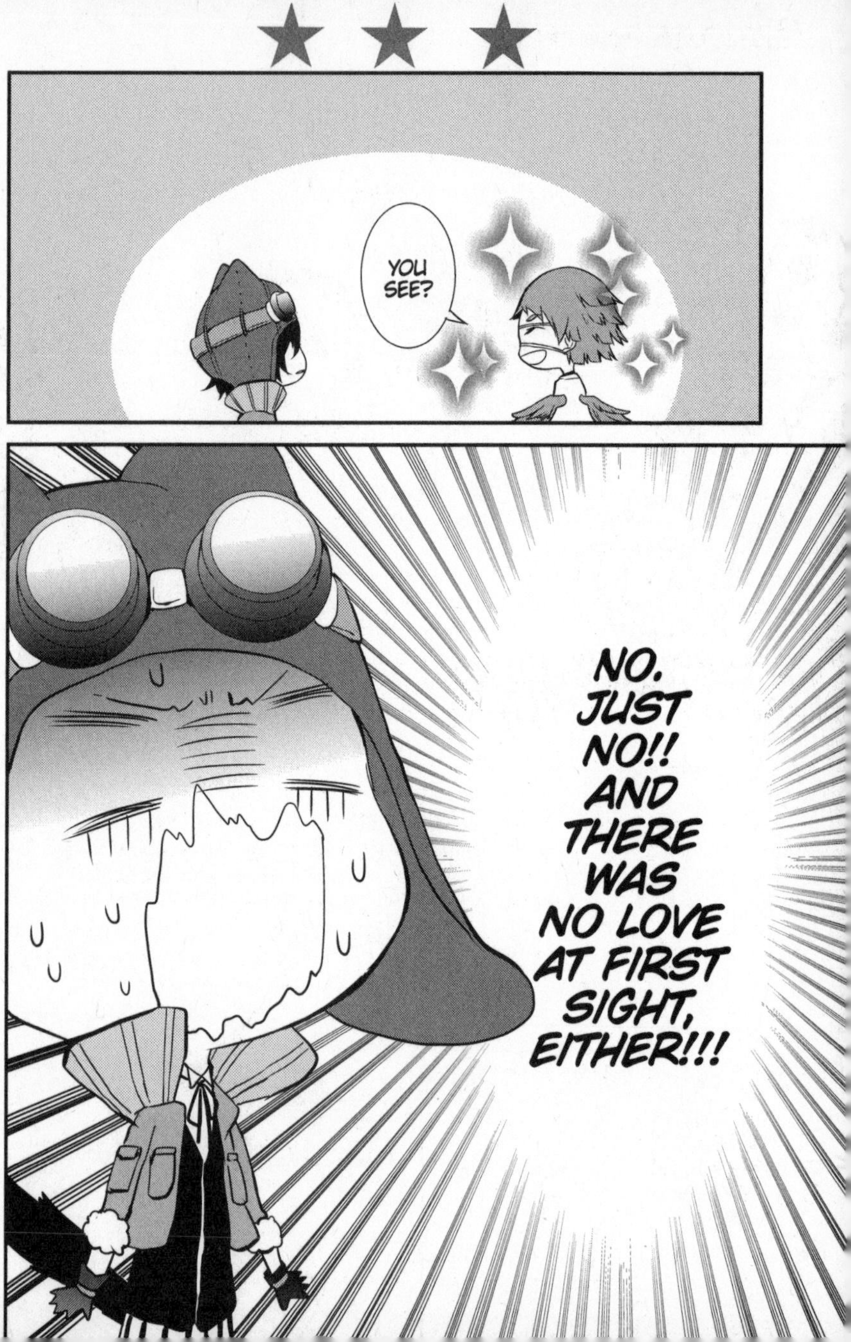
YOU SEE?
NO. JUST NO!! AND THERE WAS NO LOVE AT FIRST SIGHT, EITHER!!!

Chapter Fourteen

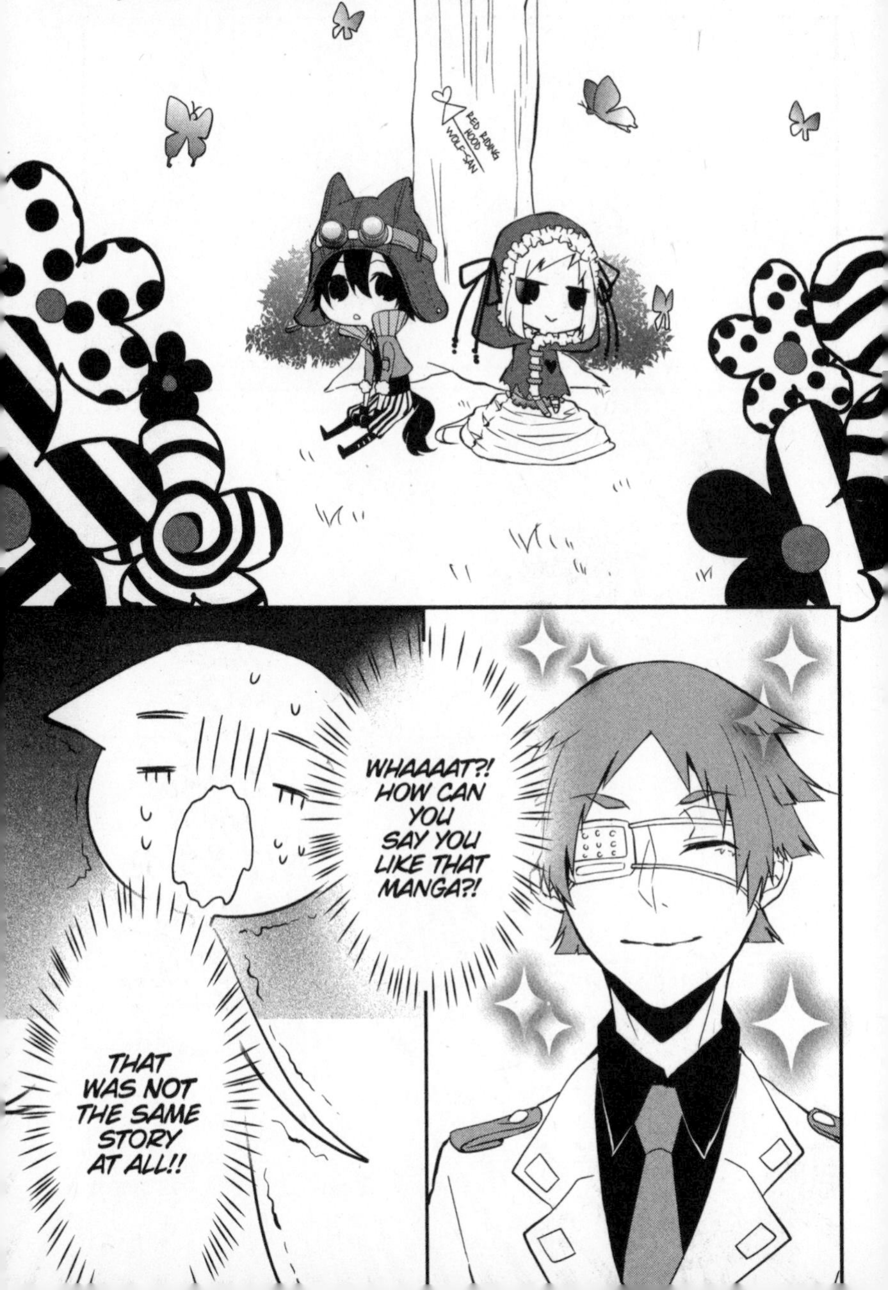
RED RIDING HOOD
WOLF-SAN
WHAAAAT?! HOW CAN YOU SAY YOU LIKE THAT MANGA?!
THAT WAS NOT THE SAME STORY AT ALL!!

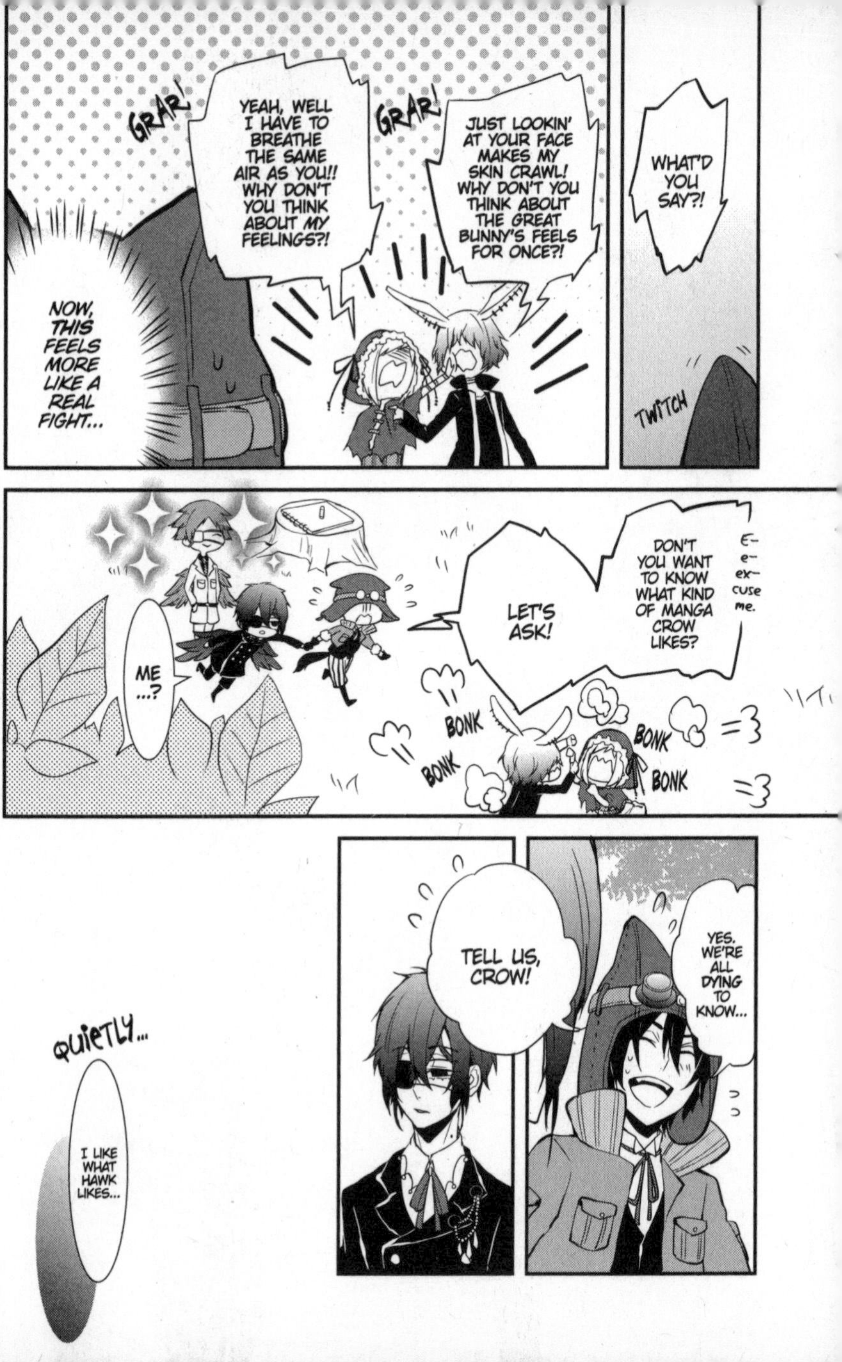
WHAT'D YOU SAY?!
TWITCH
GRAR!
JUST LOOKIN' AT YOUR FACE MAKES MY SKIN CRAWL! WHY DON'T YOU THINK ABOUT THE GREAT BUNNY'S FEELS FOR ONCE?!
GRAR!
YEAH, WELL I HAVE TO BREATHE THE SAME AIR AS YOU!! WHY DON'T YOU THINK ABOUT MY FEELINGS?!
NOW, THIS FEELS MORE LIKE A REAL FIGHT...
E-e-ex-cuse me.
DON'T YOU WANT TO KNOW WHAT KIND OF MANGA CROW LIKES?
LET'S ASK!
ME ...?
BONK
BONK
BONK
BONK
YES. WE'RE ALL DYING TO KNOW...
TELL US, CROW!
QUIETLY...
I LIKE WHAT HAWK LIKES...

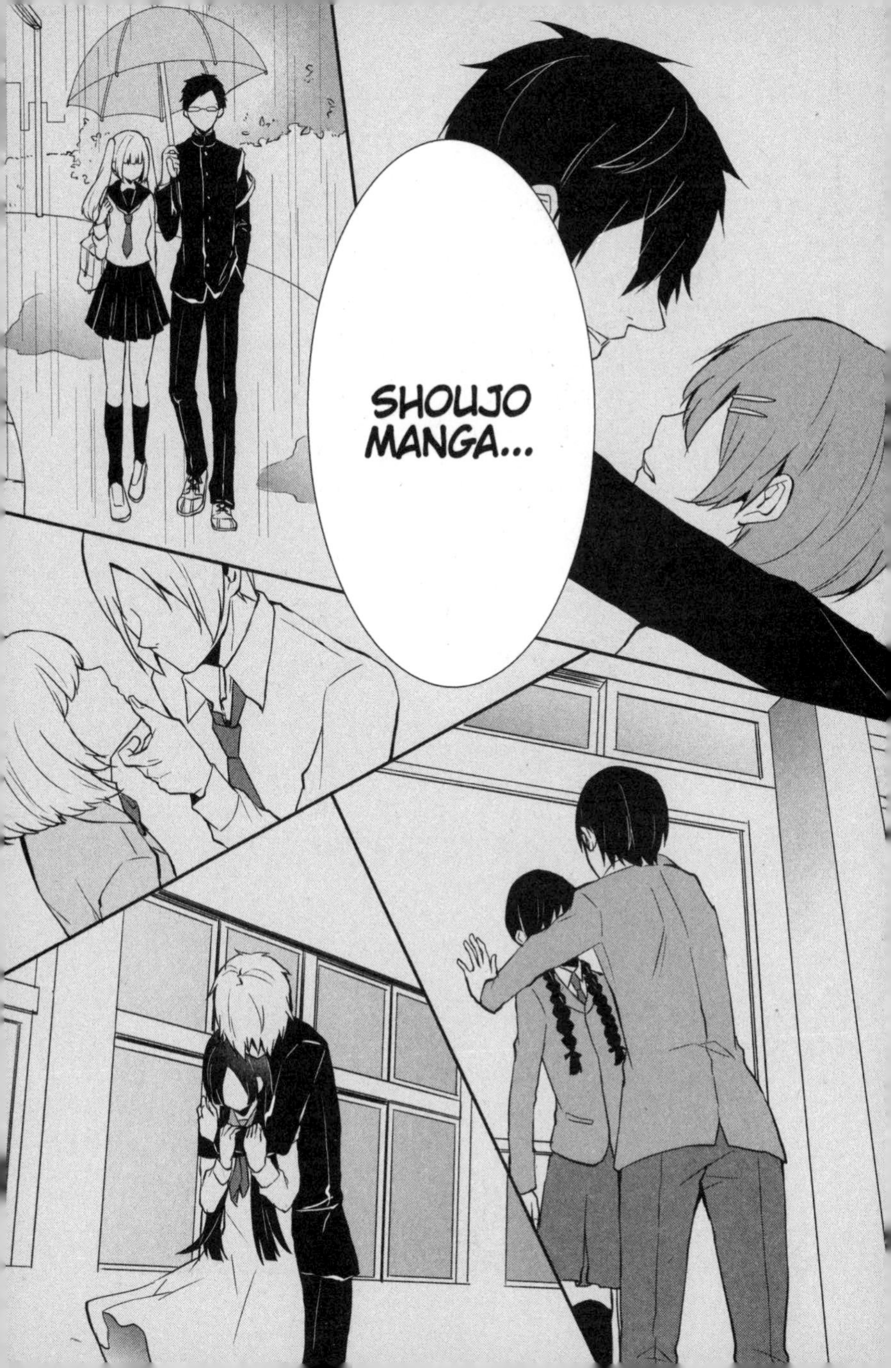
SHOUJO MANGA...

BITTER REALITY

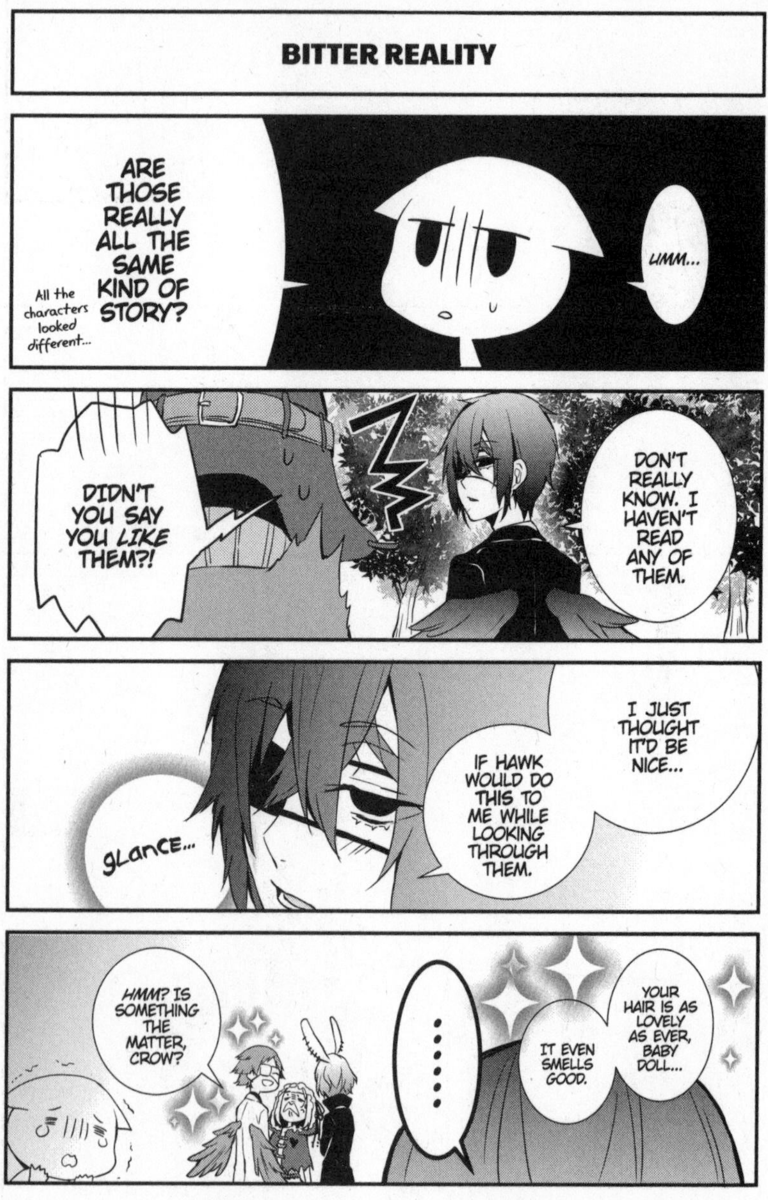
UMM...
ARE THOSE REALLY ALL THE SAME KIND OF STORY?
All the characters looked different...
DON'T REALLY KNOW. I HAVEN'T READ ANY OF THEM.
DIDN'T YOU SAY YOU LIKE THEM?!
I JUST THOUGHT IT'D BE NICE...
IF HAWK WOULD DO THIS TO ME WHILE LOOKING THROUGH THEM.
glance...
YOUR HAIR IS AS LOVELY AS EVER, BABY DOLL...
IT EVEN SMELLS GOOD.
......
HMM? IS SOMETHING THE MATTER, CROW?

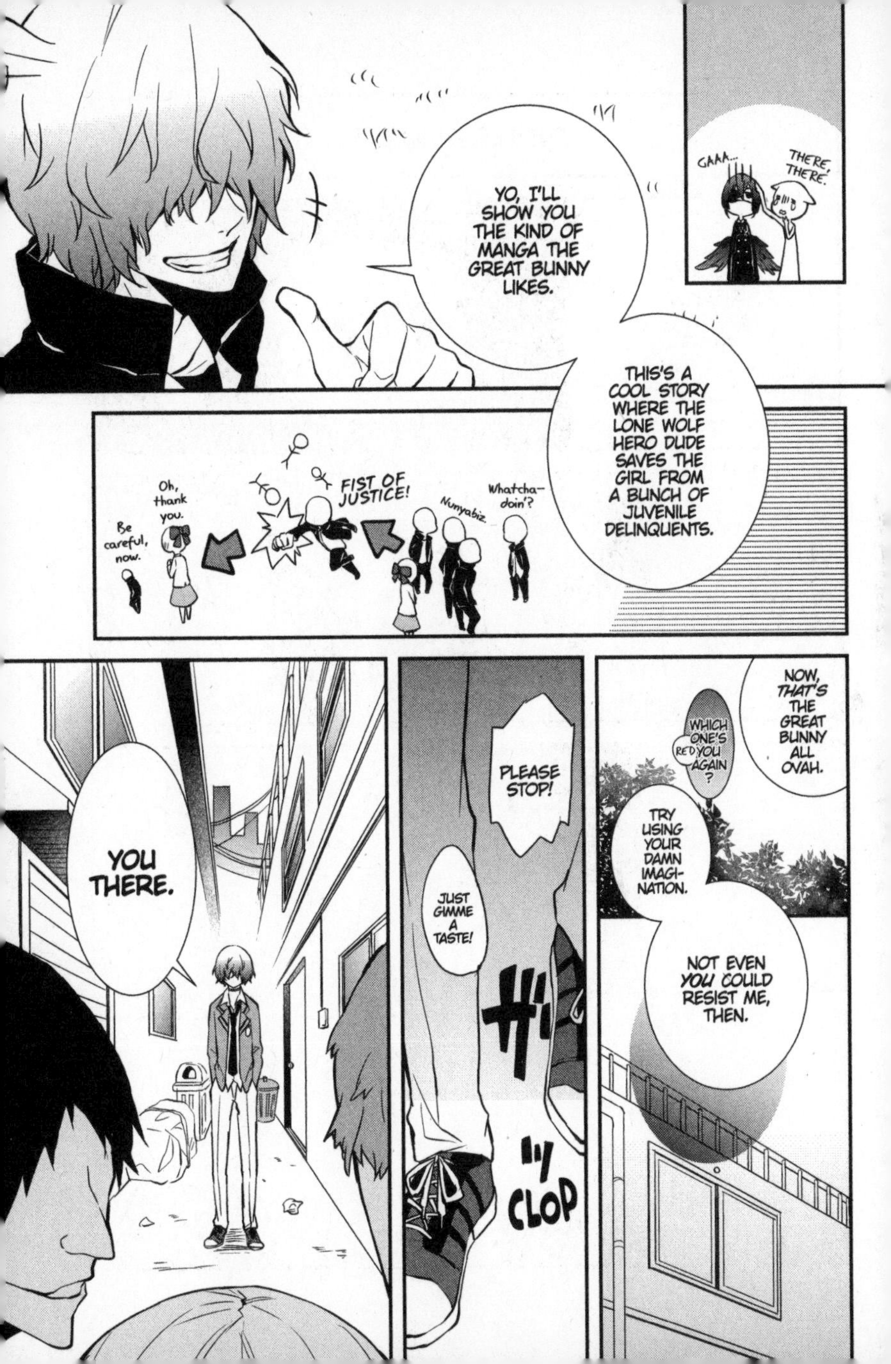
GAAA...
THERE, THERE.
YO, I'LL SHOW YOU THE KIND OF MANGA THE GREAT BUNNY LIKES.
THIS'S A COOL STORY WHERE THE LONE WOLF HERO DUDE SAVES THE GIRL FROM A BUNCH OF JUVENILE DELINQUENTS.
Whatcha-doin'?
Nunyabiz.
FIST OF JUSTICE!
Oh, thank you.
Be careful, now.
NOW, THAT'S THE GREAT BUNNY ALL OVAH.
WHICH ONE'S YOU AGAIN?
RED
TRY USING YOUR DAMN IMAGI-NATION.
NOT EVEN YOU COULD RESIST ME, THEN.
PLEASE STOP!
JUST GIMME A TASTE!
CLOP
YOU THERE.

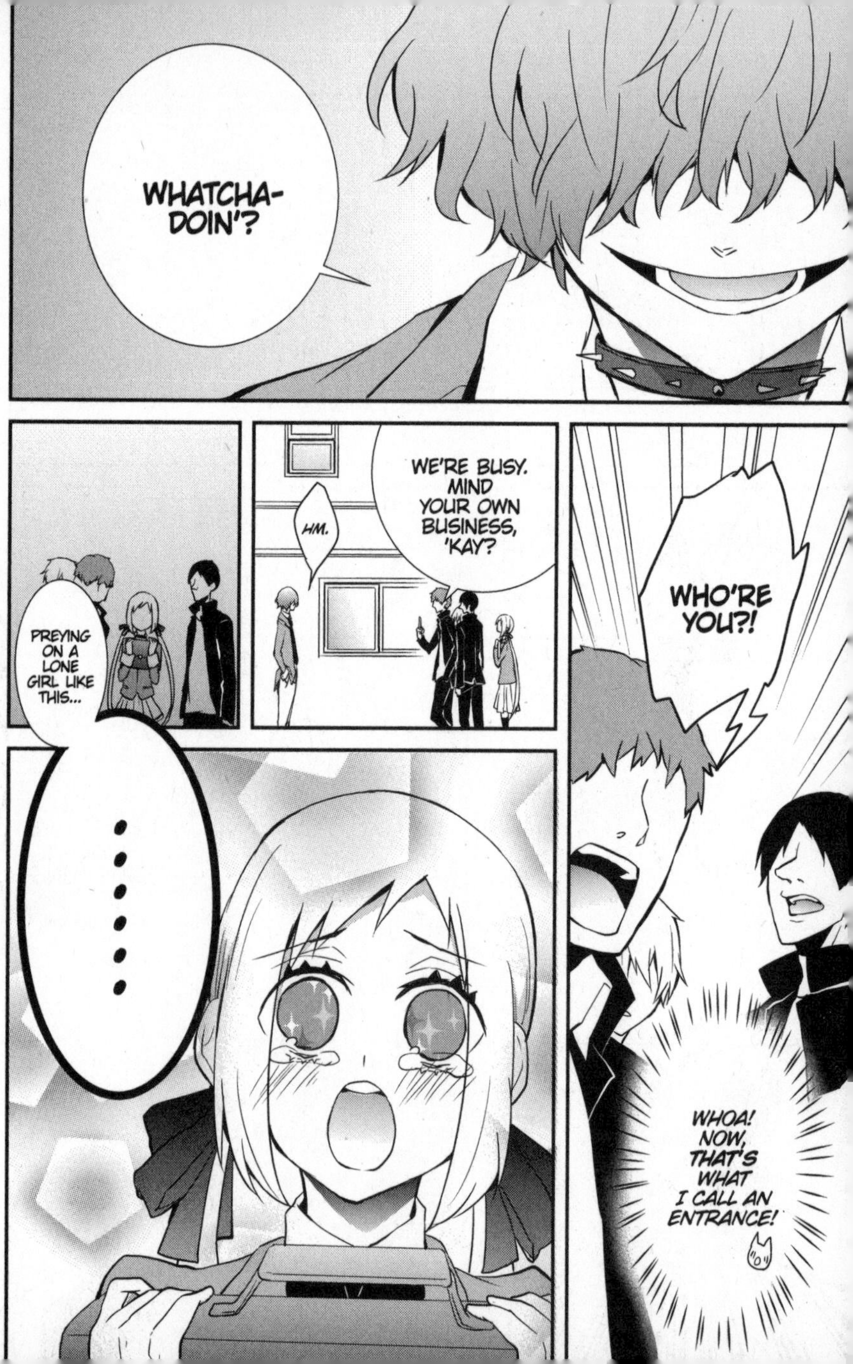
WHATCHA-DOIN'?
WHO'RE YOU?!
WHOA! NOW, THAT'S WHAT I CALL AN ENTRANCE!
WE'RE BUSY. MIND YOUR OWN BUSINESS, 'KAY?
HM.
PREYING ON A LONE GIRL LIKE THIS...
......

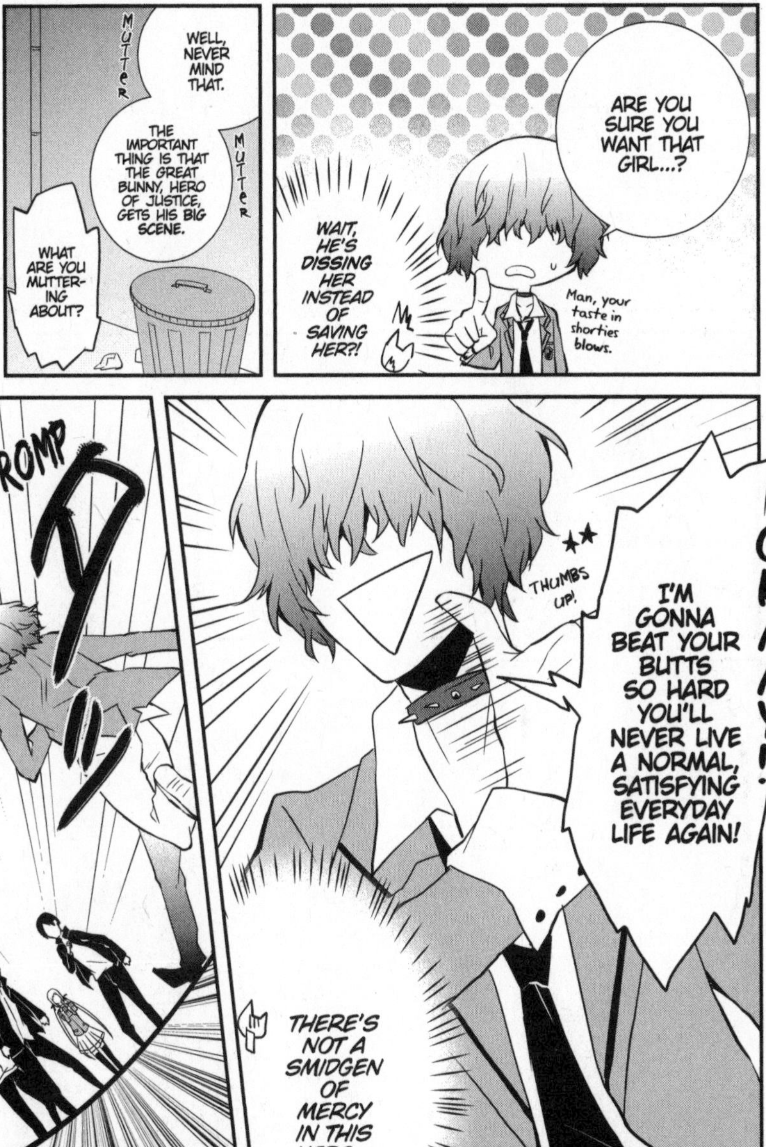
ARE YOU SURE YOU WANT THAT GIRL...?
Man, your taste in shorties blows.
WAIT, HE'S DISSING HER INSTEAD OF SAVING HER?!
MUTTER
WELL, NEVER MIND THAT.
THE IMPORTANT THING IS THAT THE GREAT BUNNY, HERO OF JUSTICE, GETS HIS BIG SCENE.
MUTTER
WHAT ARE YOU MUTTERING ABOUT?
OKAAY!!
THUMBS UP!
I'M GONNA BEAT YOUR BUTTS SO HARD YOU'LL NEVER LIVE A NORMAL, SATISFYING EVERYDAY LIFE AGAIN!
THERE'S NOT A SMIDGEN OF MERCY IN THIS HERO...
TROMP

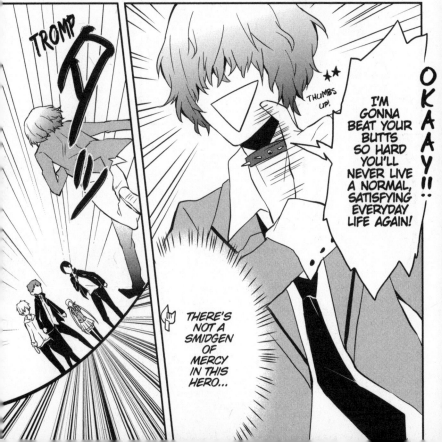

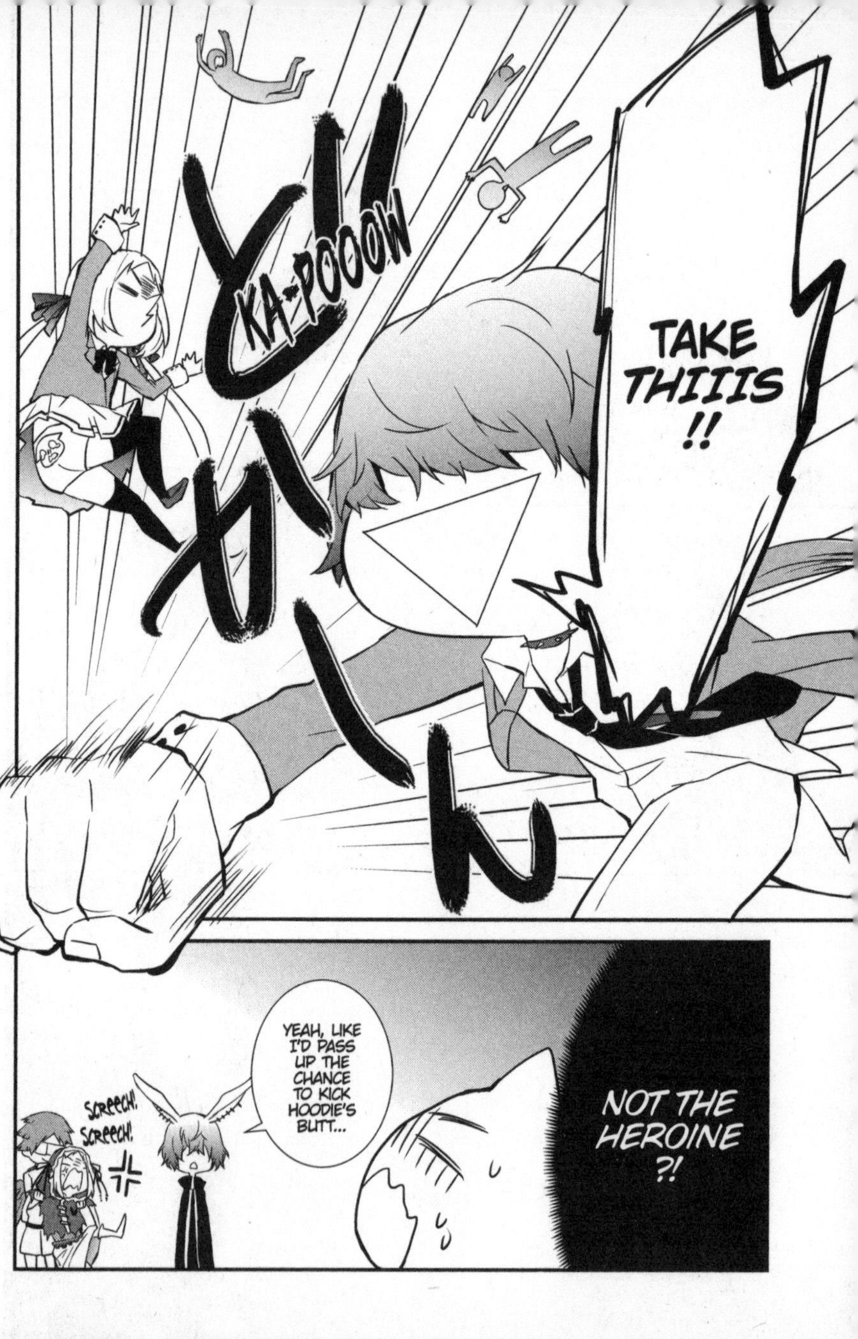
TAKE THIIIS!!
どかーん
KA-POOOW
NOT THE HEROINE?!
YEAH, LIKE I'D PASS UP THE CHANCE TO KICK HOODIE'S BUTT...
SCREECH! SCREECH!

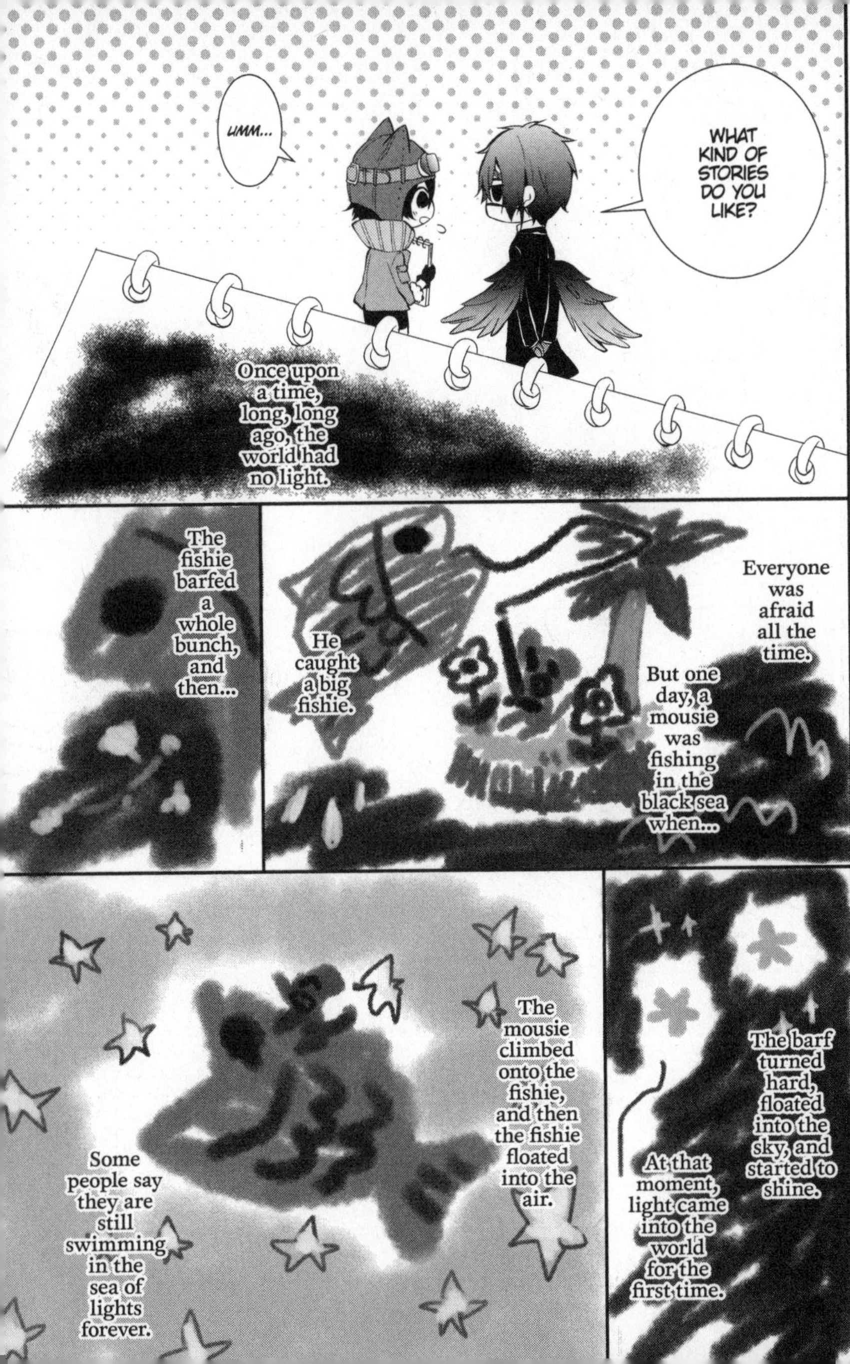
WHAT KIND OF STORIES DO YOU LIKE?
UMM...
Once upon a time, long, long ago, the world had no light.
Everyone was afraid all the time.
But one day, a mousie was fishing in the black sea when...
He caught a big fishie.
The fishie barfed a whole bunch, and then...
The barf turned hard, floated into the sky, and started to shine.
At that moment, light came into the world for the first time.
The mousie climbed onto the fishie, and then the fishie floated into the air.
Some people say they are still swimming in the sea of lights forever.

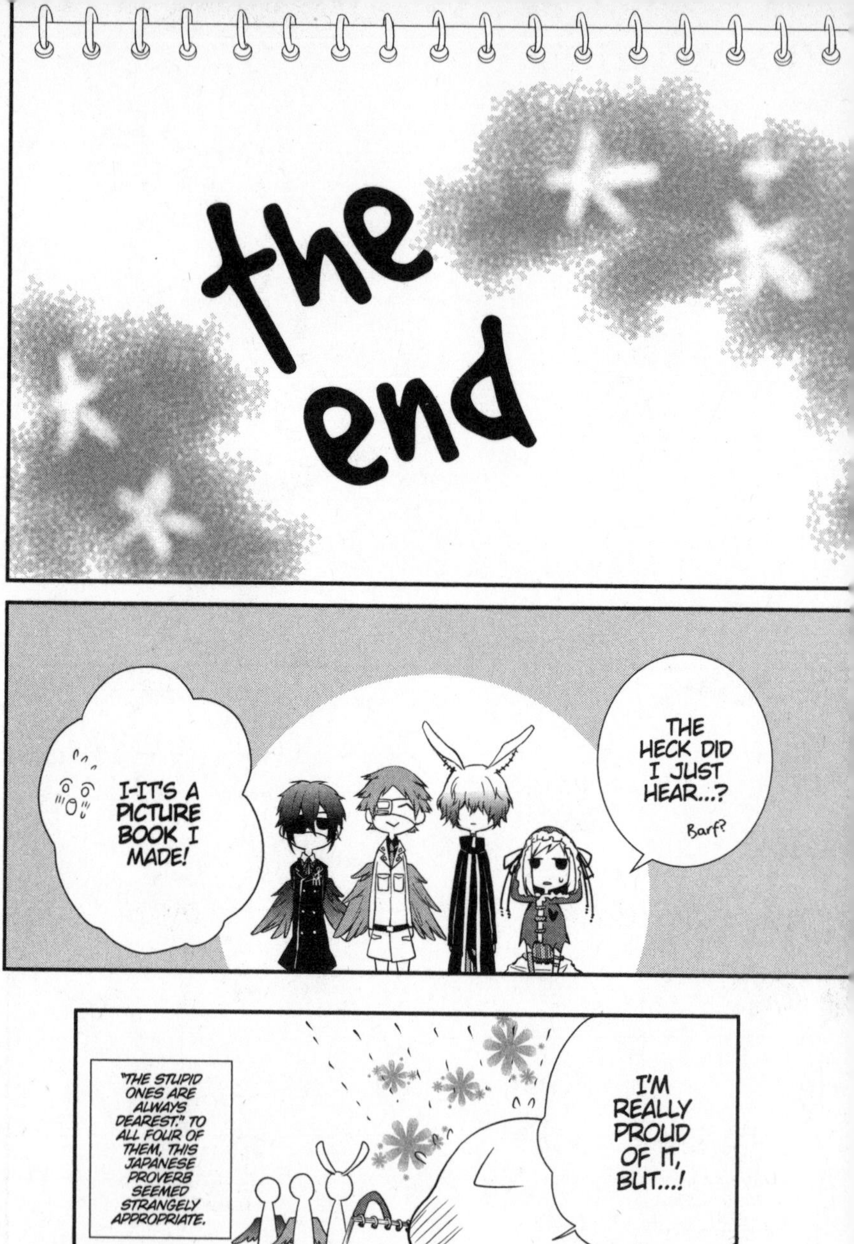
the end
THE HECK DID I JUST HEAR...?
Barf?
I-IT'S A PICTURE BOOK I MADE!
I'M REALLY PROUD OF IT, BUT...!
"THE STUPID ONES ARE ALWAYS DEAREST." TO ALL FOUR OF THEM, THIS JAPANESE PROVERB SEEMED STRANGELY APPROPRIATE.

Chapter Fifteen

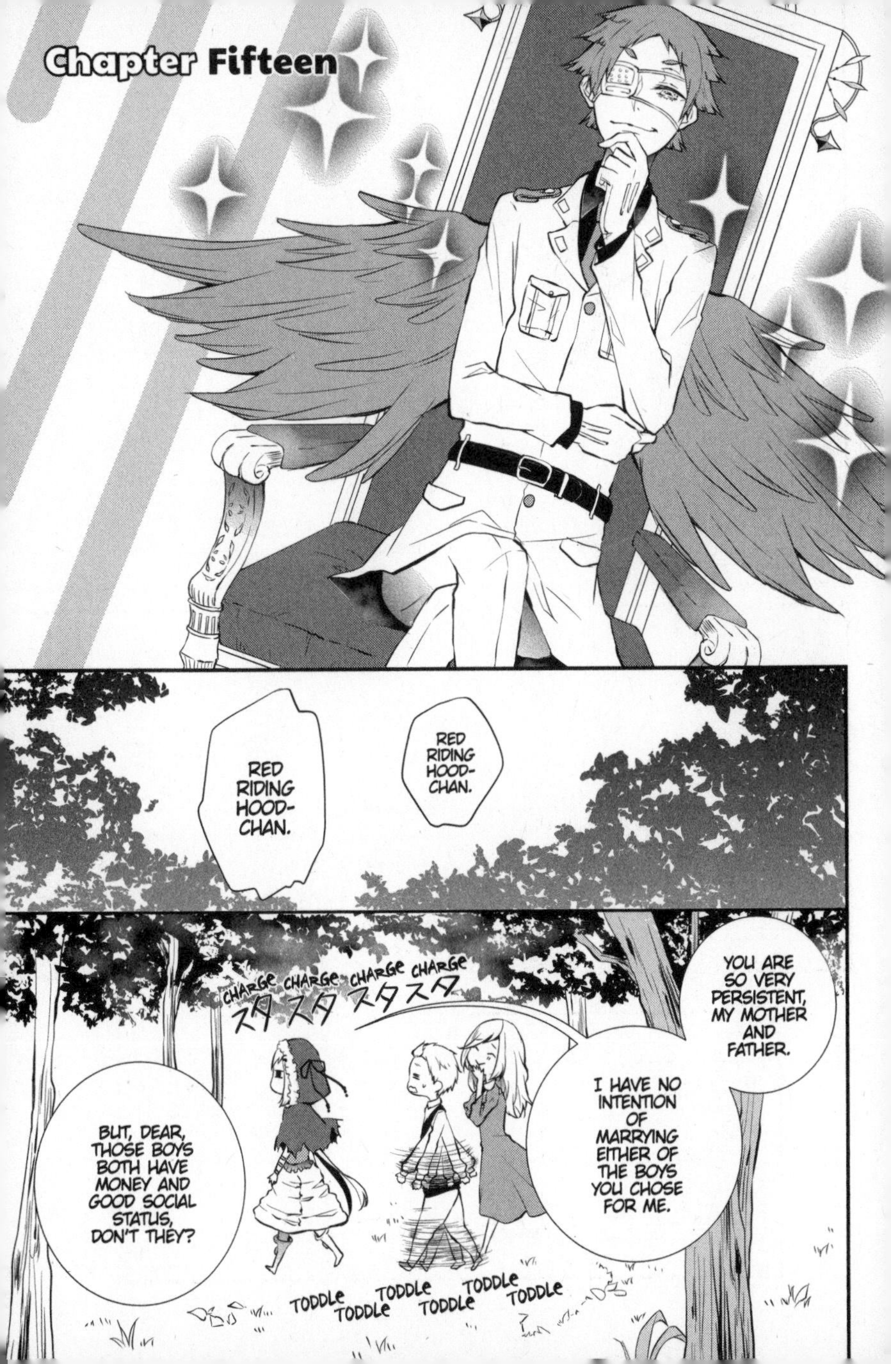
RED RIDING HOOD-CHAN.
RED RIDING HOOD-CHAN.
YOU ARE SO VERY PERSISTENT, MY MOTHER AND FATHER.
I HAVE NO INTENTION OF MARRYING EITHER OF THE BOYS YOU CHOSE FOR ME.
CHARGE CHARGE CHARGE CHARGE
スタ スタ スタスタ
BUT, DEAR, THOSE BOYS BOTH HAVE MONEY AND GOOD SOCIAL STATUS, DON'T THEY?
TODDLE TODDLE TODDLE TODDLE TODDLE TODDLE

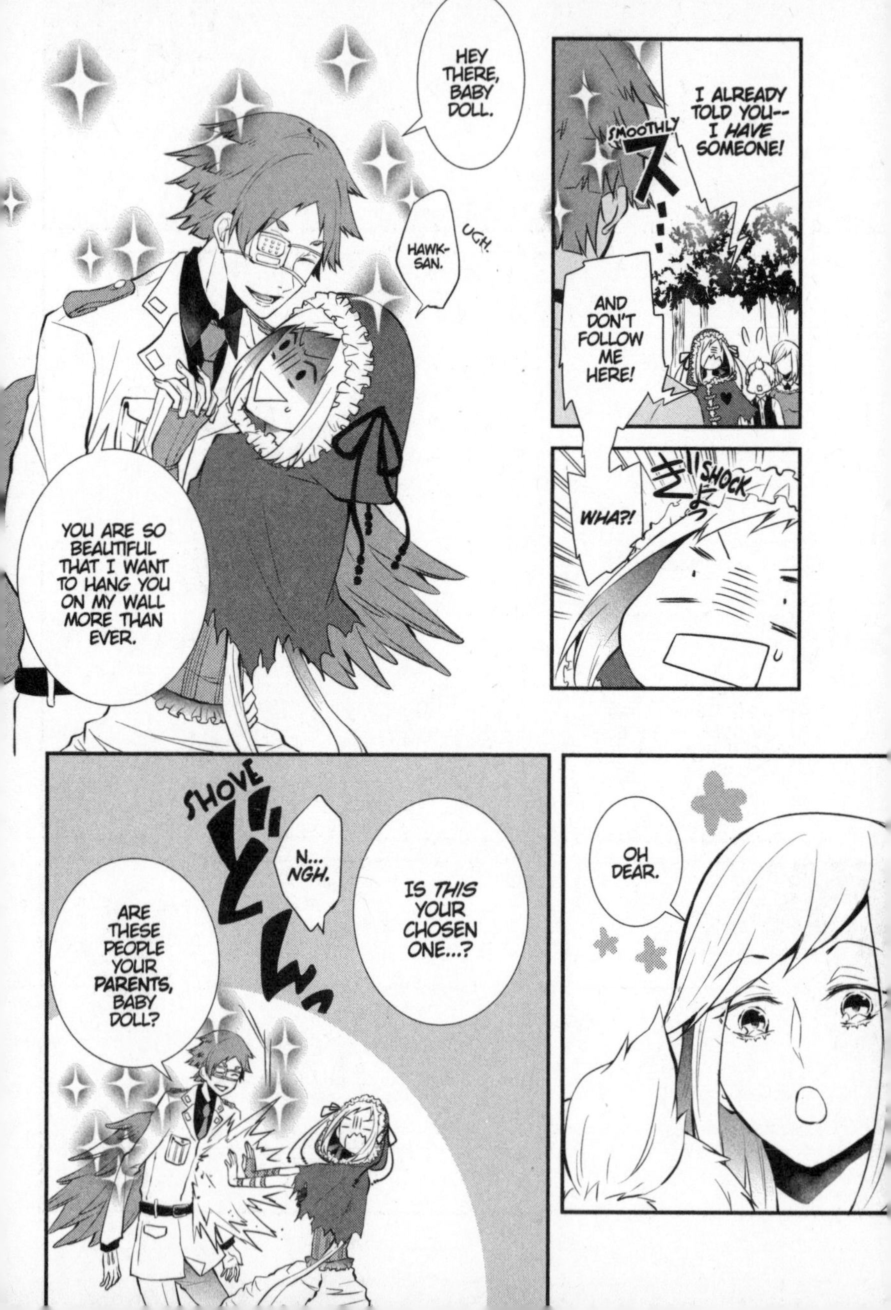
I ALREADY TOLD YOU-- I *HAVE* SOMEONE!
SMOOTHLY
AND DON'T FOLLOW ME HERE!
SHOCK
WHA?!
HEY THERE, BABY DOLL.
HAWK-SAN.
UGH.
YOU ARE SO BEAUTIFUL THAT I WANT TO HANG YOU ON MY WALL MORE THAN EVER.
OH DEAR.
IS *THIS* YOUR CHOSEN ONE...?
N... NGH.
SHOVE
ARE THESE PEOPLE YOUR PARENTS, BABY DOLL?

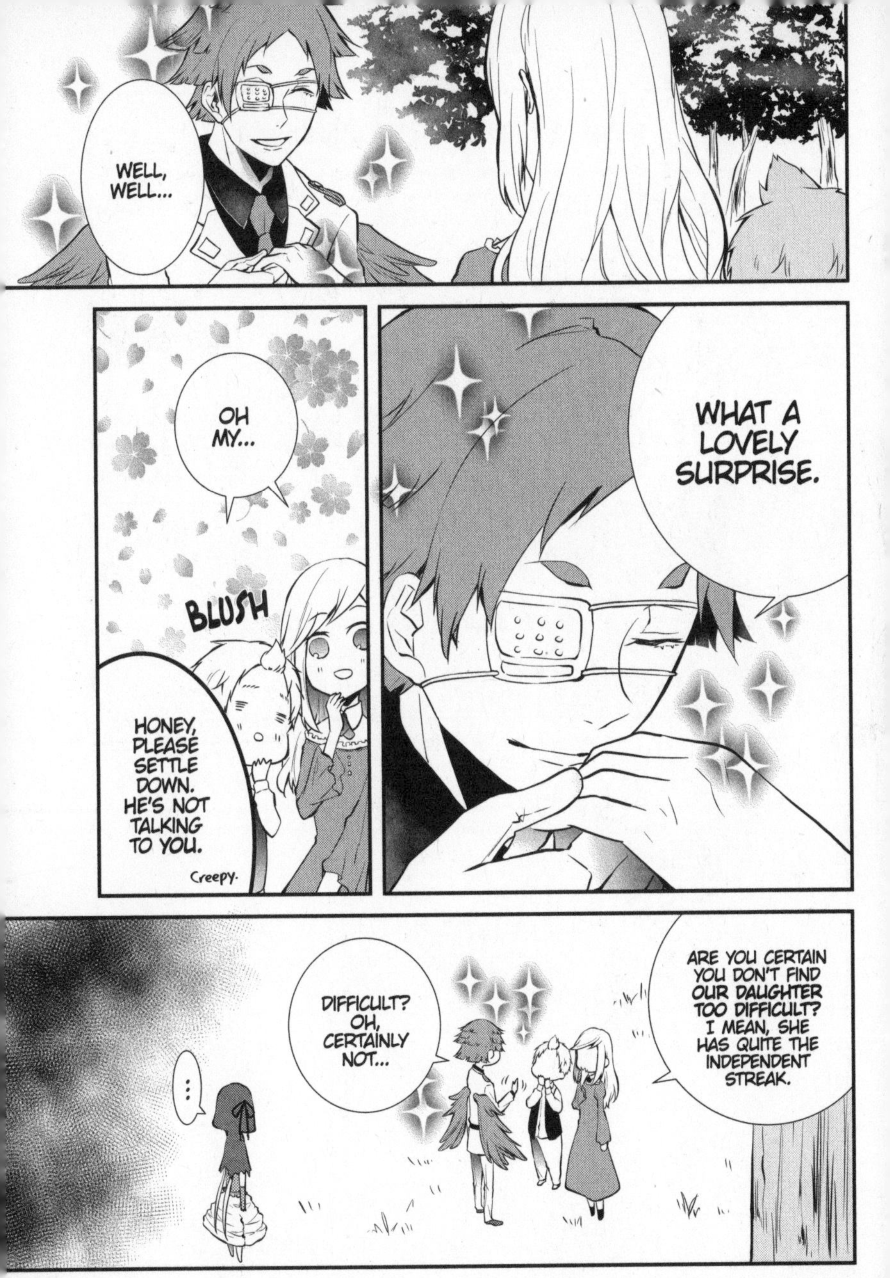

WELL, WELL...
WHAT A LOVELY SURPRISE.
OH MY...
BLUSH
HONEY, PLEASE SETTLE DOWN. HE'S NOT TALKING TO YOU.
Creepy.
ARE YOU CERTAIN YOU DON'T FIND OUR DAUGHTER TOO DIFFICULT? I MEAN, SHE HAS QUITE THE INDEPENDENT STREAK.
DIFFICULT? OH, CERTAINLY NOT...
...

READ BETWEEN THE LINES

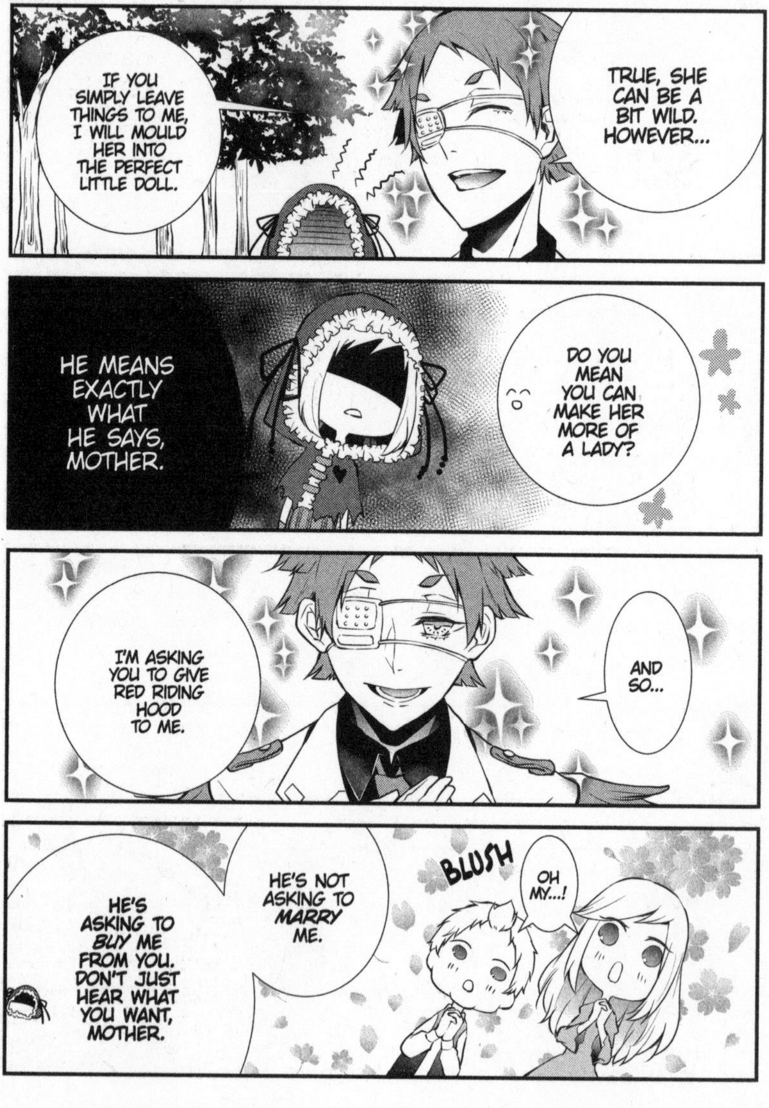
TRUE, SHE CAN BE A BIT WILD. HOWEVER...
IF YOU SIMPLY LEAVE THINGS TO ME, I WILL MOULD HER INTO THE PERFECT LITTLE DOLL.
DO YOU MEAN YOU CAN MAKE HER MORE OF A LADY?
HE MEANS EXACTLY WHAT HE SAYS, MOTHER.
AND SO...
I'M ASKING YOU TO GIVE RED RIDING HOOD TO ME.
BLUSH
OH MY...!
HE'S NOT ASKING TO *MARRY* ME.
HE'S ASKING TO *BUY* ME FROM YOU. DON'T JUST HEAR WHAT YOU WANT, MOTHER.

THE IMPOSSIBLE ACKNOWLEDGEMENT

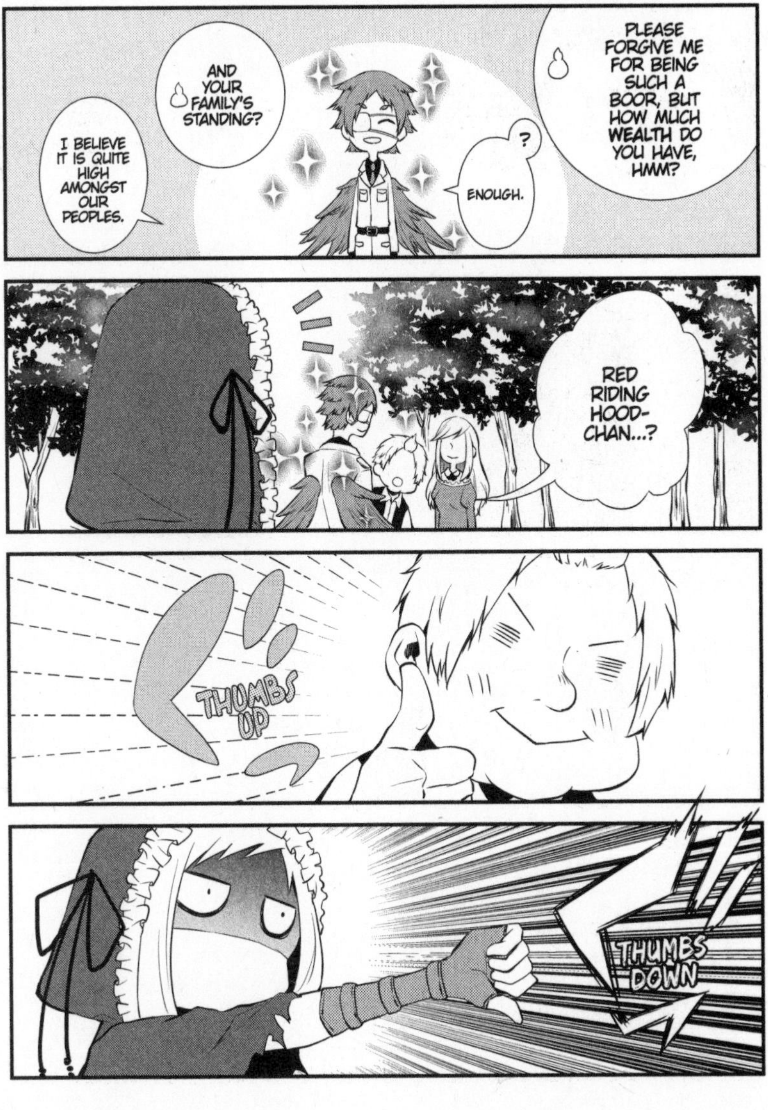
PLEASE FORGIVE ME FOR BEING SUCH A BOOR, BUT HOW MUCH WEALTH DO YOU HAVE, HMM?
?
ENOUGH.
AND YOUR FAMILY'S STANDING?
I BELIEVE IT IS QUITE HIGH AMONGST OUR PEOPLES.
RED RIDING HOOD-CHAN...?
THUMBS UP
THUMBS DOWN

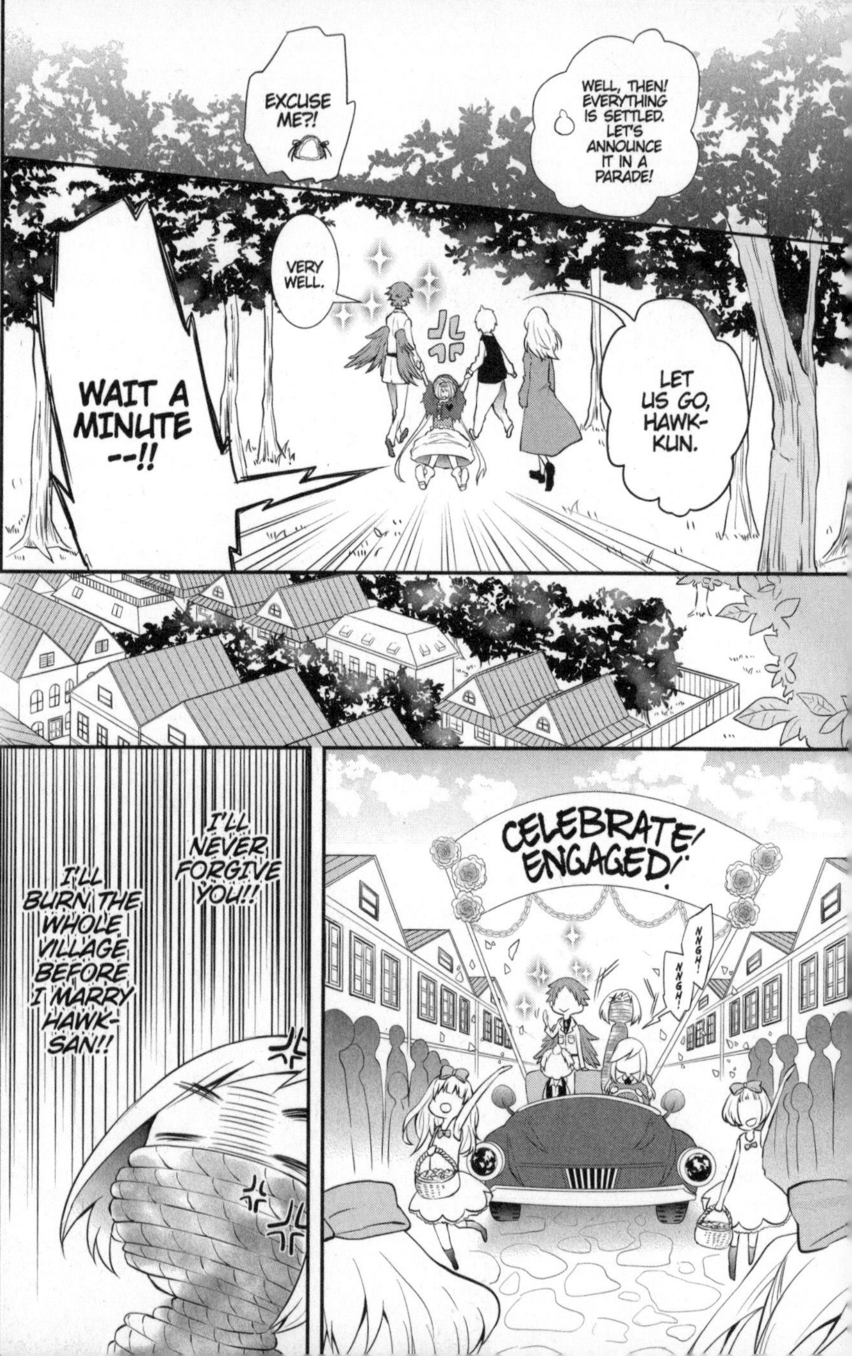
WELL, THEN! EVERYTHING IS SETTLED. LET'S ANNOUNCE IT IN A PARADE!
EXCUSE ME?!
LET US GO, HAWK-KUN.
VERY WELL.
WAIT A MINUTE --!!
CELEBRATE! ENGAGED!
NNGH! NNGH!
I'LL NEVER FORGIVE YOU!!
I'LL BURN THE WHOLE VILLAGE BEFORE I MARRY HAWK-SAN!!

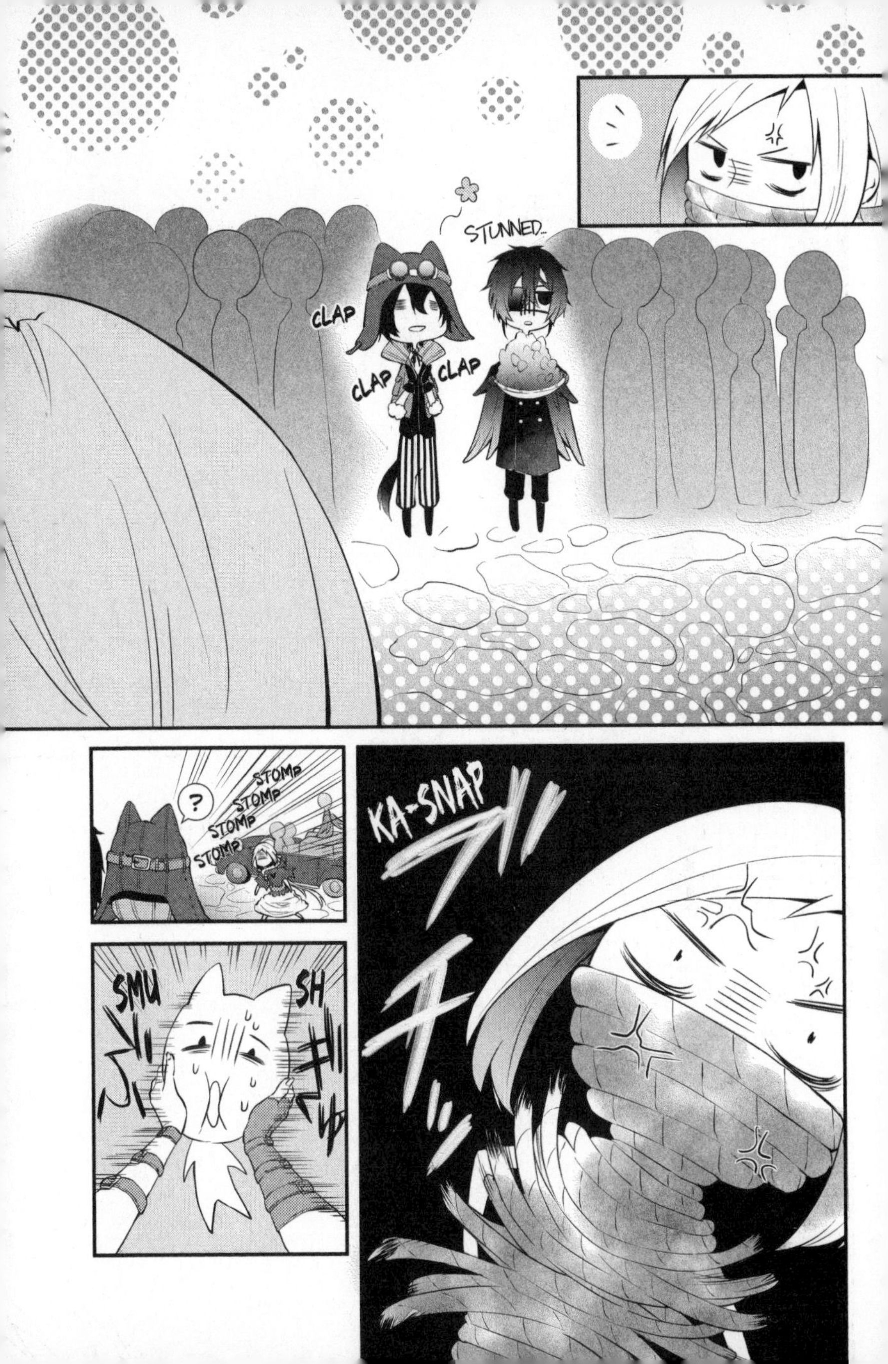
STUNNED...
CLAP
CLAP
CLAP
KA-SNAP
STOMP
STOMP
STOMP
STOMP
?
SH
SMU

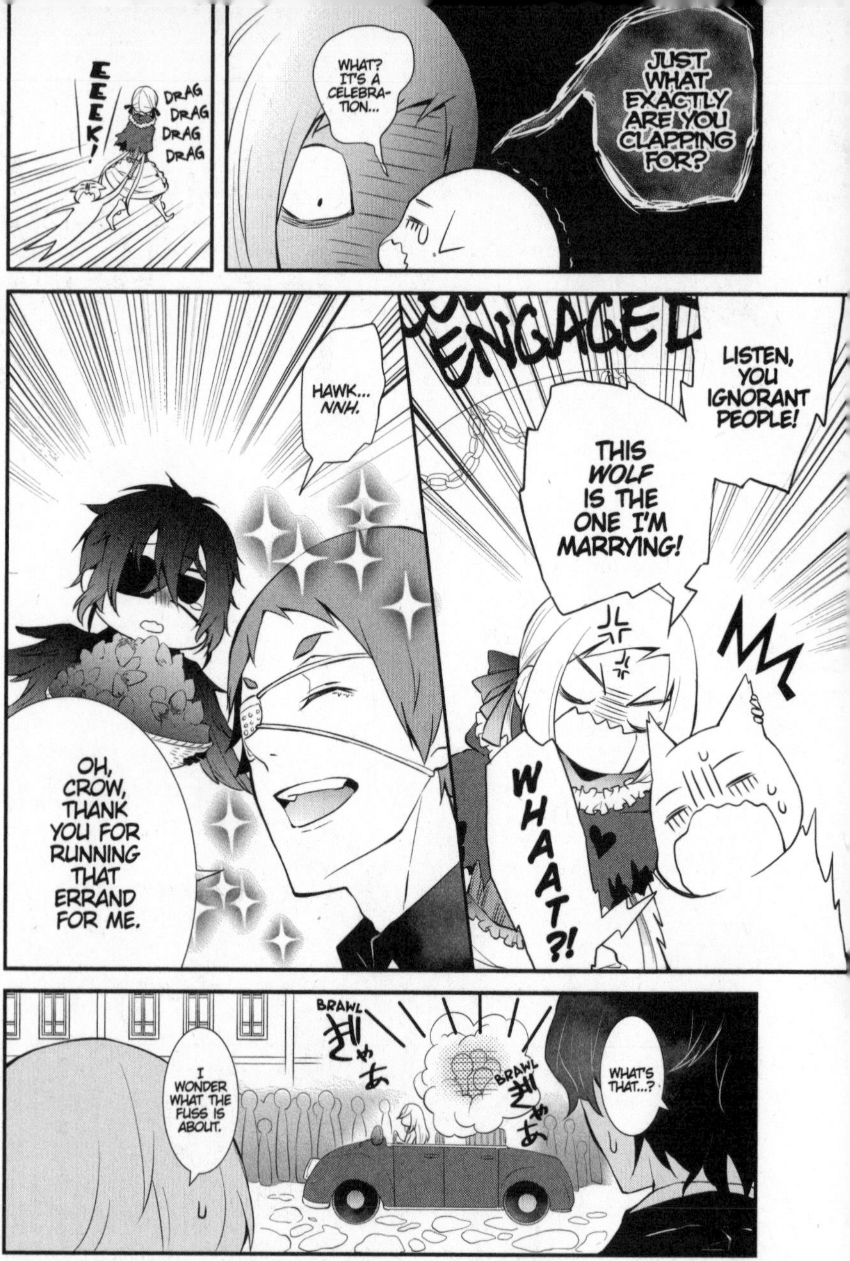
JUST WHAT EXACTLY ARE YOU CLAPPING FOR?
WHAT? IT'S A CELEBRA-TION...
EEEK!
DRAG DRAG DRAG DRAG
ENGAGED
LISTEN, YOU IGNORANT PEOPLE!
THIS WOLF IS THE ONE I'M MARRYING!
WHAAT?!
HAWK... NNH.
OH, CROW, THANK YOU FOR RUNNING THAT ERRAND FOR ME.
WHAT'S THAT...?
BRAWL
BRAWL
I WONDER WHAT THE FUSS IS ABOUT.

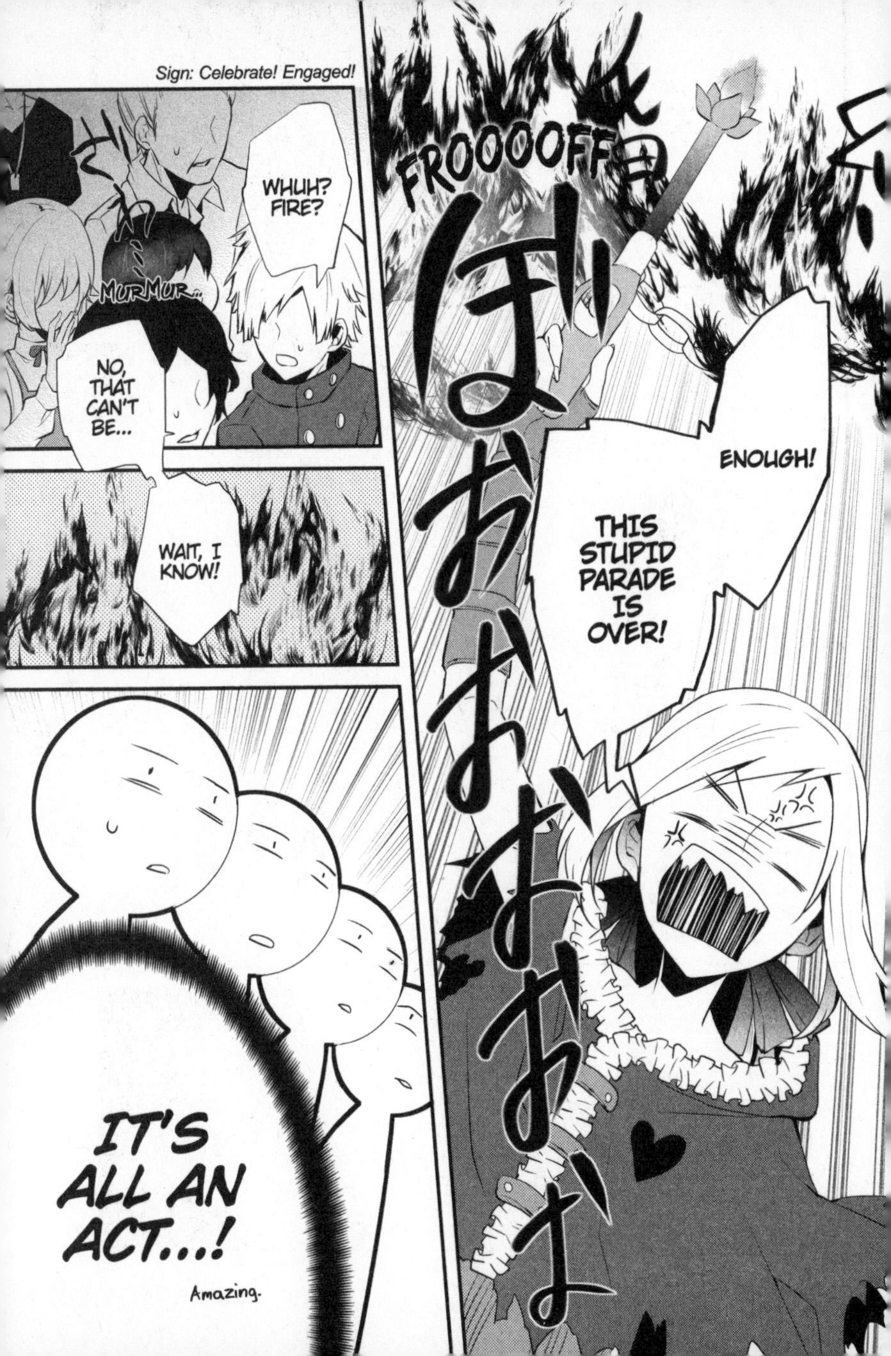
FROOOOFF
ぼおおおおおお
ENOUGH!
THIS STUPID PARADE IS OVER!
Sign: Celebrate! Engaged!
WHUH? FIRE?
MurMur...
NO, THAT CAN'T BE...
WAIT, I KNOW!
IT'S ALL AN ACT...!
Amazing.

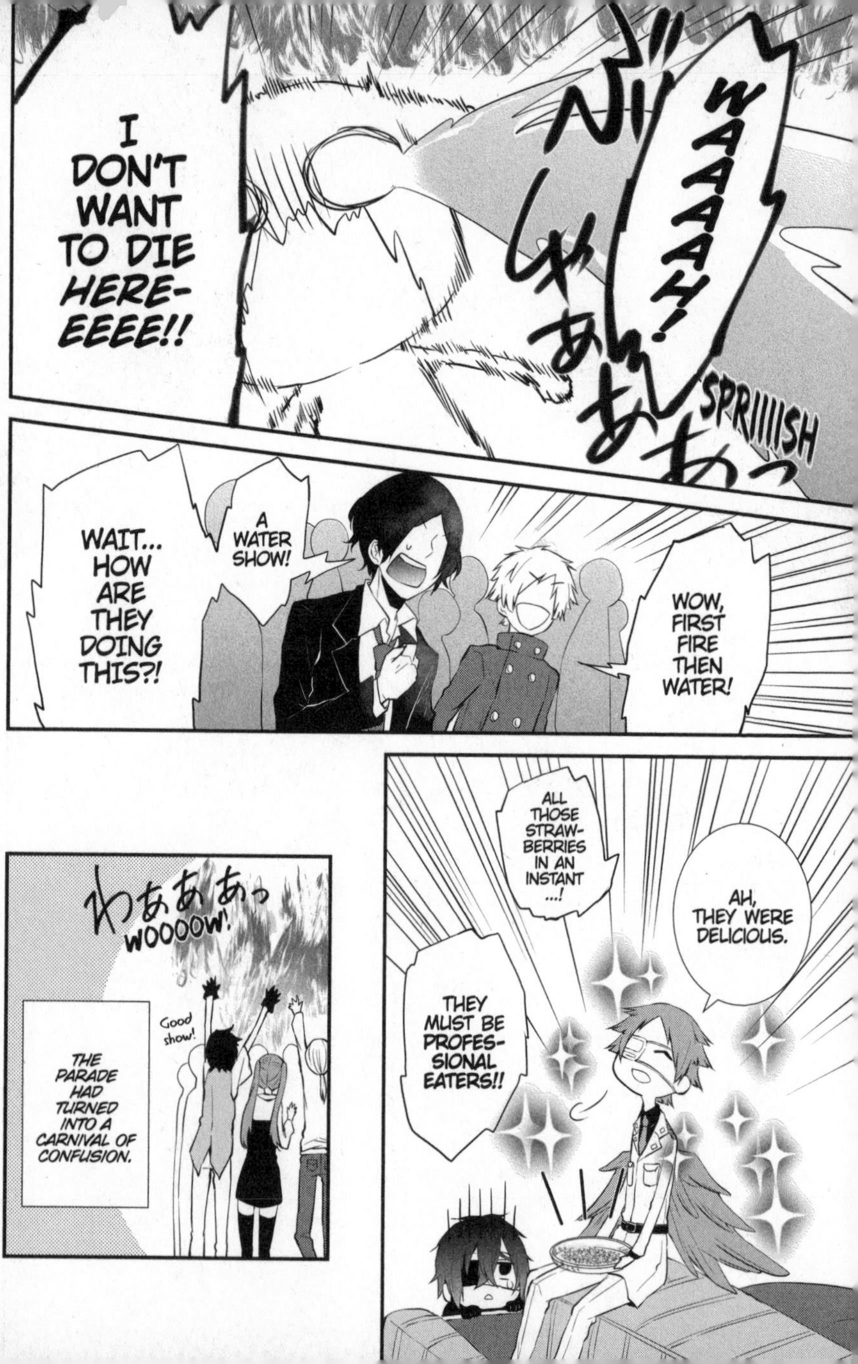
WAAAAAH!
SPRIIIISH
I DON'T WANT TO DIE HERE-EEEE!!
WOW, FIRST FIRE THEN WATER!
A WATER SHOW!
WAIT... HOW ARE THEY DOING THIS?!
ALL THOSE STRAW-BERRIES IN AN INSTANT ...!
AH, THEY WERE DELICIOUS.
THEY MUST BE PROFES-SIONAL EATERS!!
わあああっ
WOOOOW!
Good show!
THE PARADE HAD TURNED INTO A CARNIVAL OF CONFUSION.

Chapter Sixteen

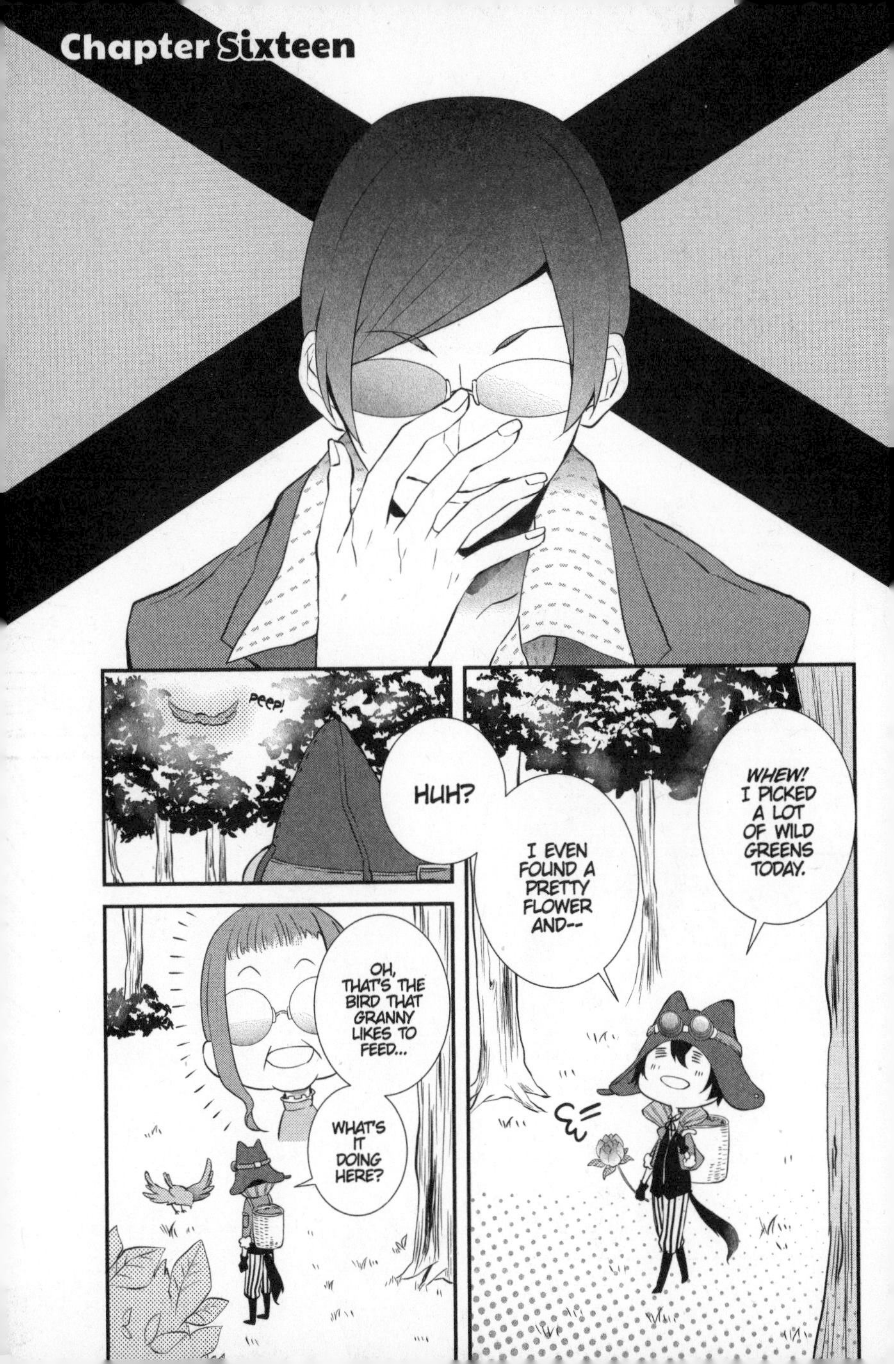
WHEW! I PICKED A LOT OF WILD GREENS TODAY.
I EVEN FOUND A PRETTY FLOWER AND--
PEEP!
HUH?
OH, THAT'S THE BIRD THAT GRANNY LIKES TO FEED...
WHAT'S IT DOING HERE?

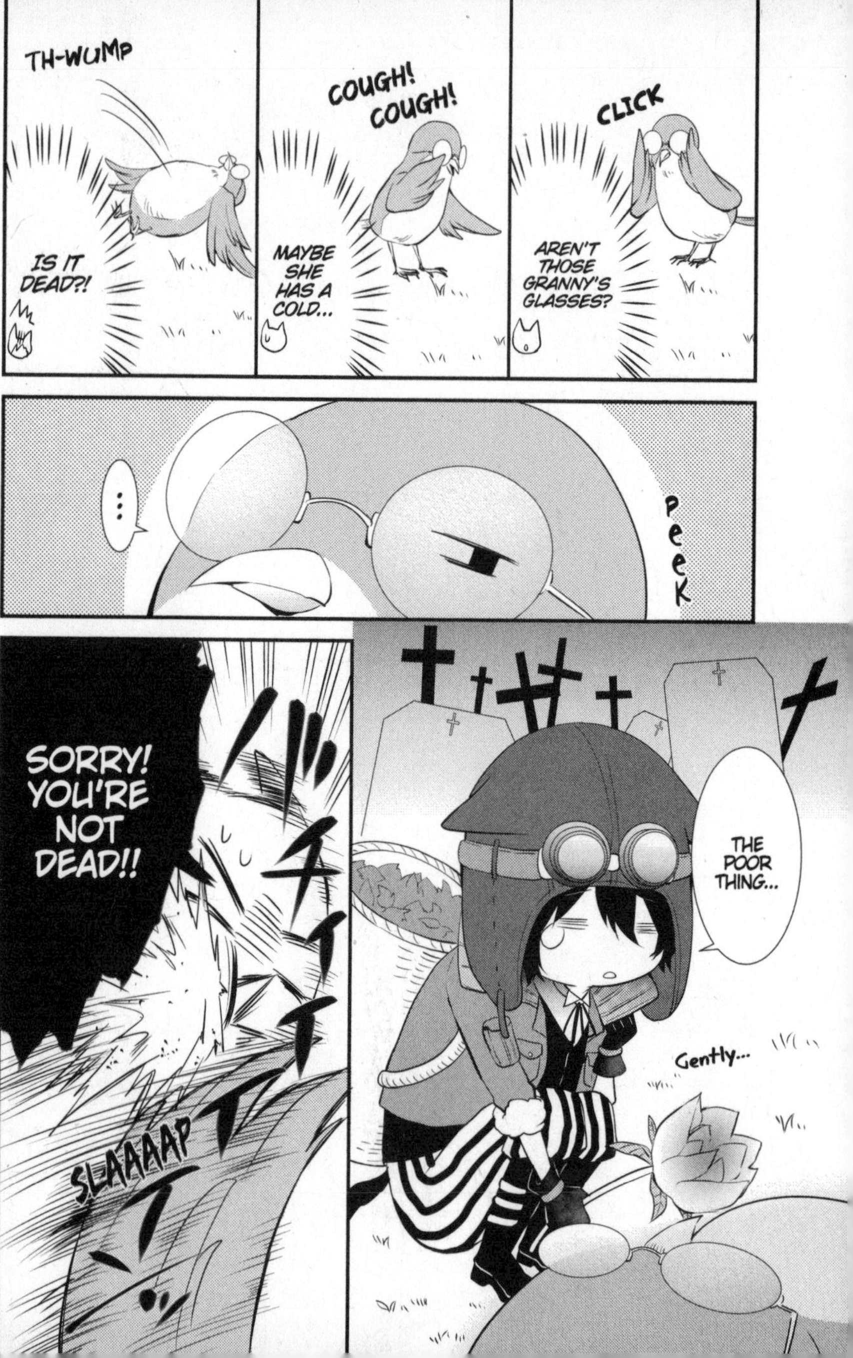
CLICK
AREN'T THOSE GRANNY'S GLASSES?
COUGH! COUGH!
MAYBE SHE HAS A COLD...
TH-WUMP
IS IT DEAD?!
...
PEEK
THE POOR THING...
Gently...
SORRY! YOU'RE NOT DEAD!!
SLAAAAP

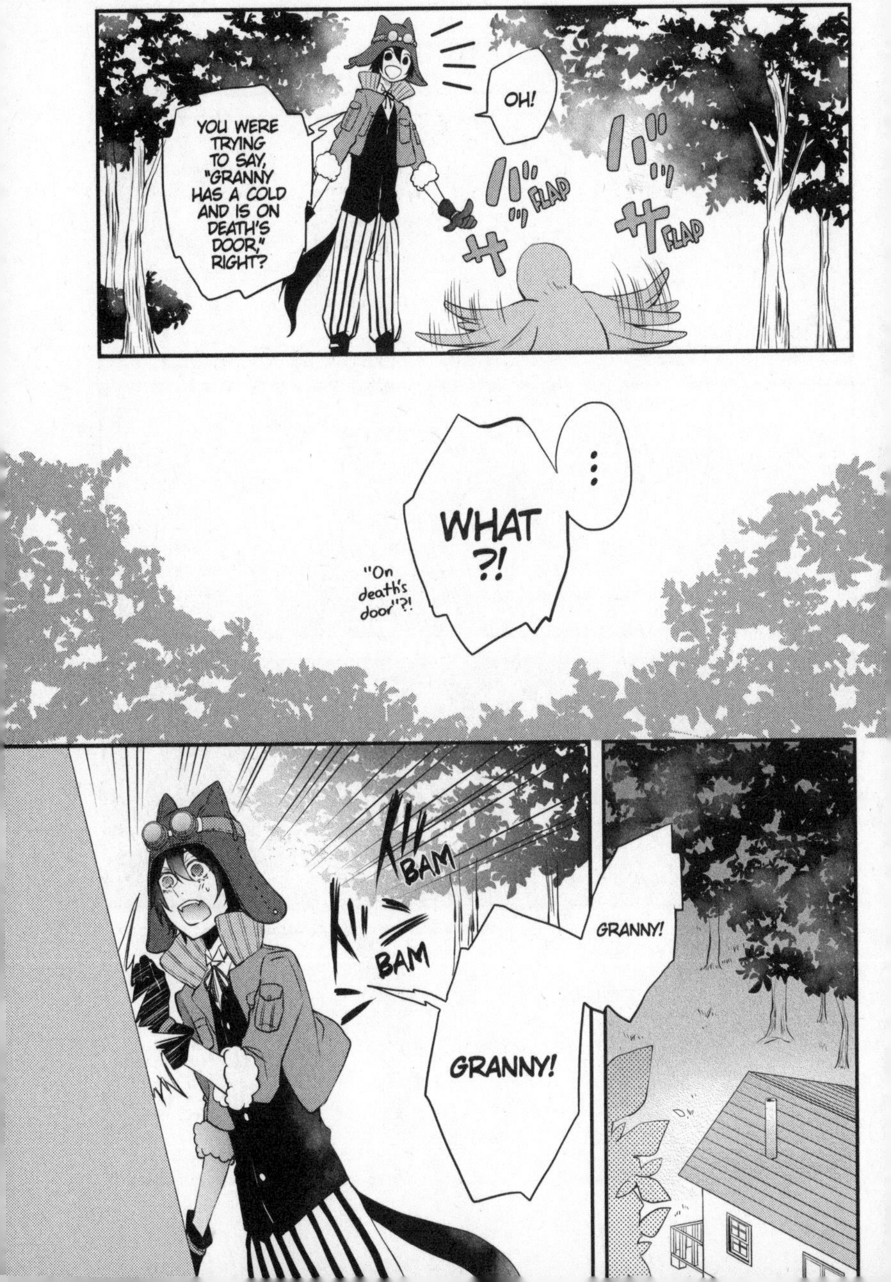
FLAP
OH!
FLAP
YOU WERE TRYING TO SAY, "GRANNY HAS A COLD AND IS ON DEATH'S DOOR," RIGHT?
...
WHAT ?!
"On death's door"?!
GRANNY!
GRANNY!
BAM
BAM

A HORROR STORY ENDING

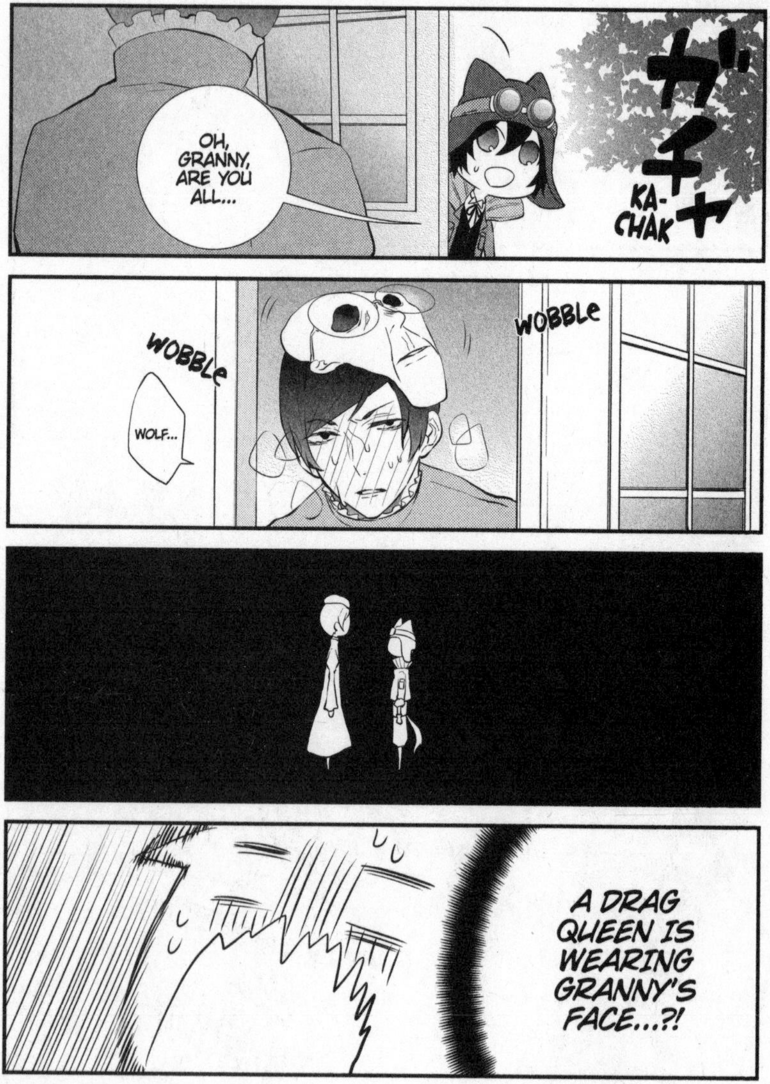
ガチャ
KA-CHAK
OH, GRANNY, ARE YOU ALL...
WOBBLE
WOBBLE
WOLF...
A DRAG QUEEN IS WEARING GRANNY'S FACE...?!

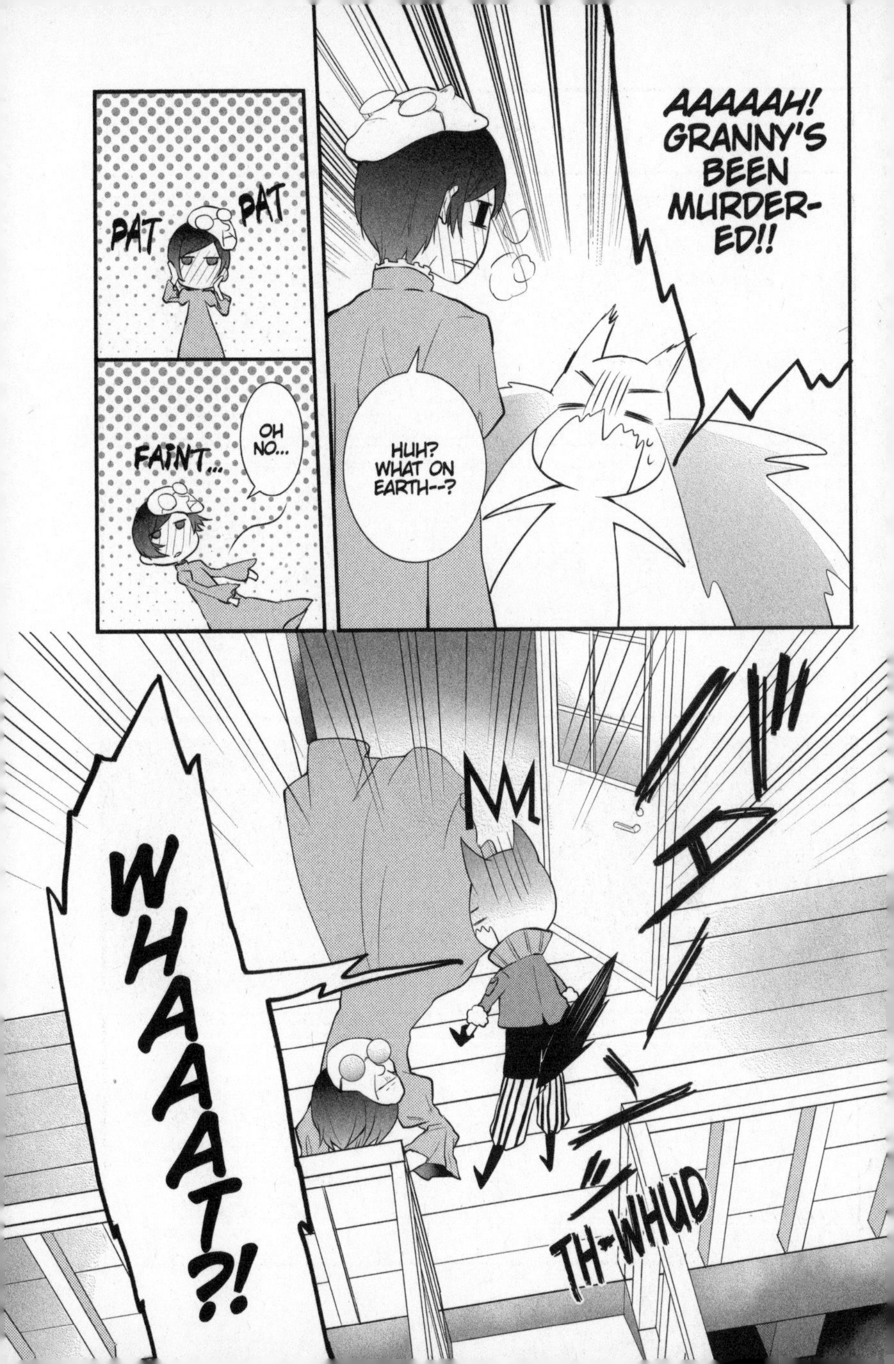
AAAAAH! GRANNY'S BEEN MURDER-ED!!
HUH? WHAT ON EARTH--?
PAT PAT
FAINT...
OH NO...
TH-WHUD
WHAAAT?!

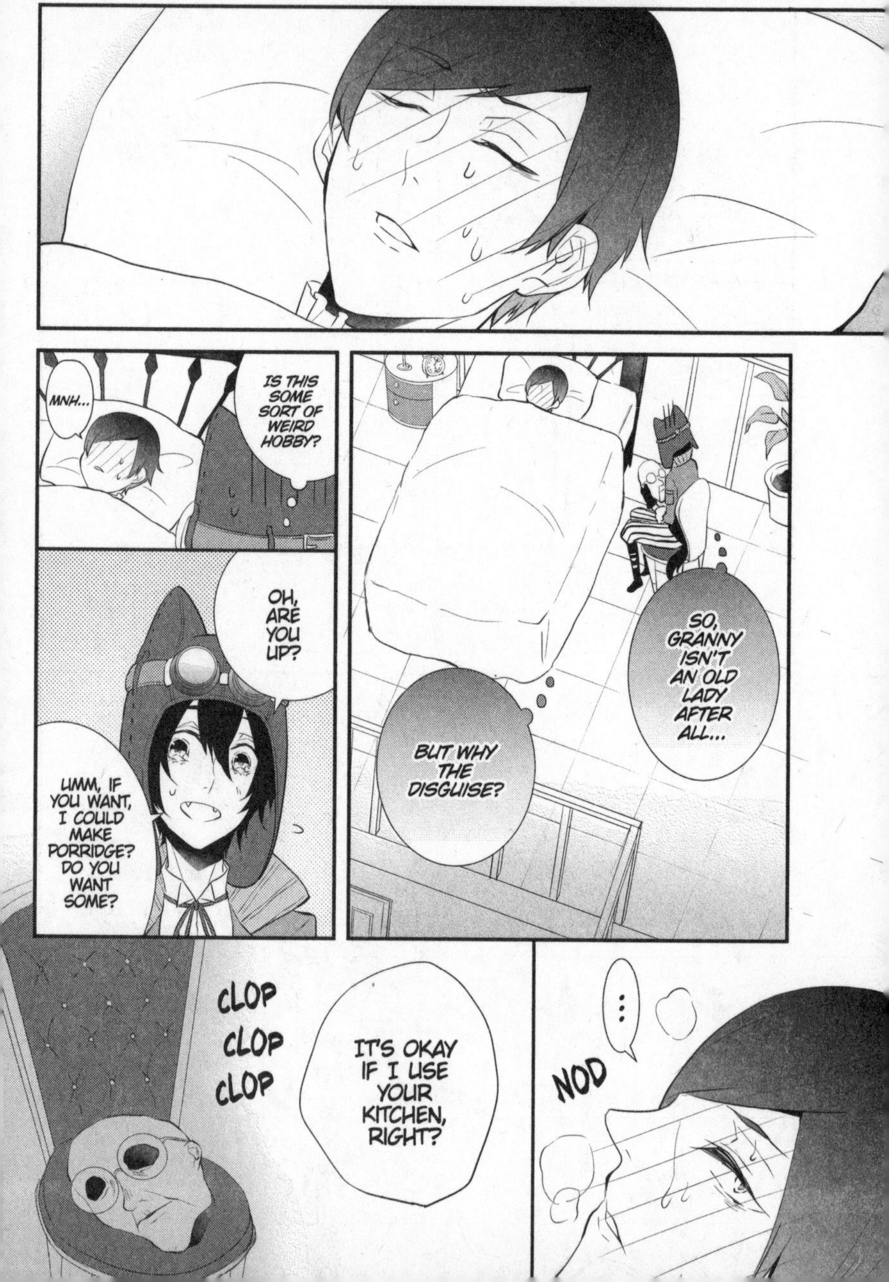
SO, GRANNY ISN'T AN OLD LADY AFTER ALL...
BUT WHY THE DISGUISE?
IS THIS SOME SORT OF WEIRD HOBBY?
MNH...
OH, ARE YOU UP?
UMM, IF YOU WANT, I COULD MAKE PORRIDGE? DO YOU WANT SOME?
...
NOD
IT'S OKAY IF I USE YOUR KITCHEN, RIGHT?
CLOP CLOP CLOP

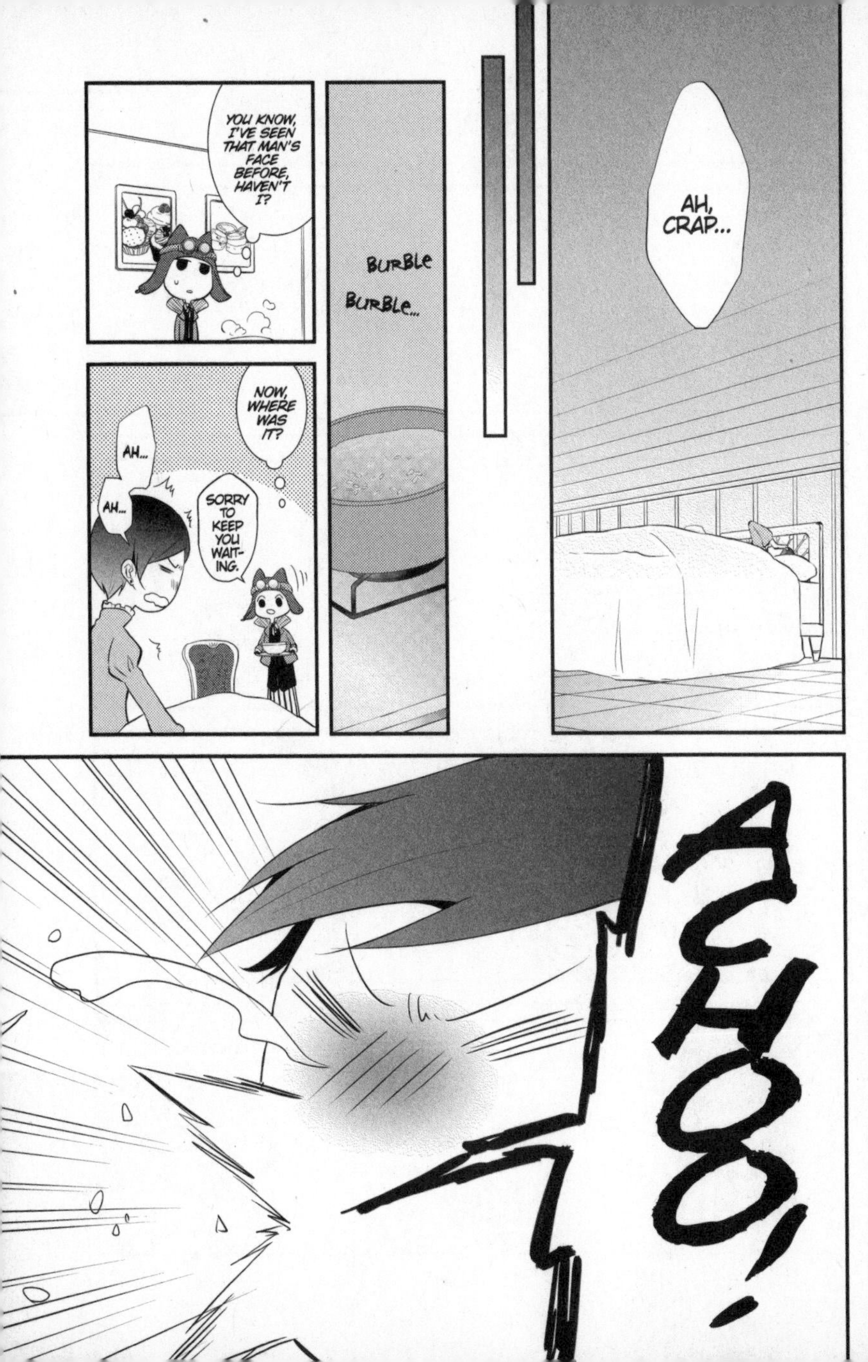
AH, CRAP...
BURBLE
BURBLE...
YOU KNOW, I'VE SEEN THAT MAN'S FACE BEFORE, HAVEN'T I?
NOW, WHERE WAS IT?
SORRY TO KEEP YOU WAIT-ING.
AH...
AH...
ACHOO!

SUCCESS AND FAILURE

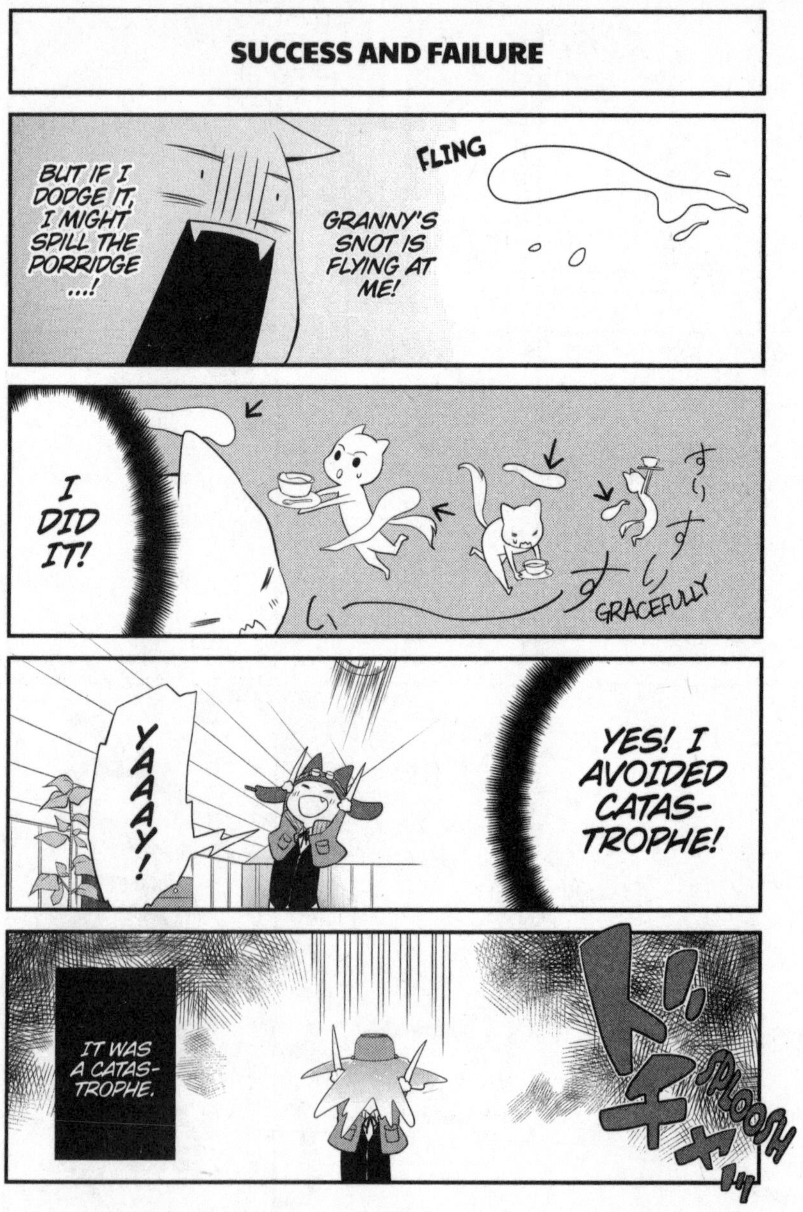
FLING
GRANNY'S SNOT IS FLYING AT ME!
BUT IF I DODGE IT, I MIGHT SPILL THE PORRIDGE ...!
すりすりすい
GRACEFULLY
I DID IT!
YES! I AVOIDED CATAS-TROPHE!
YAAAAY!
ドチャッ
SPLOOSH
IT WAS A CATAS-TROPHE.

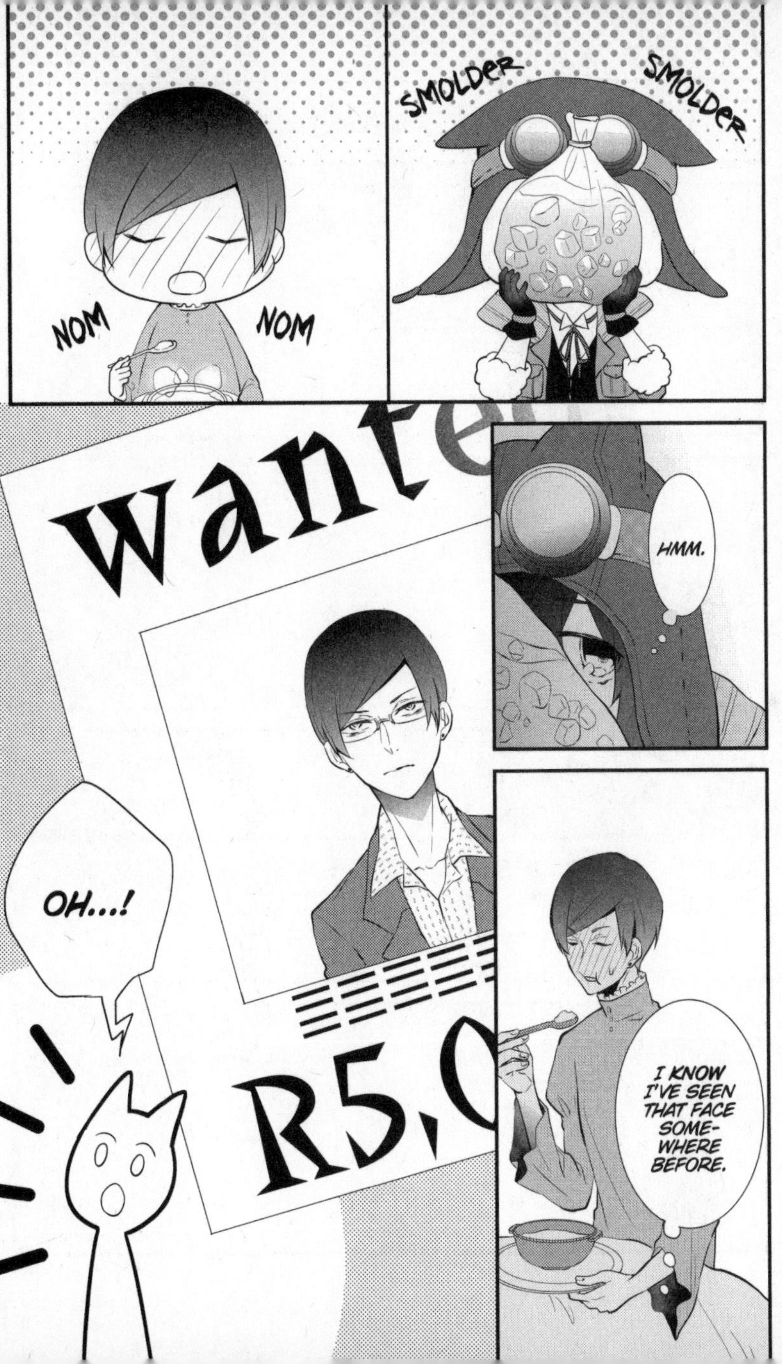
SMOLDER
SMOLDER
NOM
NOM
HMM.
I KNOW I'VE SEEN THAT FACE SOME-WHERE BEFORE.
wante
R5,0
OH...!

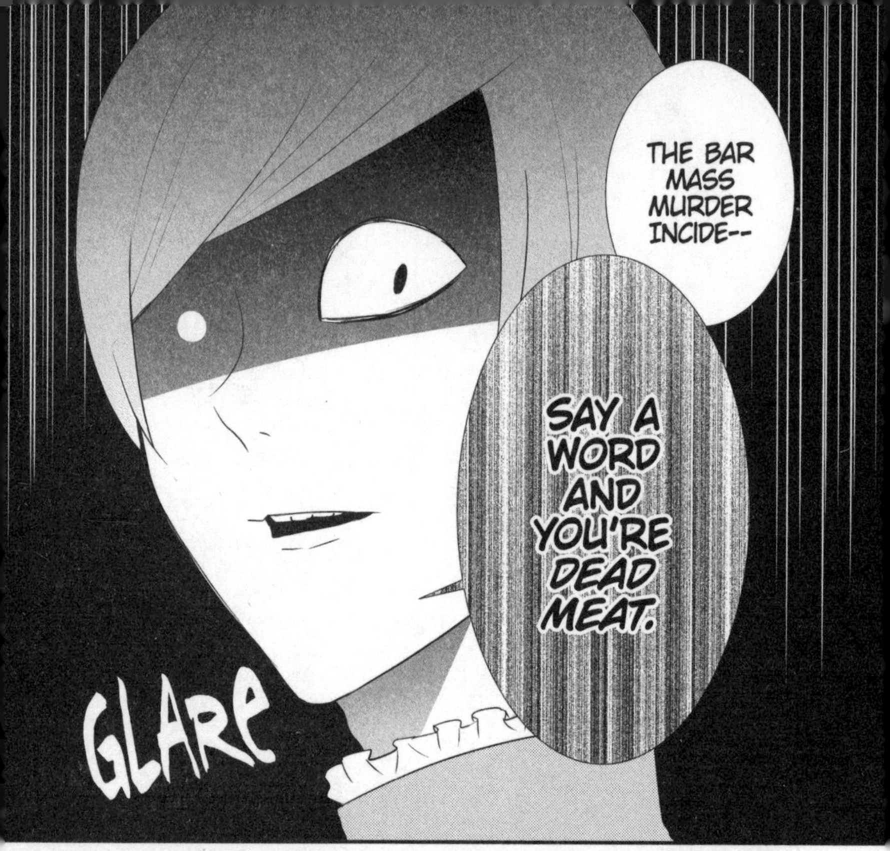
THE BAR MASS MURDER INCIDE--
SAY A WORD AND YOU'RE DEAD MEAT.
GLARE

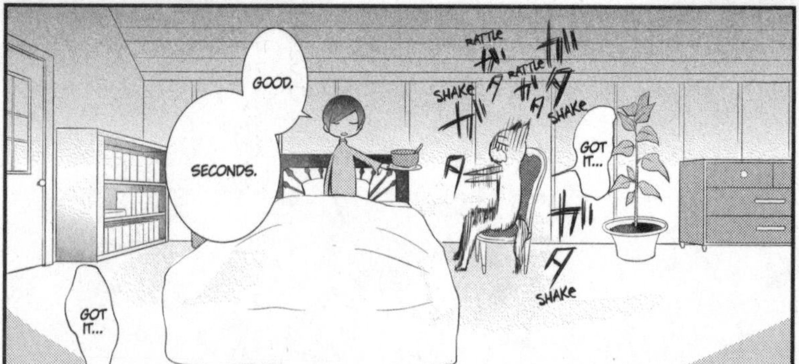
RATTLE
RATTLE
SHAKE
SHAKE
GOT IT...
GOOD.
SECONDS.
SHAKE
GOT IT...

Chapter Seventeen

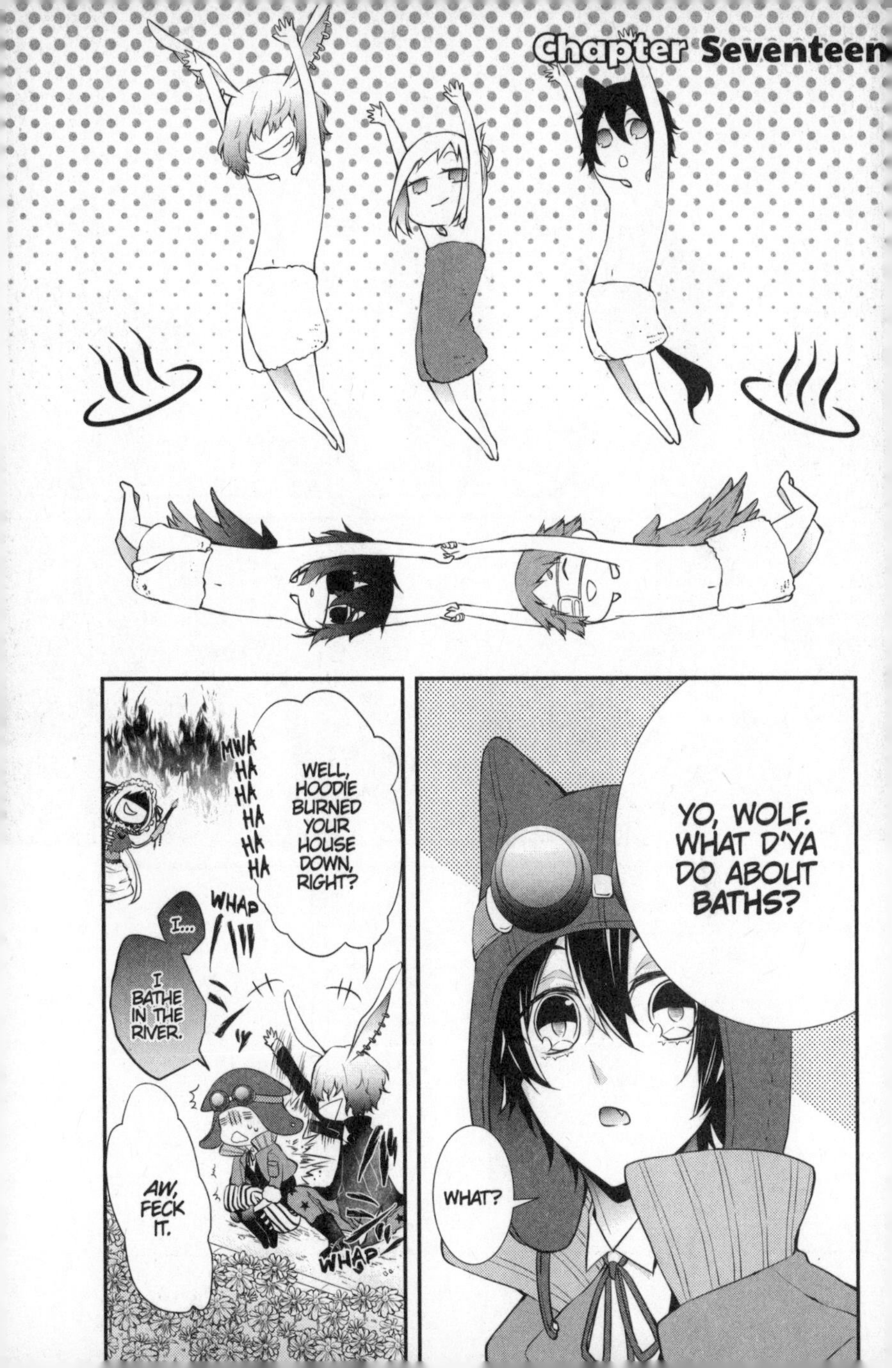
YO, WOLF. WHAT D'YA DO ABOUT BATHS?
WHAT?
WELL, HOODIE BURNED YOUR HOUSE DOWN, RIGHT?
MWA HA HA HA HA HA
WHAP
I...
I BATHE IN THE RIVER.
AW, FECK IT.
WHAP

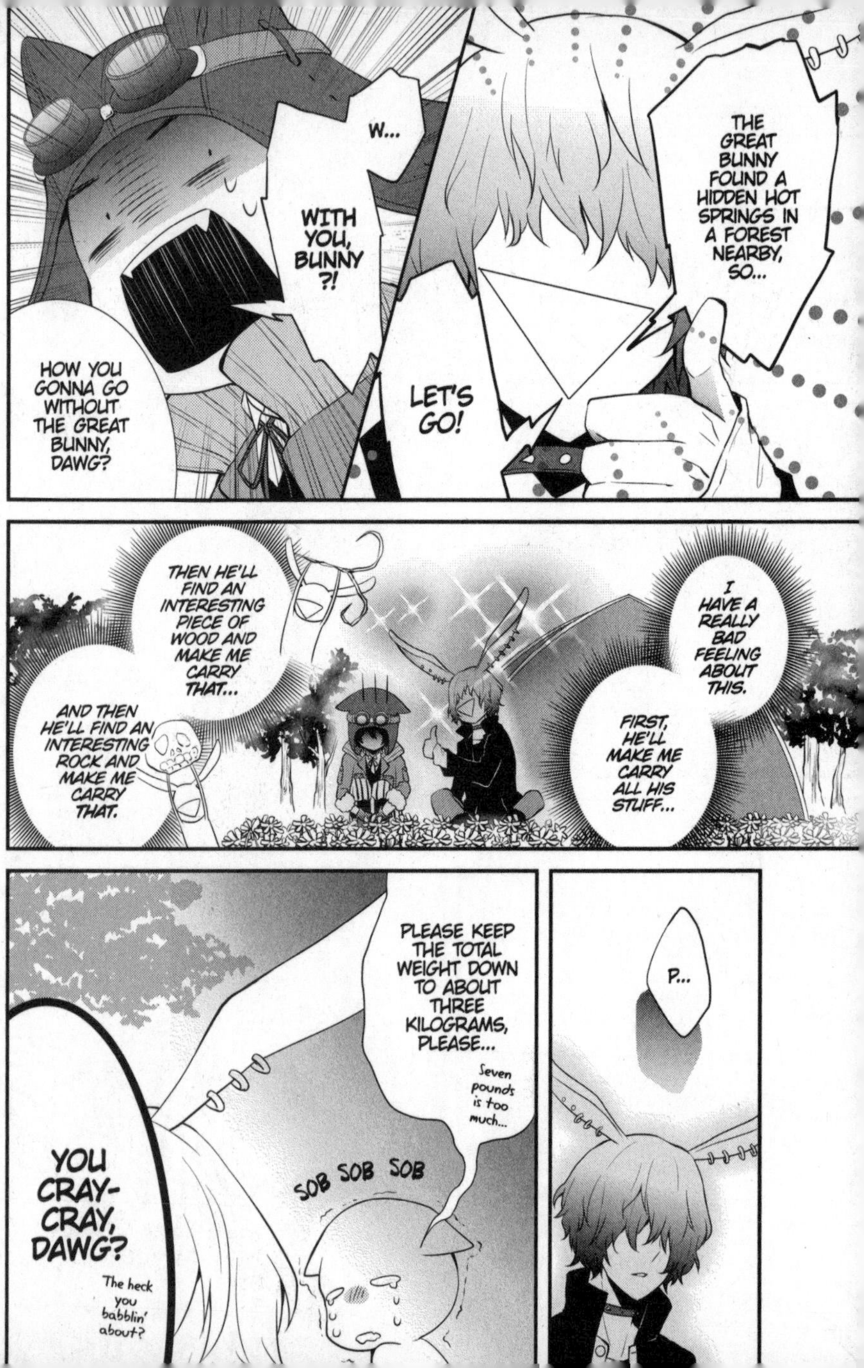
THE GREAT BUNNY FOUND A HIDDEN HOT SPRINGS IN A FOREST NEARBY, SO...
LET'S GO!
W...
WITH YOU, BUNNY?!
HOW YOU GONNA GO WITHOUT THE GREAT BUNNY, DAWG?
I HAVE A REALLY BAD FEELING ABOUT THIS.
FIRST, HE'LL MAKE ME CARRY ALL HIS STUFF...
THEN HE'LL FIND AN INTERESTING PIECE OF WOOD AND MAKE ME CARRY THAT...
AND THEN HE'LL FIND AN INTERESTING ROCK AND MAKE ME CARRY THAT.
P...
PLEASE KEEP THE TOTAL WEIGHT DOWN TO ABOUT THREE KILOGRAMS, PLEASE...
Seven pounds is too much...
SOB SOB SOB
YOU CRAY-CRAY, DAWG?
The heck you babblin' about?

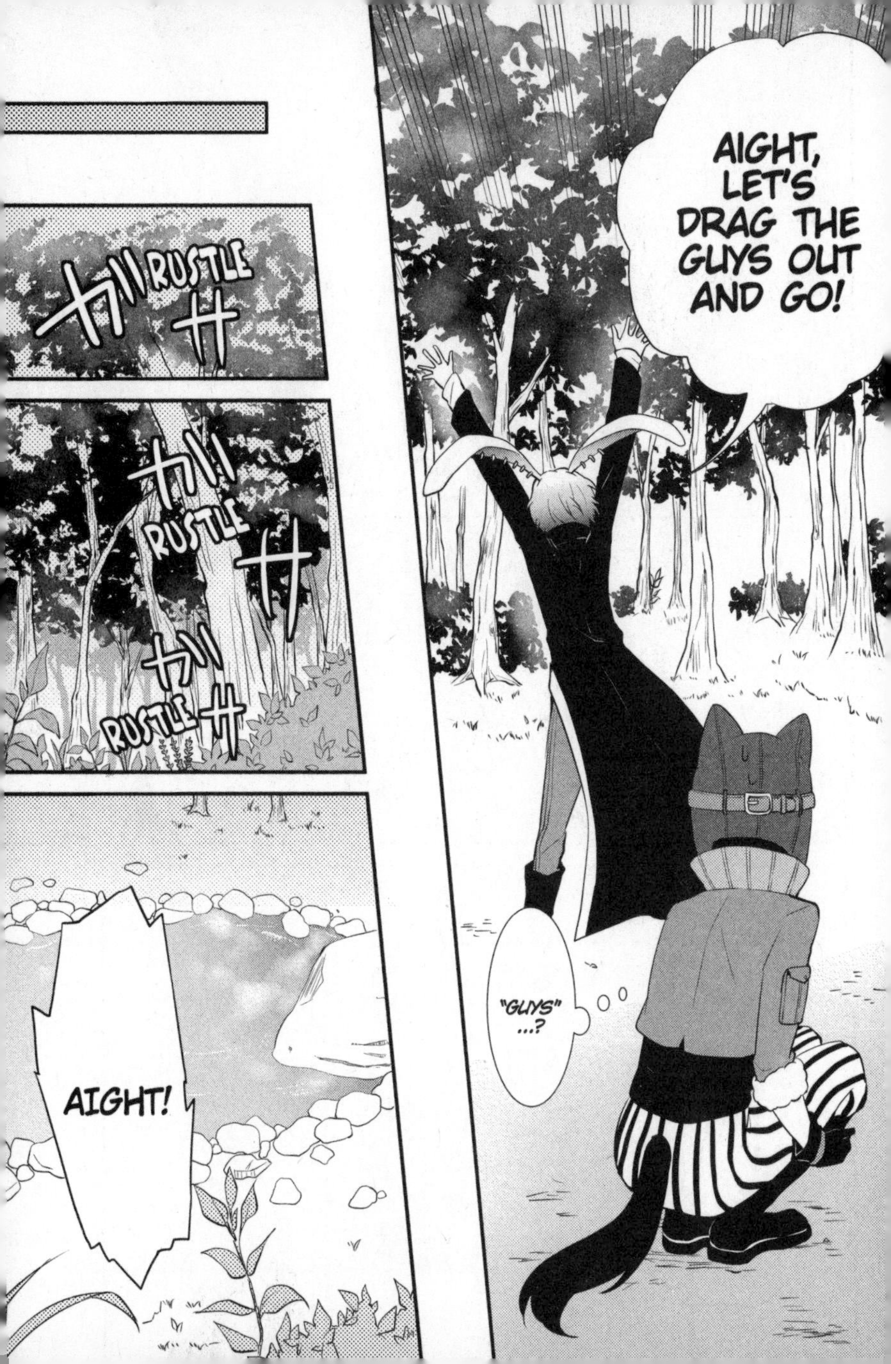
AIGHT, LET'S DRAG THE GUYS OUT AND GO!
"GUYS" ...?
RUSTLE
RUSTLE
RUSTLE
AIGHT!

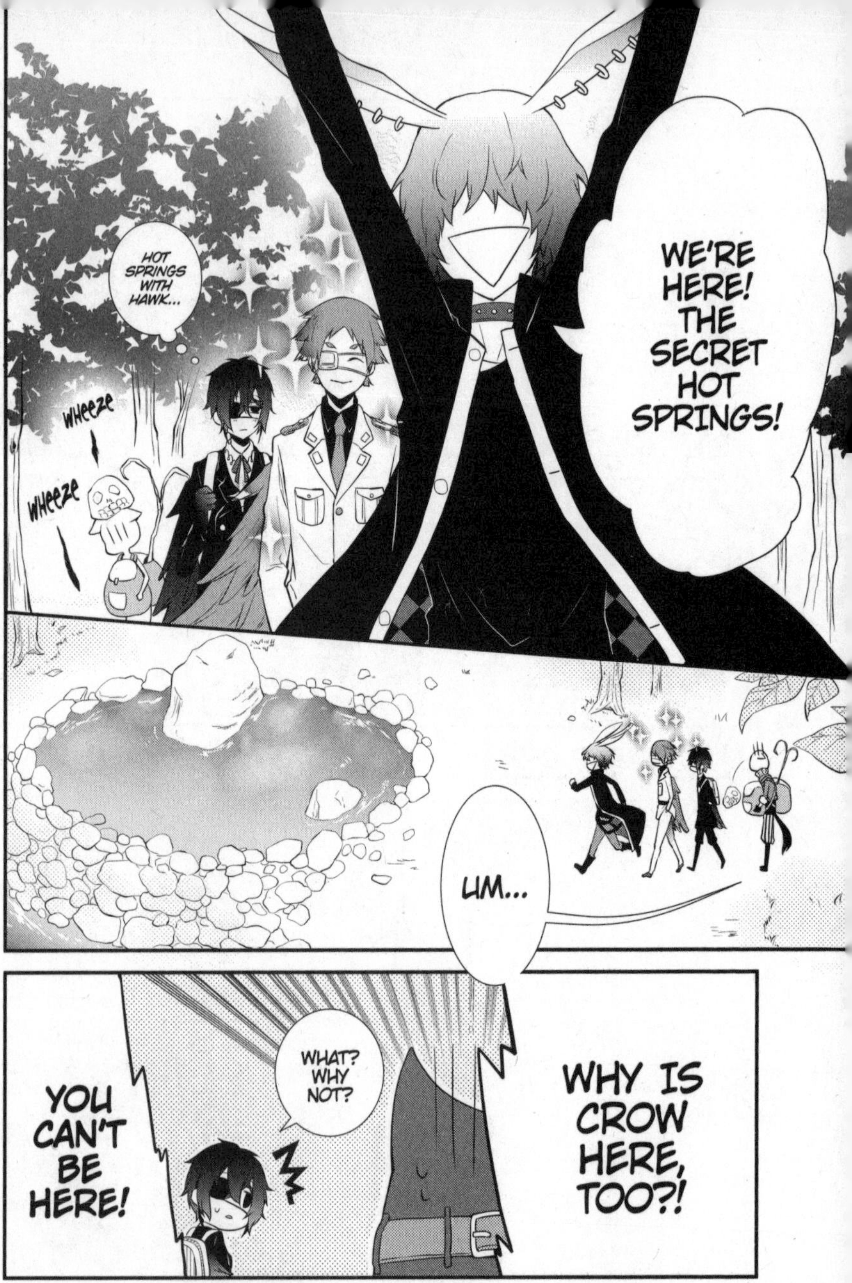
WE'RE HERE! THE SECRET HOT SPRINGS!
HOT SPRINGS WITH HAWK...
WHEEZE
WHEEZE
UM...
WHY IS CROW HERE, TOO?!
WHAT? WHY NOT?
YOU CAN'T BE HERE!

CLEARING THINGS UP

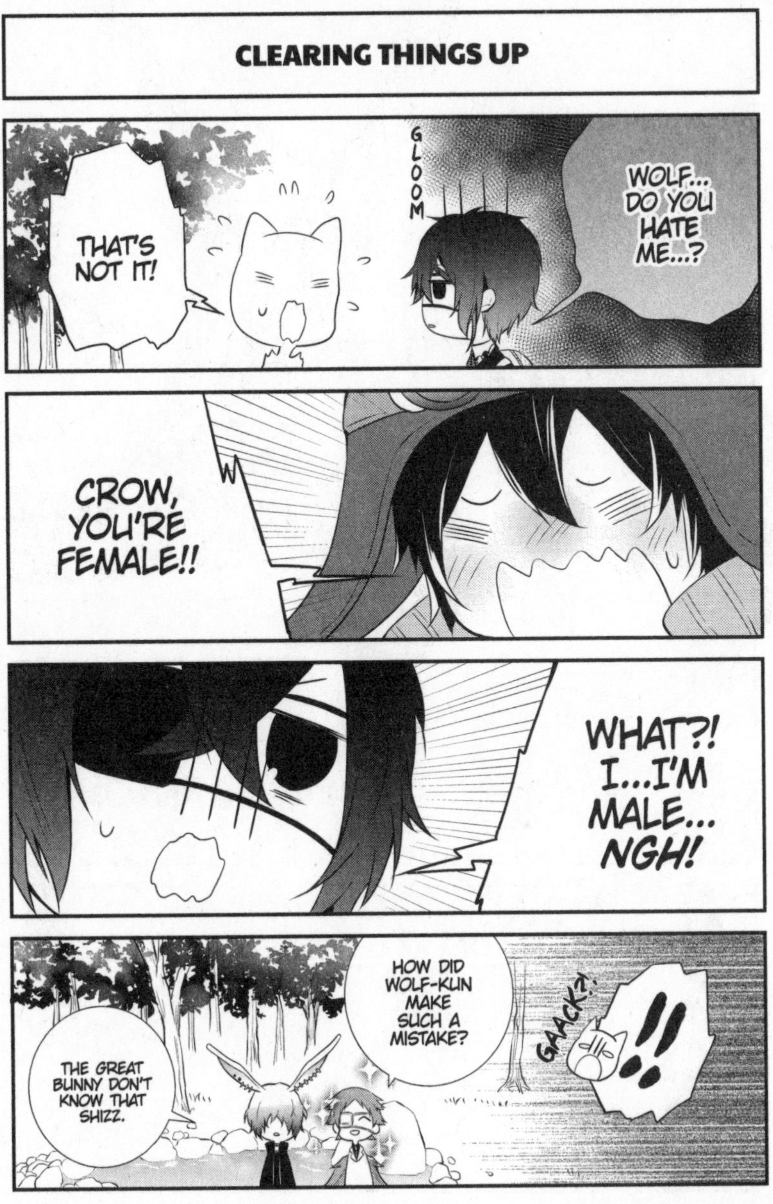
WOLF... DO YOU HATE ME...?
GLOOM
THAT'S NOT IT!
CROW, YOU'RE FEMALE!!
WHAT?! I...I'M MALE... NGH!
GAACK?!
!!
HOW DID WOLF-KUN MAKE SUCH A MISTAKE?
THE GREAT BUNNY DON'T KNOW THAT SHIZZ.

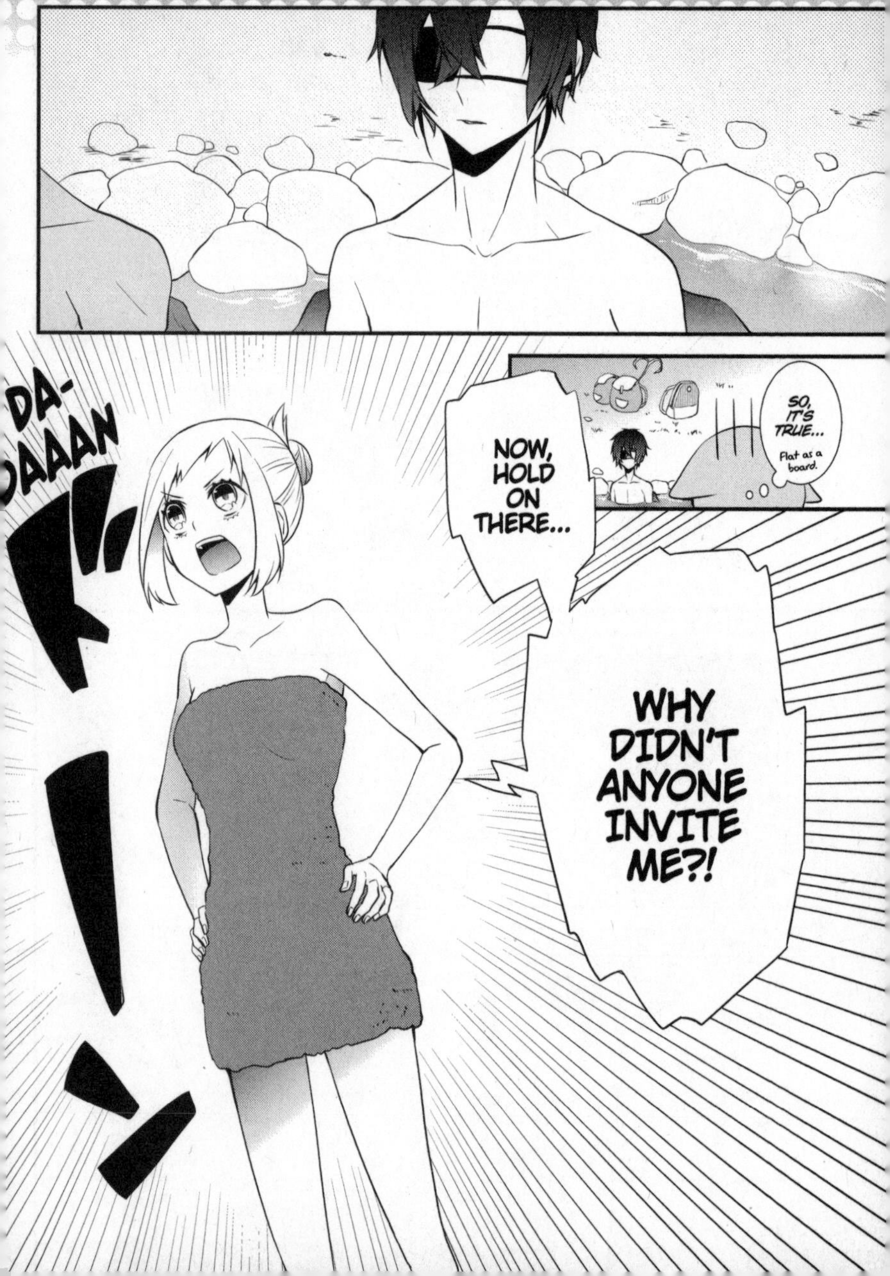
SO, IT'S TRUE...
Flat as a board.
NOW, HOLD ON THERE...
WHY DIDN'T ANYONE INVITE ME?!
DA-DAAAN

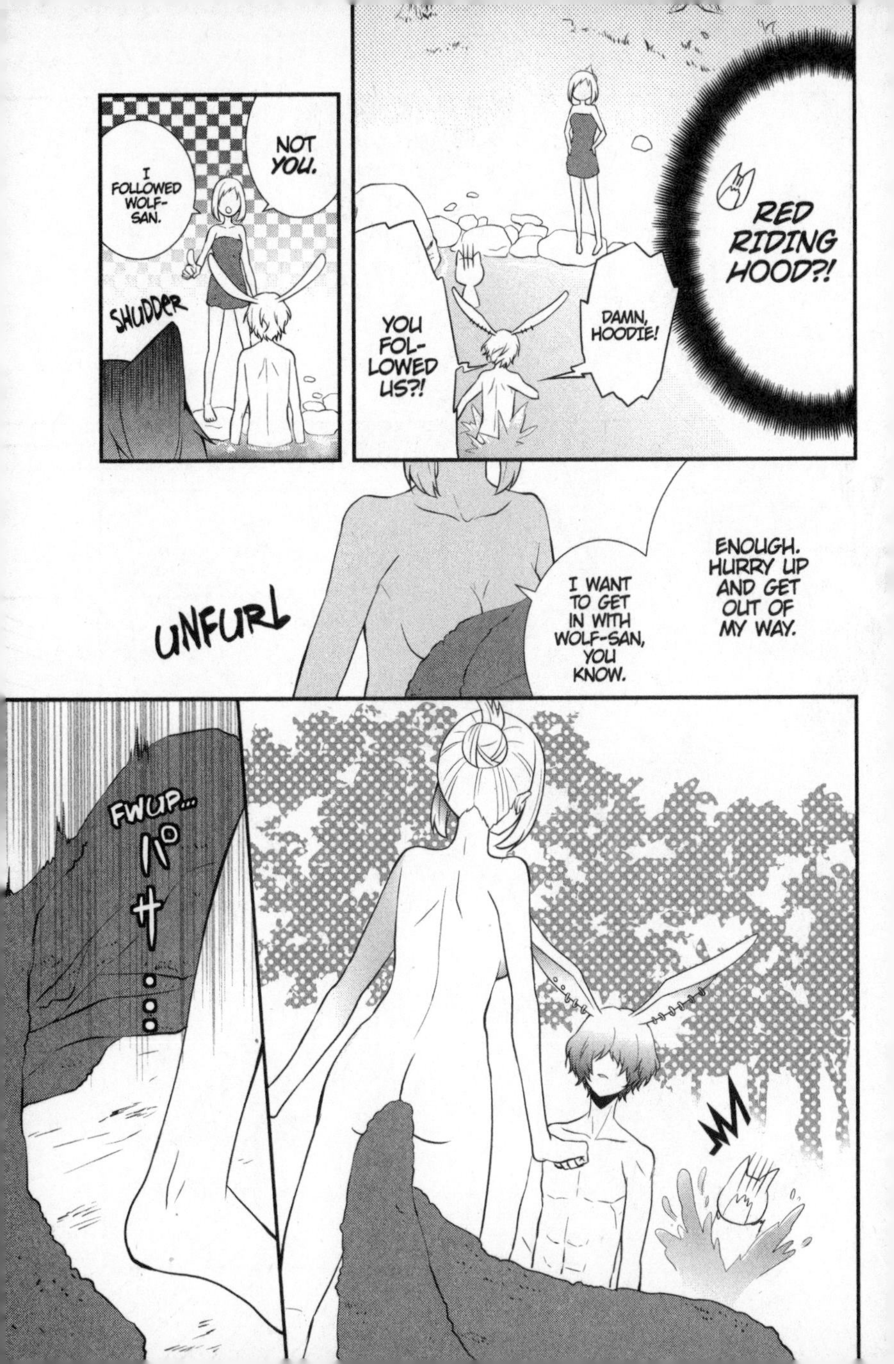
RED RIDING HOOD?!
DAMN, HOODIE!
YOU FOL-LOWED US?!
NOT YOU.
I FOLLOWED WOLF-SAN.
SHUDDER
ENOUGH. HURRY UP AND GET OUT OF MY WAY.
I WANT TO GET IN WITH WOLF-SAN, YOU KNOW.
UNFURL
FWUP...
パサ...

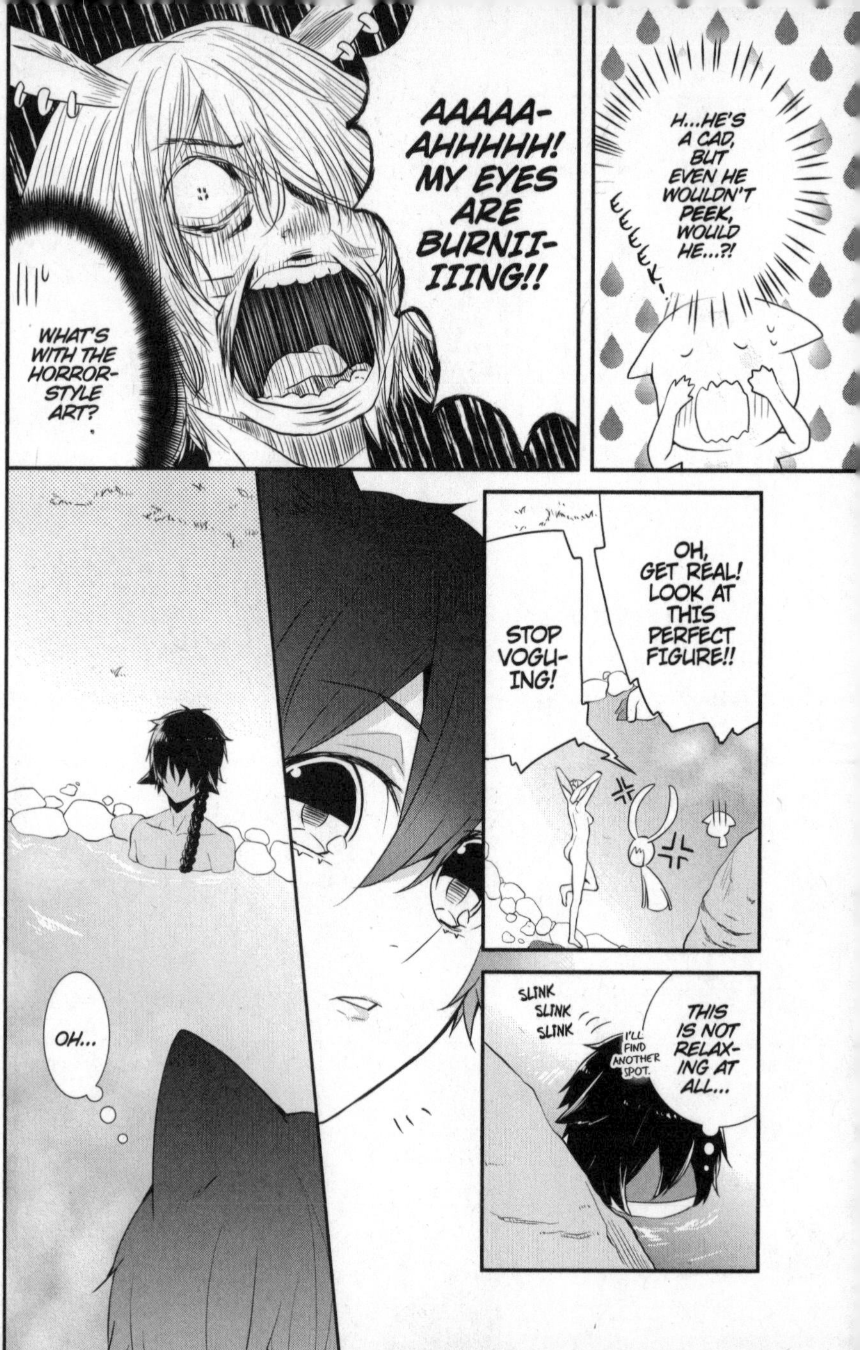
H...HE'S A CAD, BUT EVEN HE WOULDN'T PEEK, WOULD HE...?!
EEEEEK!
AAAAA-AHHHHH! MY EYES ARE BURNII-IIING!!
WHAT'S WITH THE HORROR-STYLE ART?
OH, GET REAL! LOOK AT THIS PERFECT FIGURE!!
STOP VOGU-ING!
THIS IS NOT RELAX-ING AT ALL...
SLINK SLINK SLINK
I'LL FIND ANOTHER SPOT.
OH...

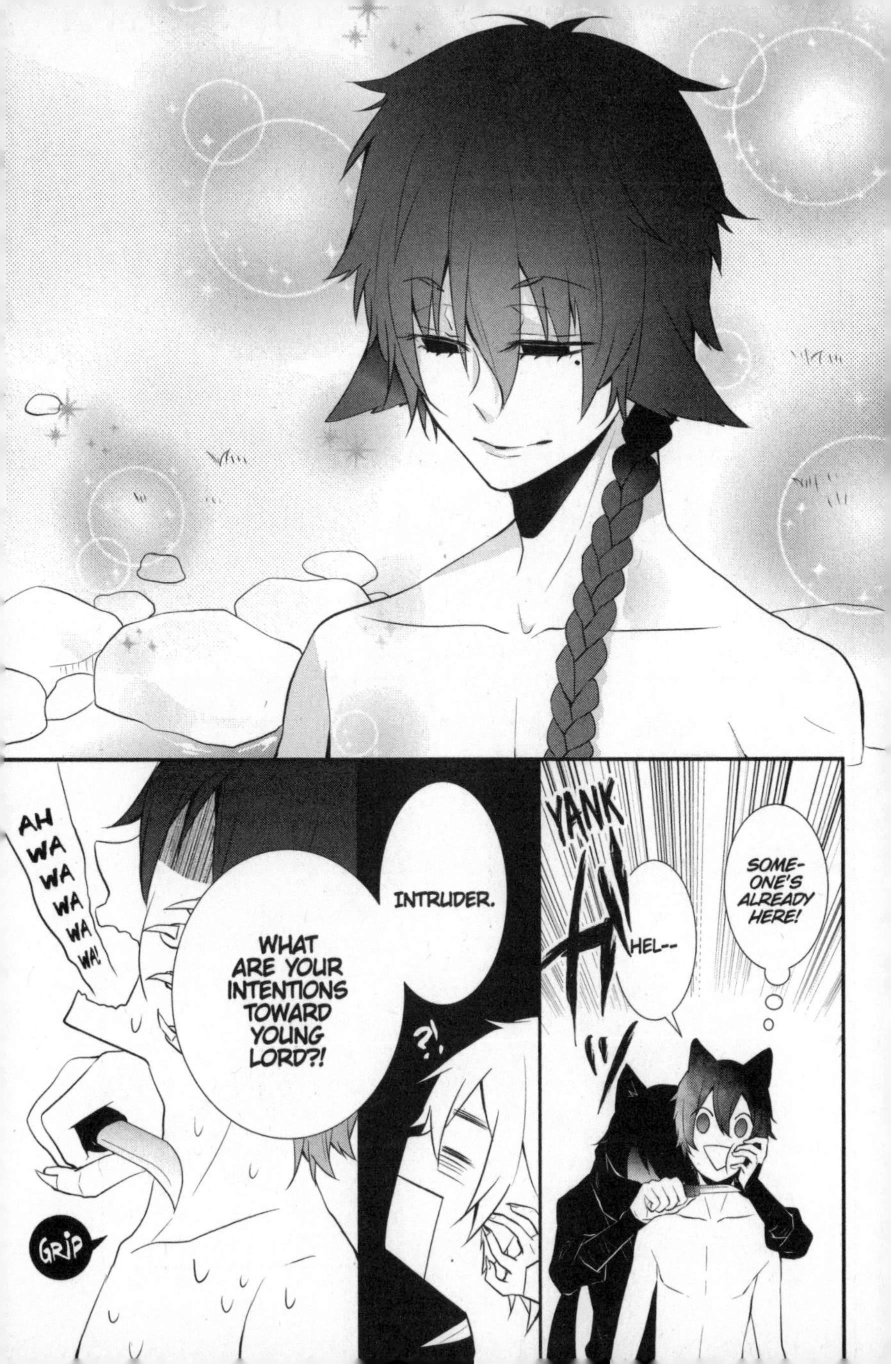
SOME-ONE'S ALREADY HERE!
HEL--
YANK
INTRUDER.
WHAT ARE YOUR INTENTIONS TOWARD YOUNG LORD?!
?!
AH WA WA WA WA WA WA!
GRIP

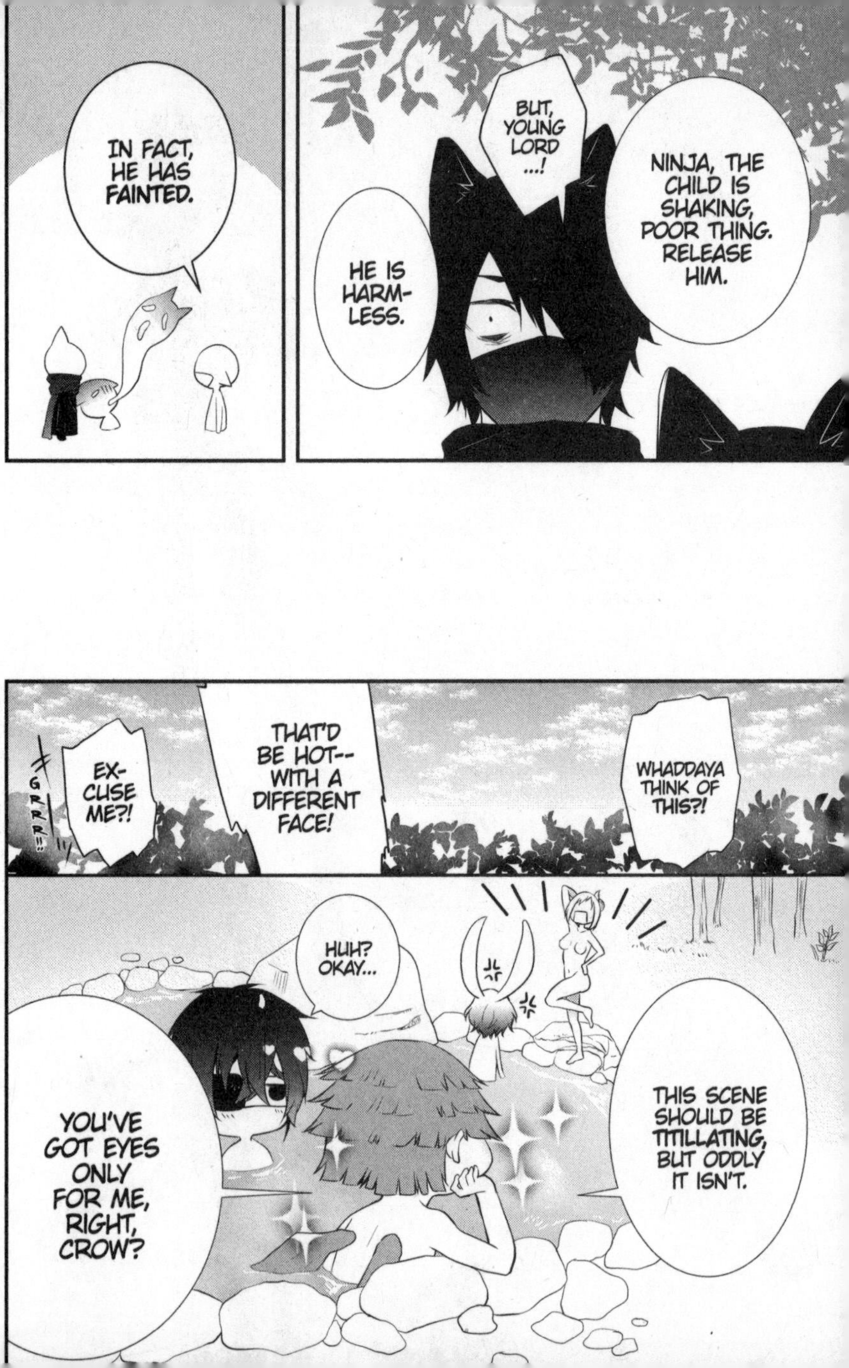
NINJA, THE CHILD IS SHAKING, POOR THING. RELEASE HIM.
BUT, YOUNG LORD ...!
HE IS HARM-LESS.
IN FACT, HE HAS FAINTED.
WHADDAYA THINK OF THIS?!
THAT'D BE HOT-- WITH A DIFFERENT FACE!
EX-CUSE ME?!
GRRR!!
THIS SCENE SHOULD BE TITILLATING, BUT ODDLY IT ISN'T.
HUH? OKAY...
YOU'VE GOT EYES ONLY FOR ME, RIGHT, CROW?

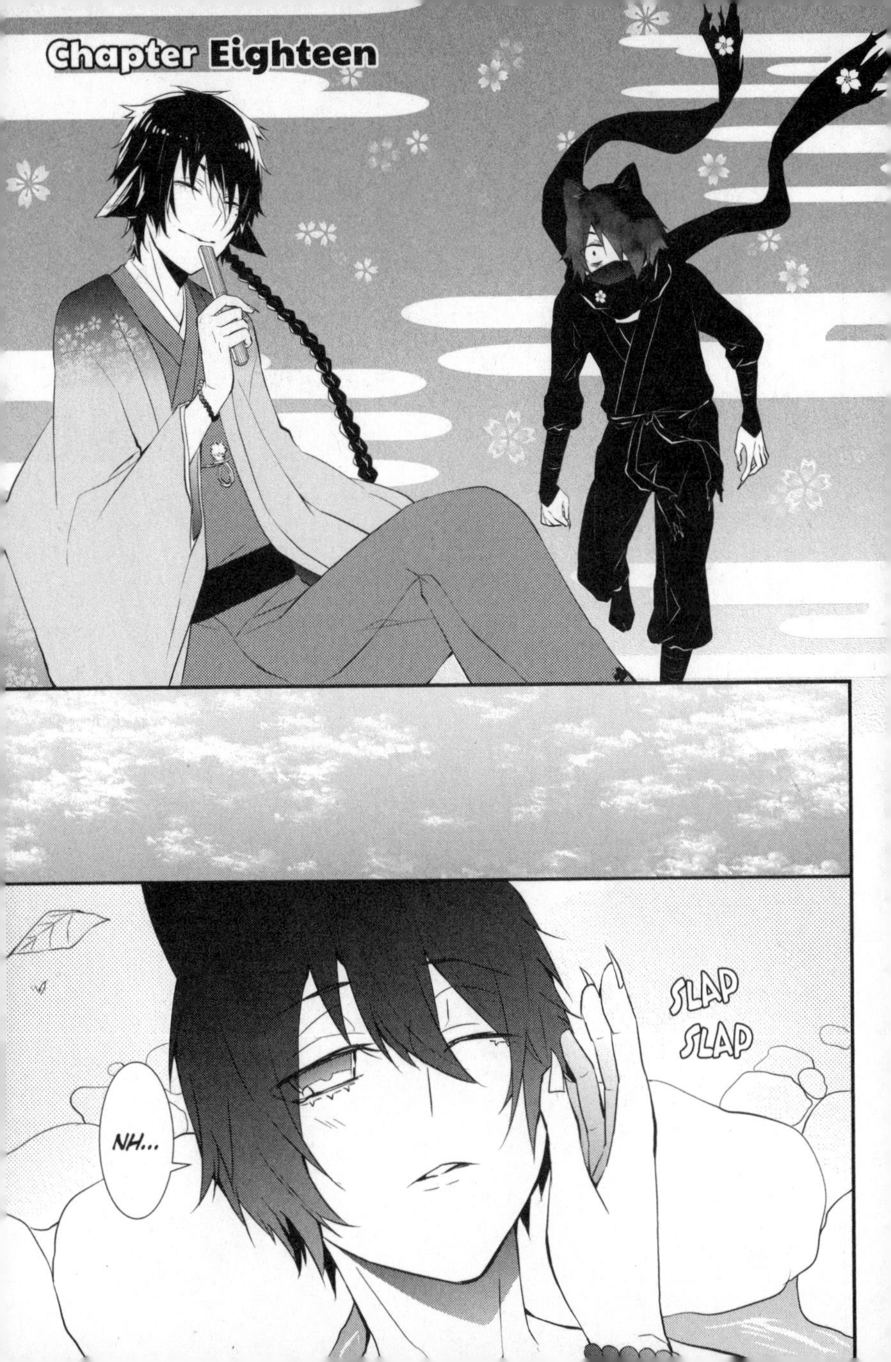
Chapter Eighteen
SLAP SLAP
NH...

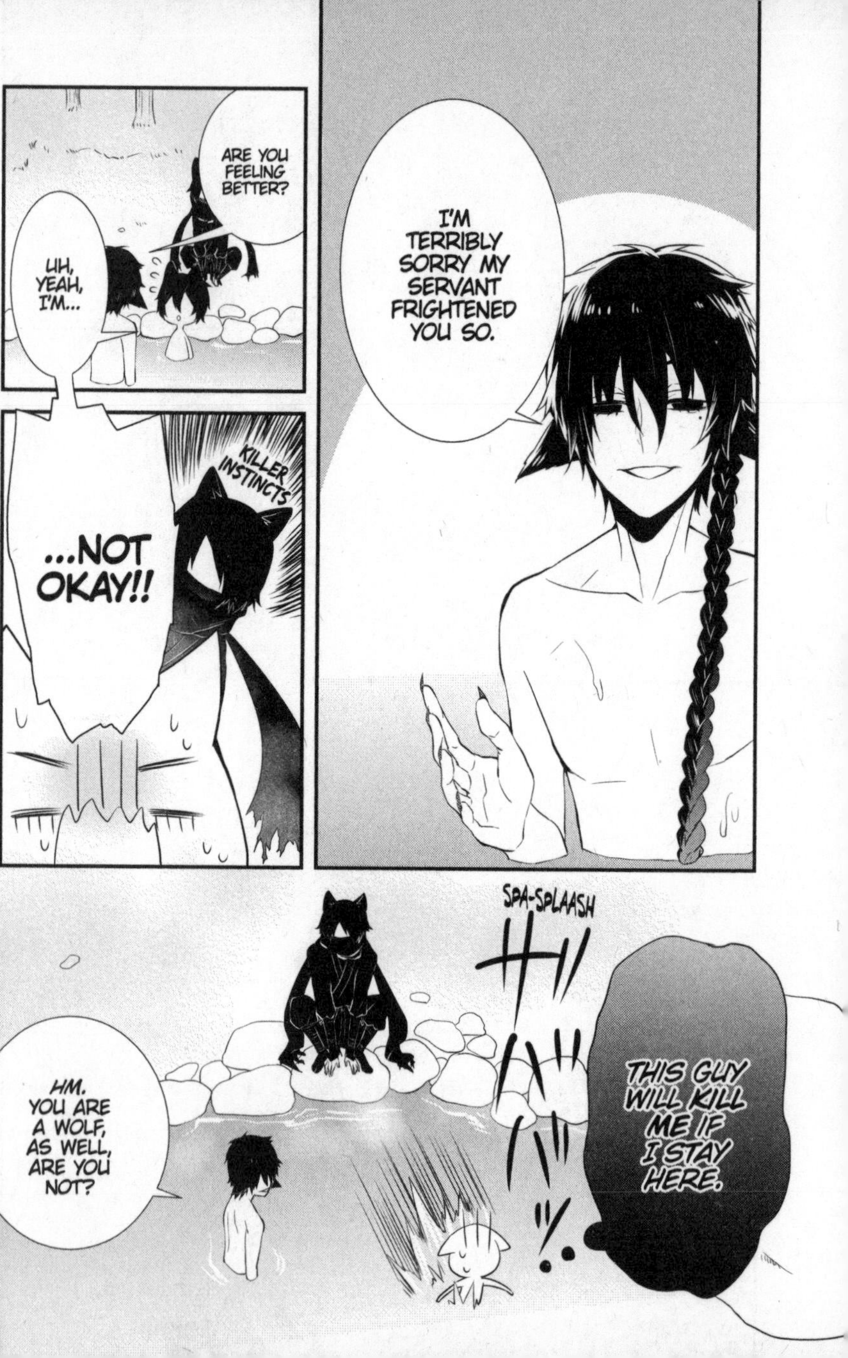
I'M TERRIBLY SORRY MY SERVANT FRIGHTENED YOU SO.
ARE YOU FEELING BETTER?
UH, YEAH, I'M...
KILLER INSTINCTS
...NOT OKAY!!
SPA-SPLAASH
THIS GUY WILL KILL ME IF I STAY HERE.
HM. YOU ARE A WOLF, AS WELL, ARE YOU NOT?

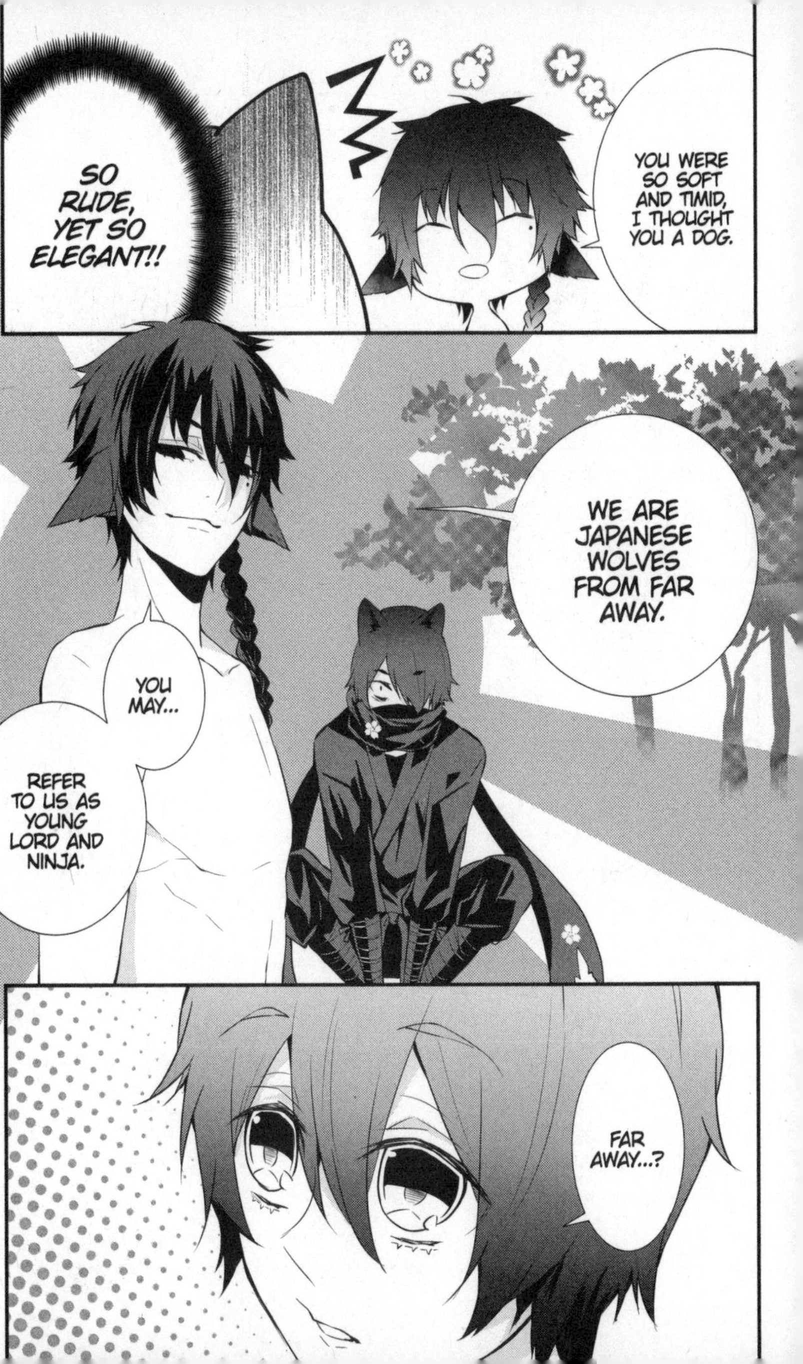
YOU WERE SO SOFT AND TIMID, I THOUGHT YOU A DOG.
SO RUDE, YET SO ELEGANT!!
WE ARE JAPANESE WOLVES FROM FAR AWAY.
YOU MAY...
REFER TO US AS YOUNG LORD AND NINJA.
FAR AWAY...?

MUCH TOO WEIGHTY A SITUATION

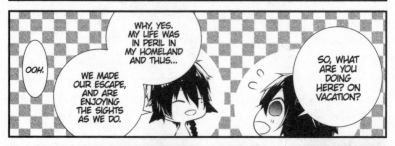

SO, WHAT ARE YOU DOING HERE? ON VACATION?
WHY, YES. MY LIFE WAS IN PERIL IN MY HOMELAND AND THUS...
WE MADE OUR ESCAPE, AND ARE ENJOYING THE SIGHTS AS WE DO.
OOH.
HUH...?
YOU SEE, MY FAMILY IS A LARGE AND INFLUENTIAL IN THE WORLD OF ORGANIZED CRIME...
HOWEVER, OF LATE, WE HAVE BECOME DIVIDED INTO TWO FACTIONS, WHICH LED TO A BLOODY FEUD.
MY LORD FATHER, THE LEADER OF HIS FACTION, WAS MURDERED...
AND, AS MY OWN LIFE WAS IN GRAVE DANGER, I ESCAPED AND FLED TO THIS PLACE.
THE WOLF HAD NO WORDS.

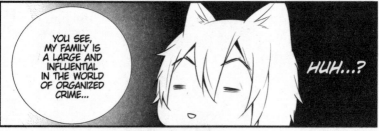

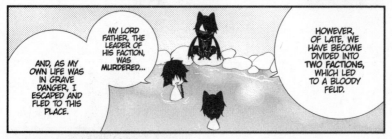

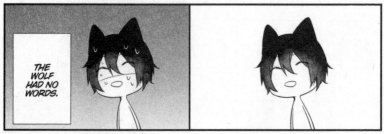

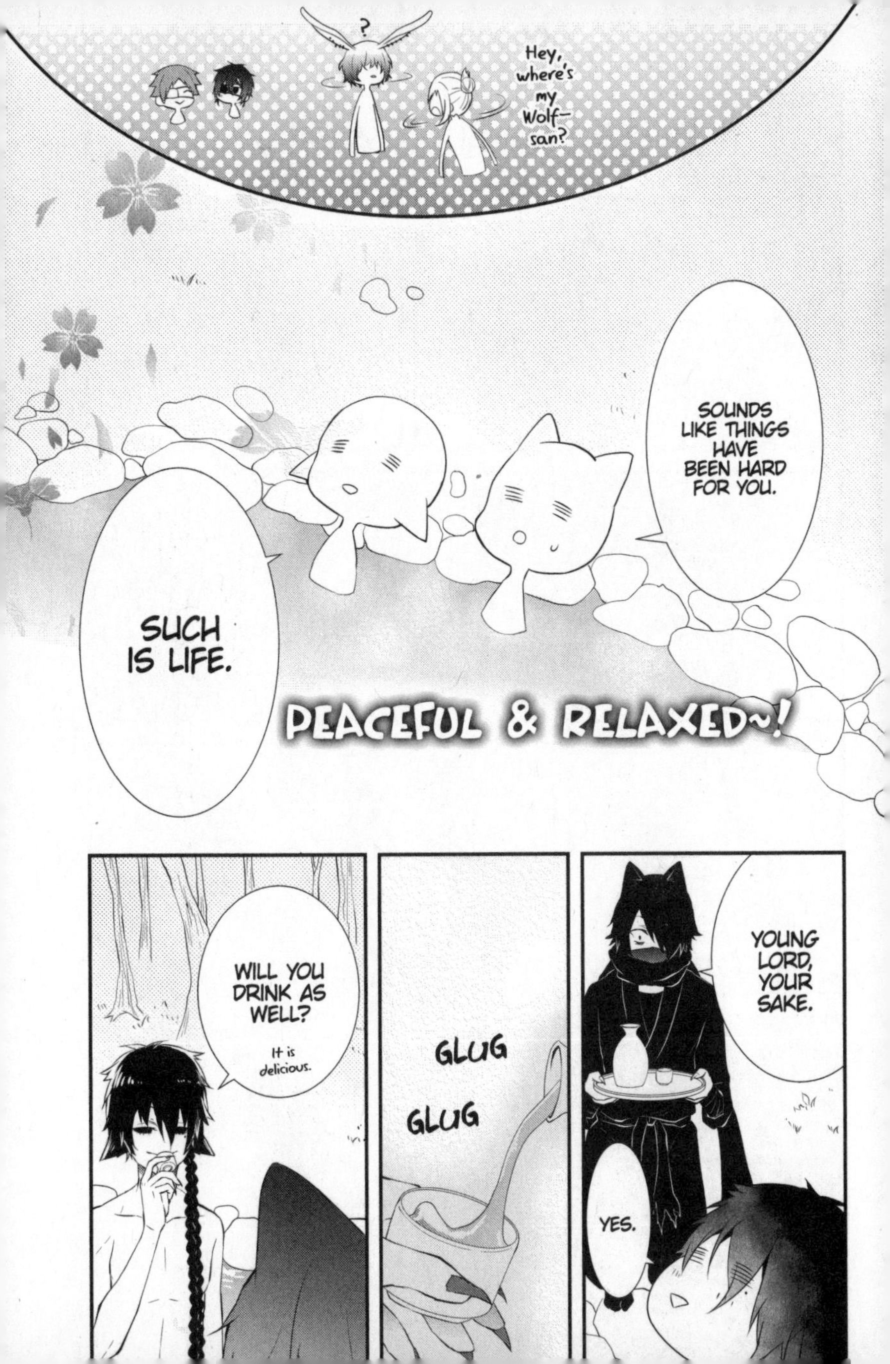
Hey, where's my Wolf-san?
SOUNDS LIKE THINGS HAVE BEEN HARD FOR YOU.
SUCH IS LIFE.
PEACEFUL & RELAXED~!
YOUNG LORD, YOUR SAKE.
YES.
GLUG
GLUG
WILL YOU DRINK AS WELL?
It is delicious.

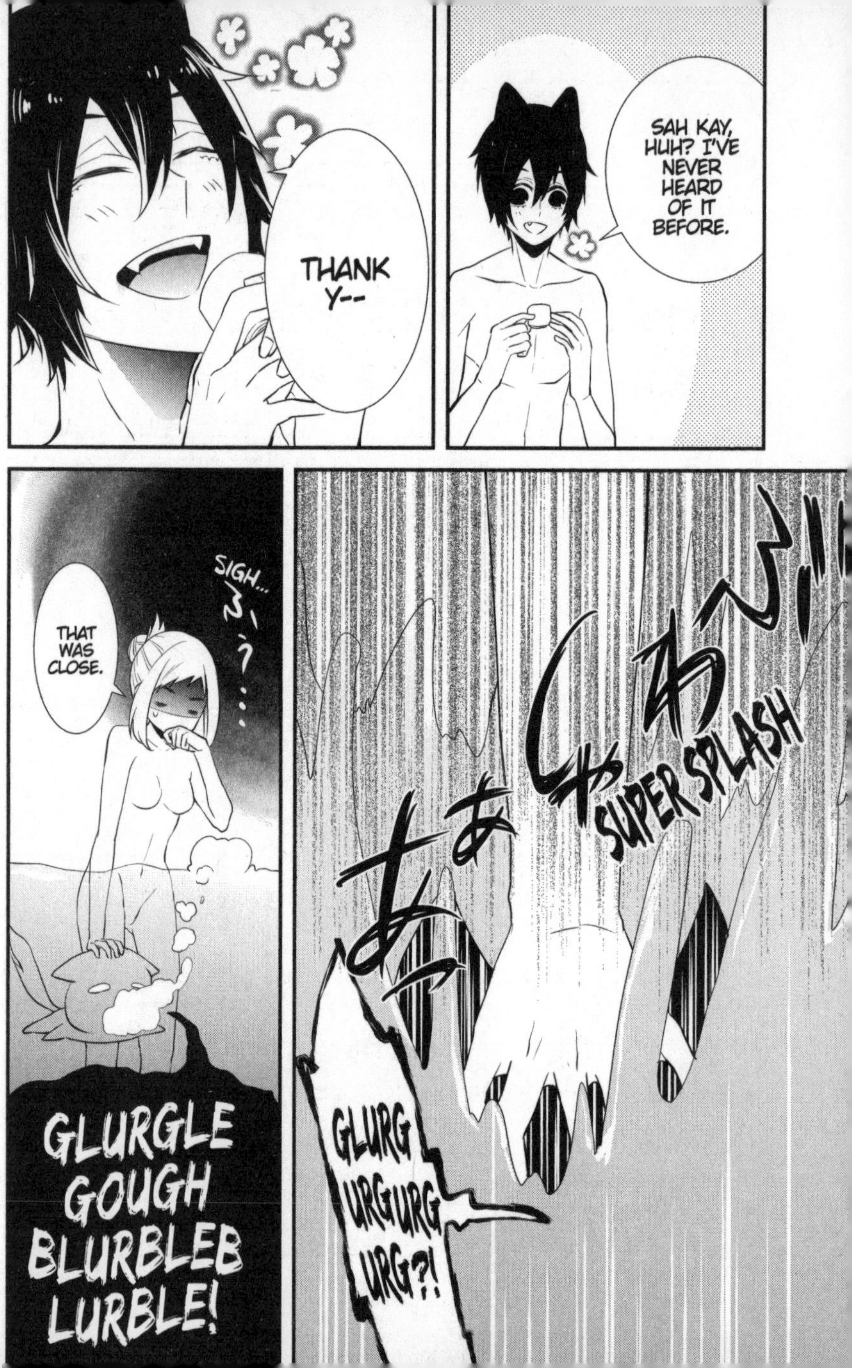
SAH KAY, HUH? I'VE NEVER HEARD OF IT BEFORE.
THANK Y--
SUPER SPLASH
GLURG URGURG URG?!
SIGH... ふぅ...
THAT WAS CLOSE.
GLURGLE GOUGH BLURBLEB LURBLE!

ENCORE

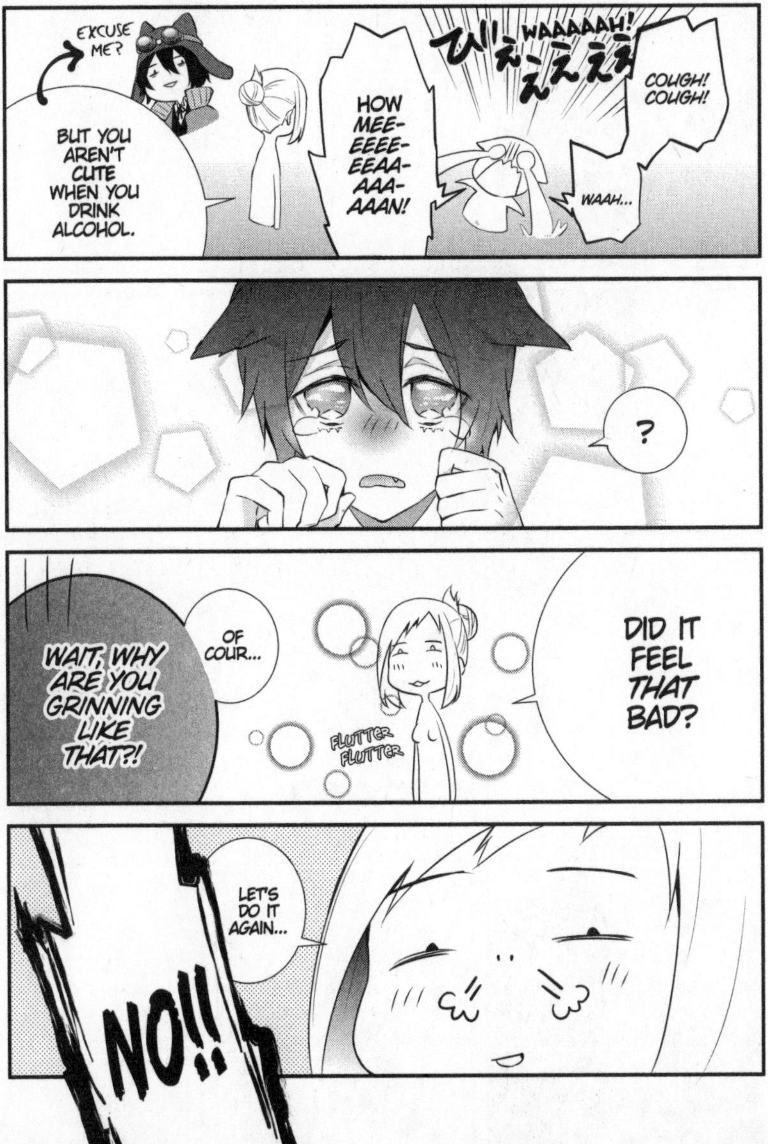
COUGH! COUGH!
WAAAAAH!
WAAH...
HOW MEE-EEEE-EEAA-AAA-AAAN!
EXCUSE ME?
BUT YOU AREN'T CUTE WHEN YOU DRINK ALCOHOL.
?
DID IT FEEL THAT BAD?
OF COUR...
FLUTTER FLUTTER
WAIT, WHY ARE YOU GRINNING LIKE THAT?!
LET'S DO IT AGAIN...
NO!!

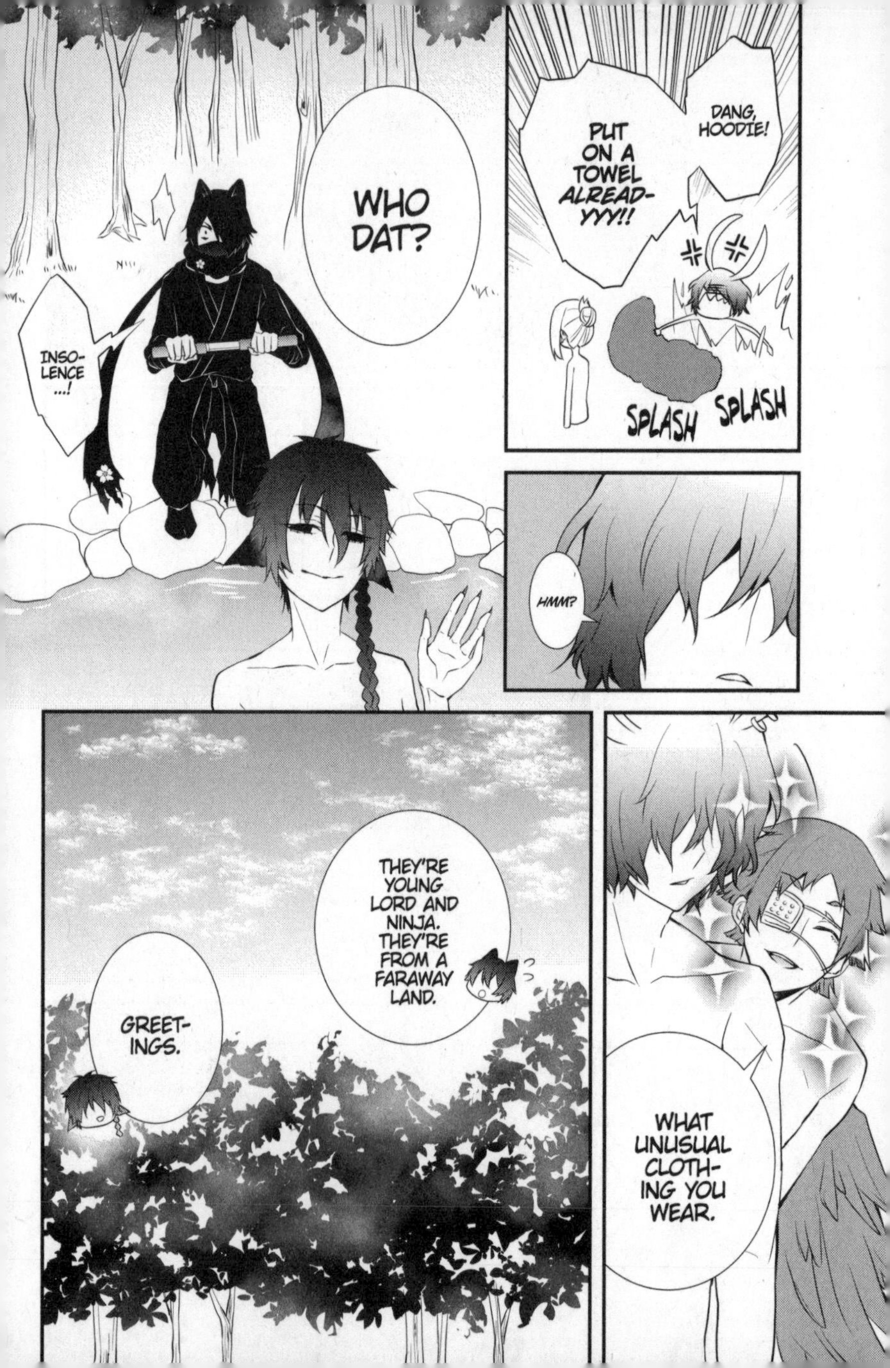
DANG, HOODIE!
PUT ON A TOWEL ALREAD-YYY!!
SPLASH
SPLASH
HMM?
WHO DAT?
INSO-LENCE ...!
WHAT UNUSUAL CLOTH-ING YOU WEAR.
THEY'RE YOUNG LORD AND NINJA. THEY'RE FROM A FARAWAY LAND.
GREET-INGS.

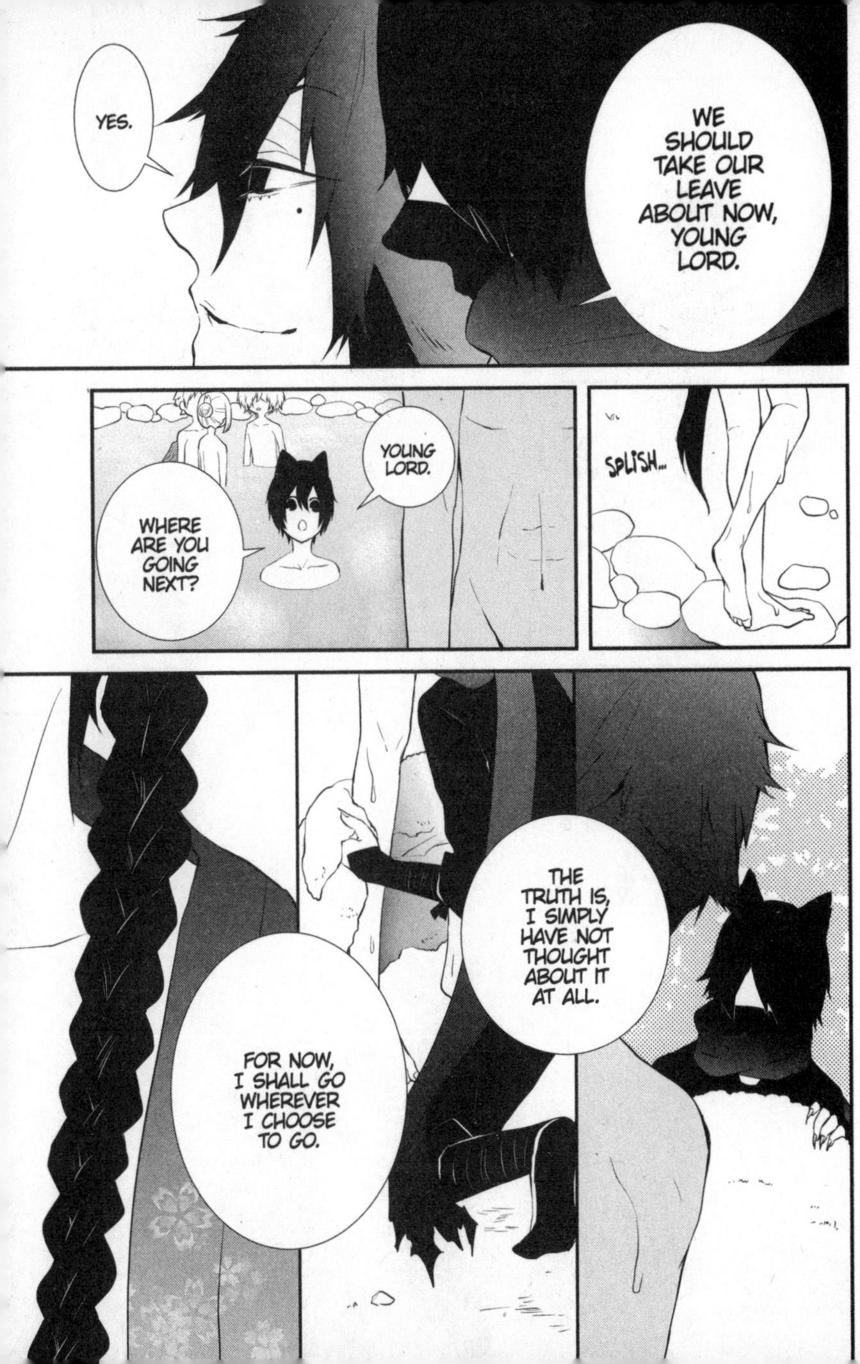
WE SHOULD TAKE OUR LEAVE ABOUT NOW, YOUNG LORD.
YES.
SPLISH...
YOUNG LORD.
WHERE ARE YOU GOING NEXT?
THE TRUTH IS, I SIMPLY HAVE NOT THOUGHT ABOUT IT AT ALL.
FOR NOW, I SHALL GO WHEREVER I CHOOSE TO GO.

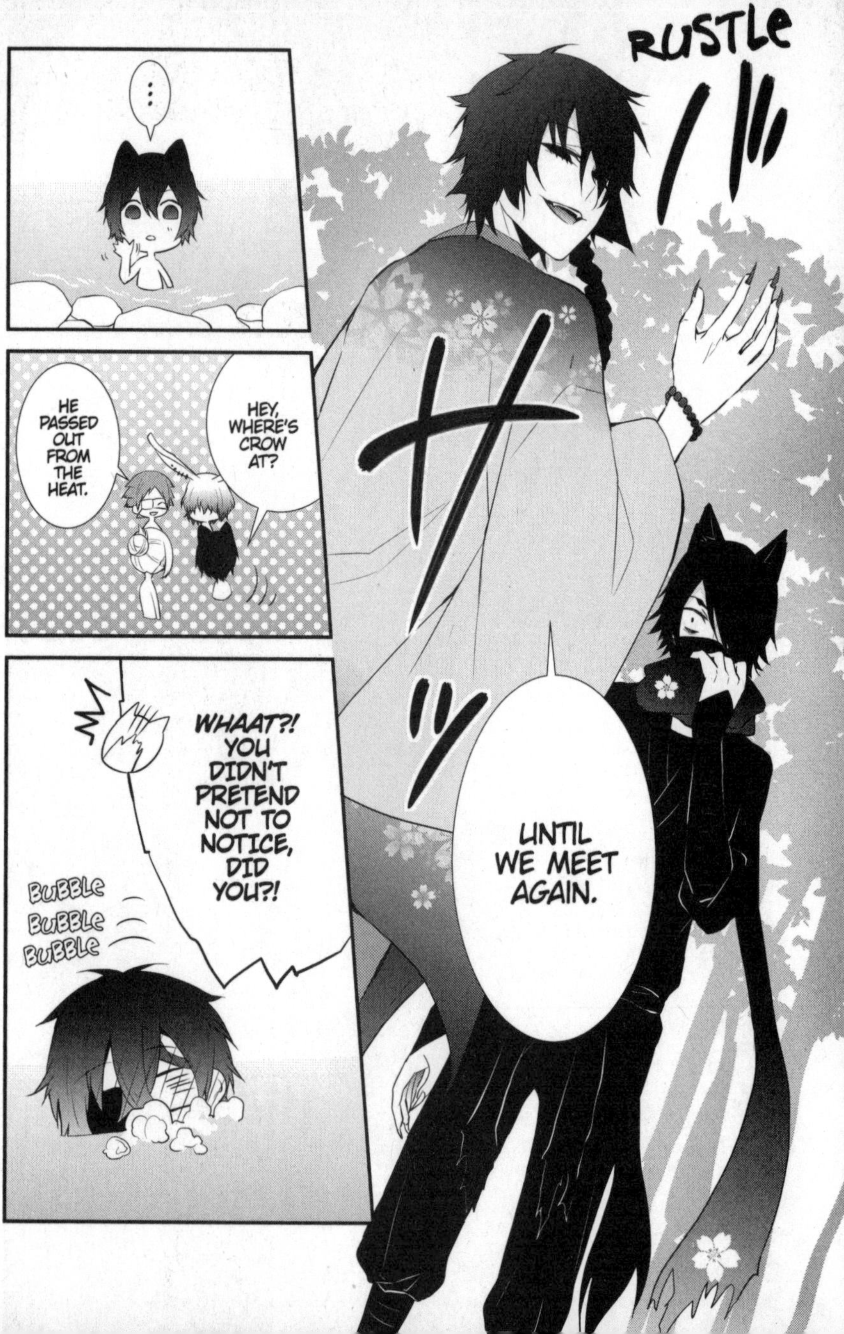
RUSTLE
UNTIL WE MEET AGAIN.
...
HEY, WHERE'S CROW AT?
HE PASSED OUT FROM THE HEAT.
WHAAT?! YOU DIDN'T PRETEND NOT TO NOTICE, DID YOU?!
BUBBLE
BUBBLE
BUBBLE

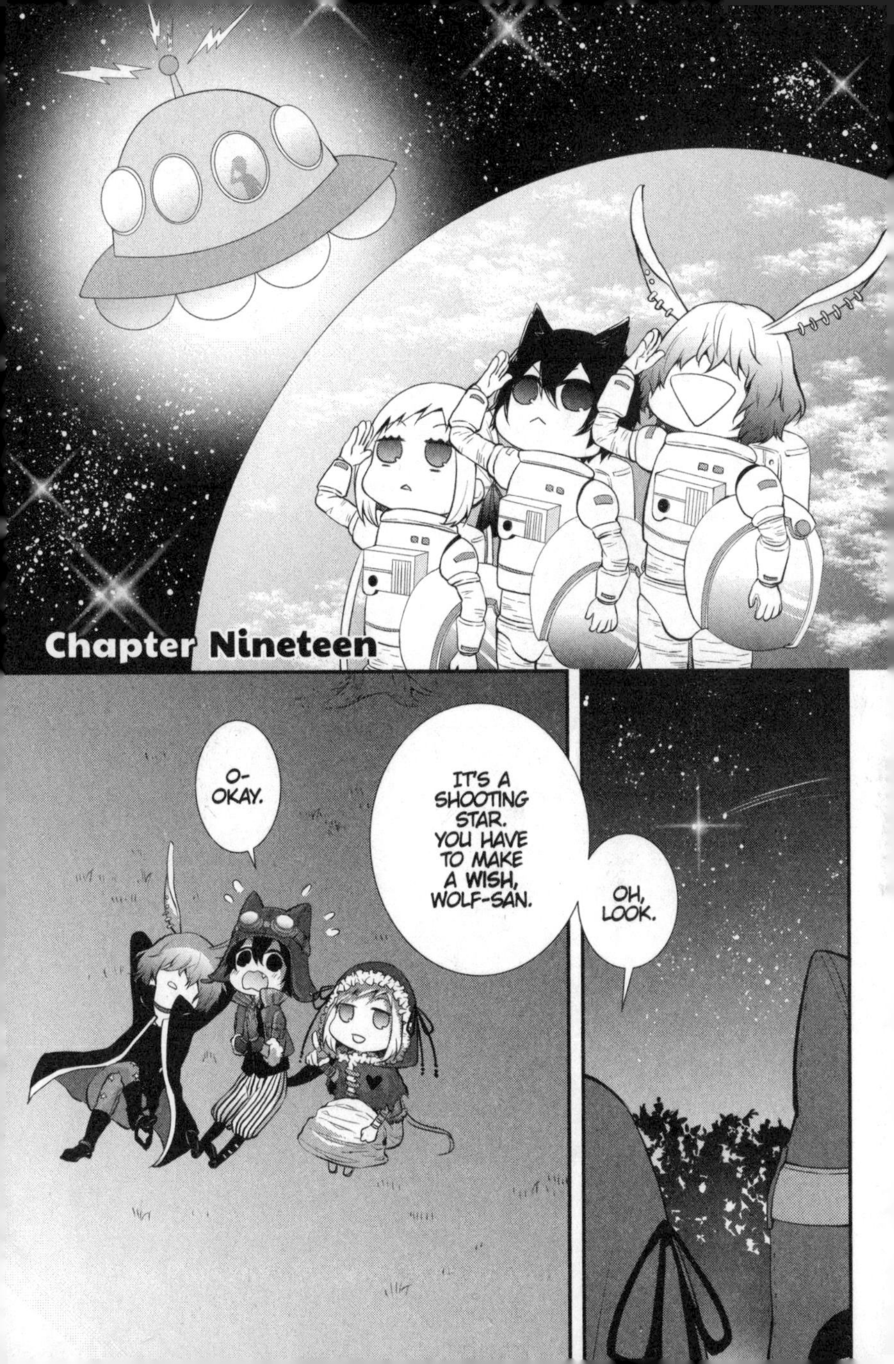
Chapter Nineteen
OH, LOOK.
IT'S A SHOOTING STAR. YOU HAVE TO MAKE A WISH, WOLF-SAN.
O-OKAY.

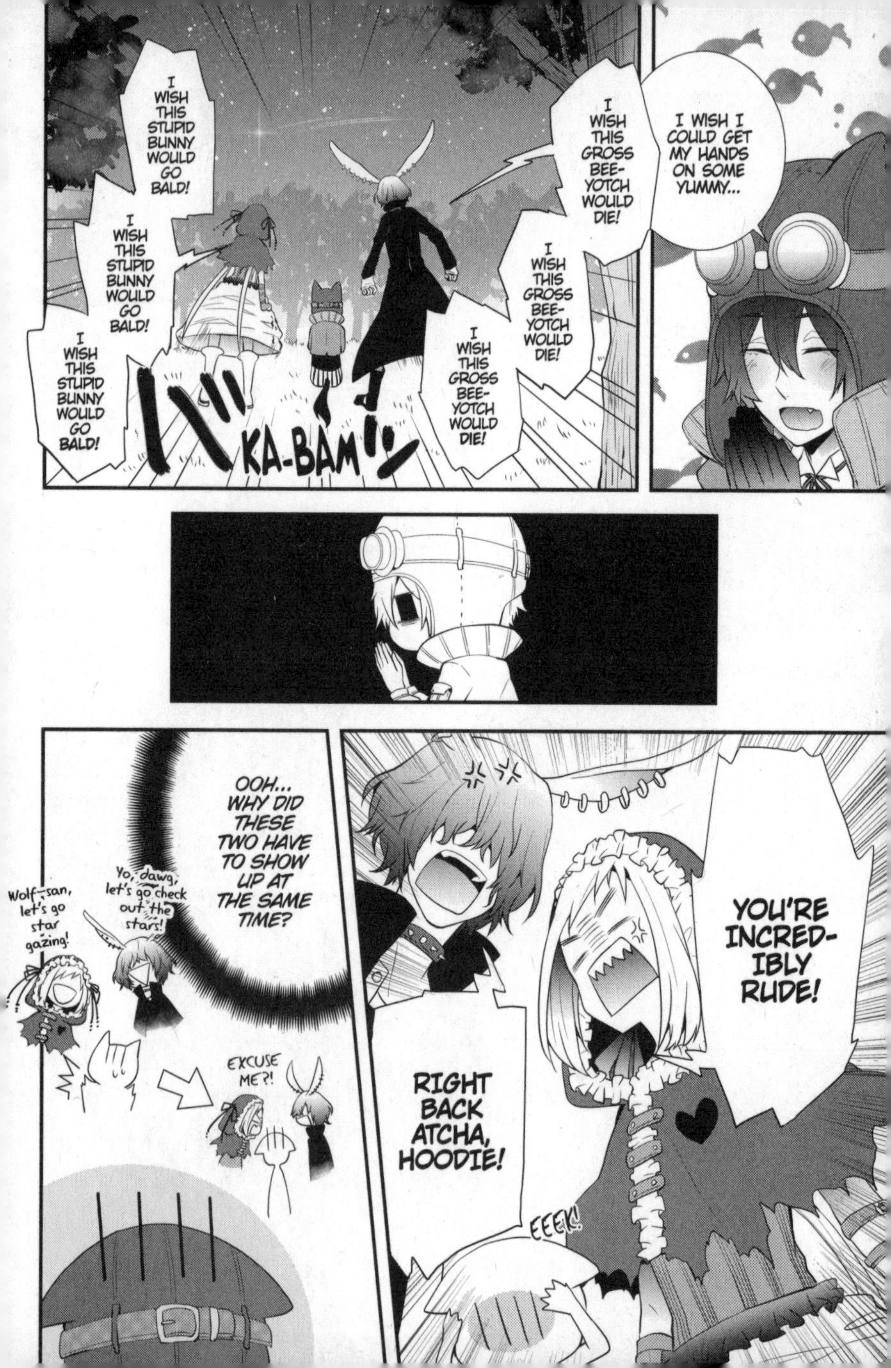
I WISH I COULD GET MY HANDS ON SOME YUMMY...
I WISH THIS GROSS BEE-YOTCH WOULD DIE!
I WISH THIS GROSS BEE-YOTCH WOULD DIE!
I WISH THIS GROSS BEE-YOTCH WOULD DIE!
I WISH THIS STUPID BUNNY WOULD GO BALD!
I WISH THIS STUPID BUNNY WOULD GO BALD!
I WISH THIS STUPID BUNNY WOULD GO BALD!
KA-BAM
YOU'RE INCREDIBLY RUDE!
RIGHT BACK ATCHA, HOODIE!
EEEK!
OOH... WHY DID THESE TWO HAVE TO SHOW UP AT THE SAME TIME?
Yo, dawg, let's go check out the stars!
Wolf-san, let's go star gazing!
EXCUSE ME?!

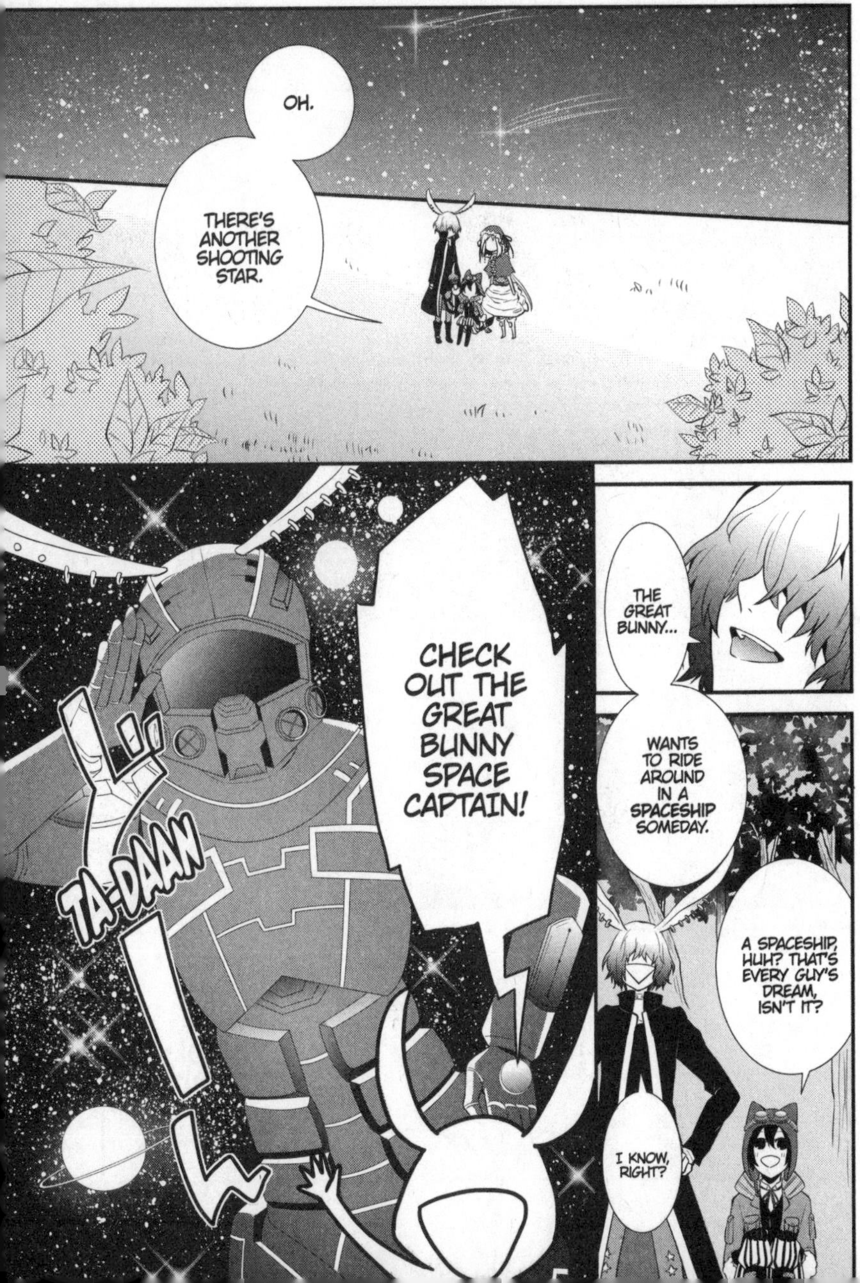
OH.
THERE'S ANOTHER SHOOTING STAR.
THE GREAT BUNNY...
WANTS TO RIDE AROUND IN A SPACESHIP SOMEDAY.
A SPACESHIP, HUH? THAT'S EVERY GUY'S DREAM, ISN'T IT?
I KNOW, RIGHT?
CHECK OUT THE GREAT BUNNY SPACE CAPTAIN!
TA-DAAN

LOST IN SPACE

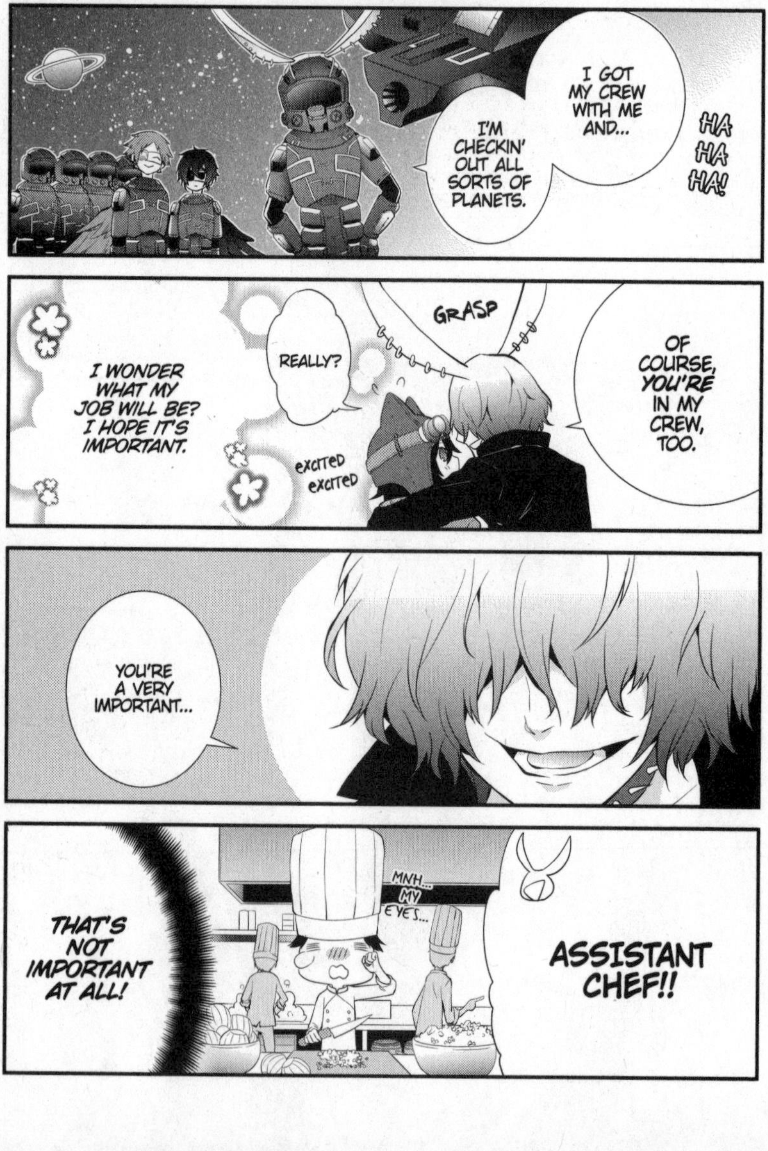
HA HA HA!
I GOT MY CREW WITH ME AND...
I'M CHECKIN' OUT ALL SORTS OF PLANETS.
OF COURSE, YOU'RE IN MY CREW, TOO.
GRASP
REALLY?
excited excited
I WONDER WHAT MY JOB WILL BE? I HOPE IT'S IMPORTANT.
YOU'RE A VERY IMPORTANT...
ASSISTANT CHEF!!
MNH... MY EYES...
THAT'S NOT IMPORTANT AT ALL!

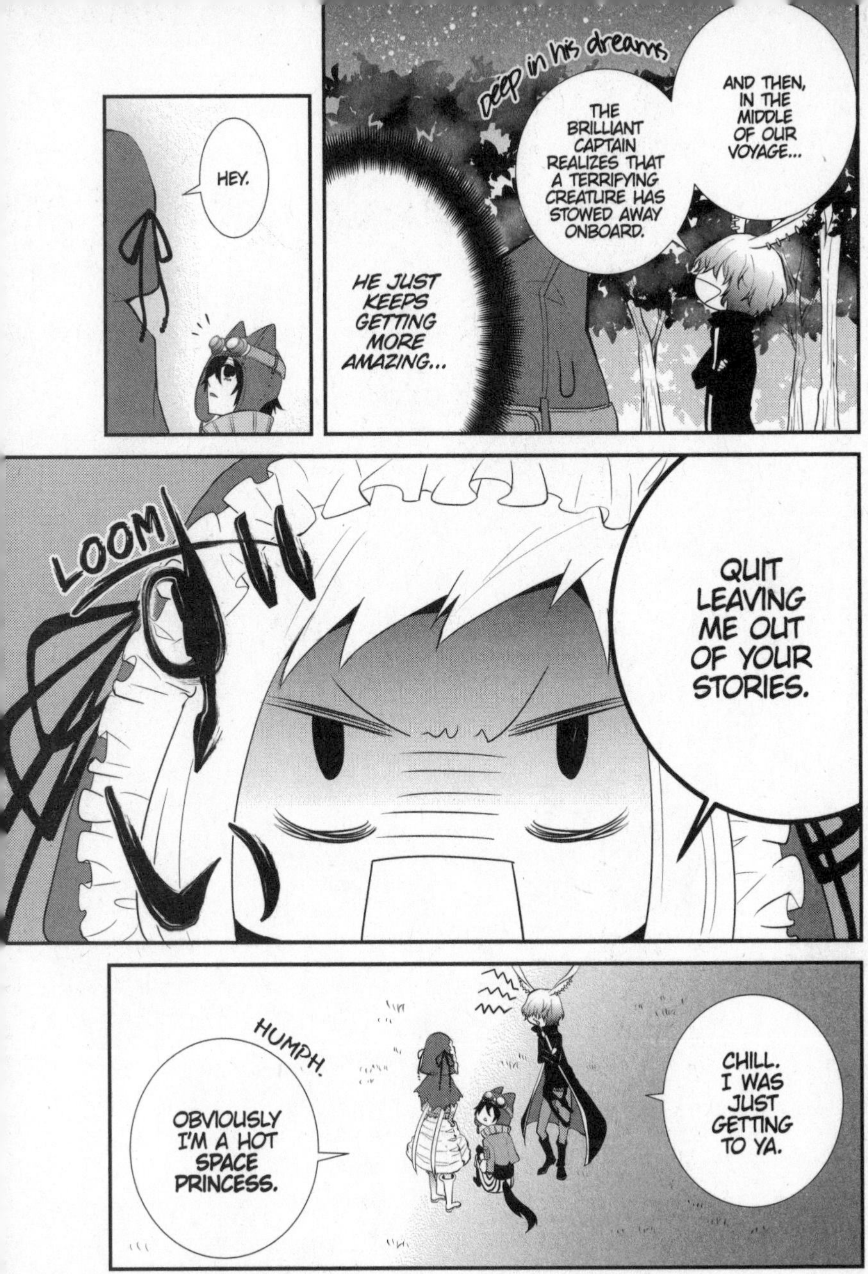
deep in his dreams
AND THEN, IN THE MIDDLE OF OUR VOYAGE...
THE BRILLIANT CAPTAIN REALIZES THAT A TERRIFYING CREATURE HAS STOWED AWAY ONBOARD.
HE JUST KEEPS GETTING MORE AMAZING...
HEY.
QUIT LEAVING ME OUT OF YOUR STORIES.
LOOM
CHILL. I WAS JUST GETTING TO YA.
HUMPH.
OBVIOUSLY I'M A HOT SPACE PRINCESS.

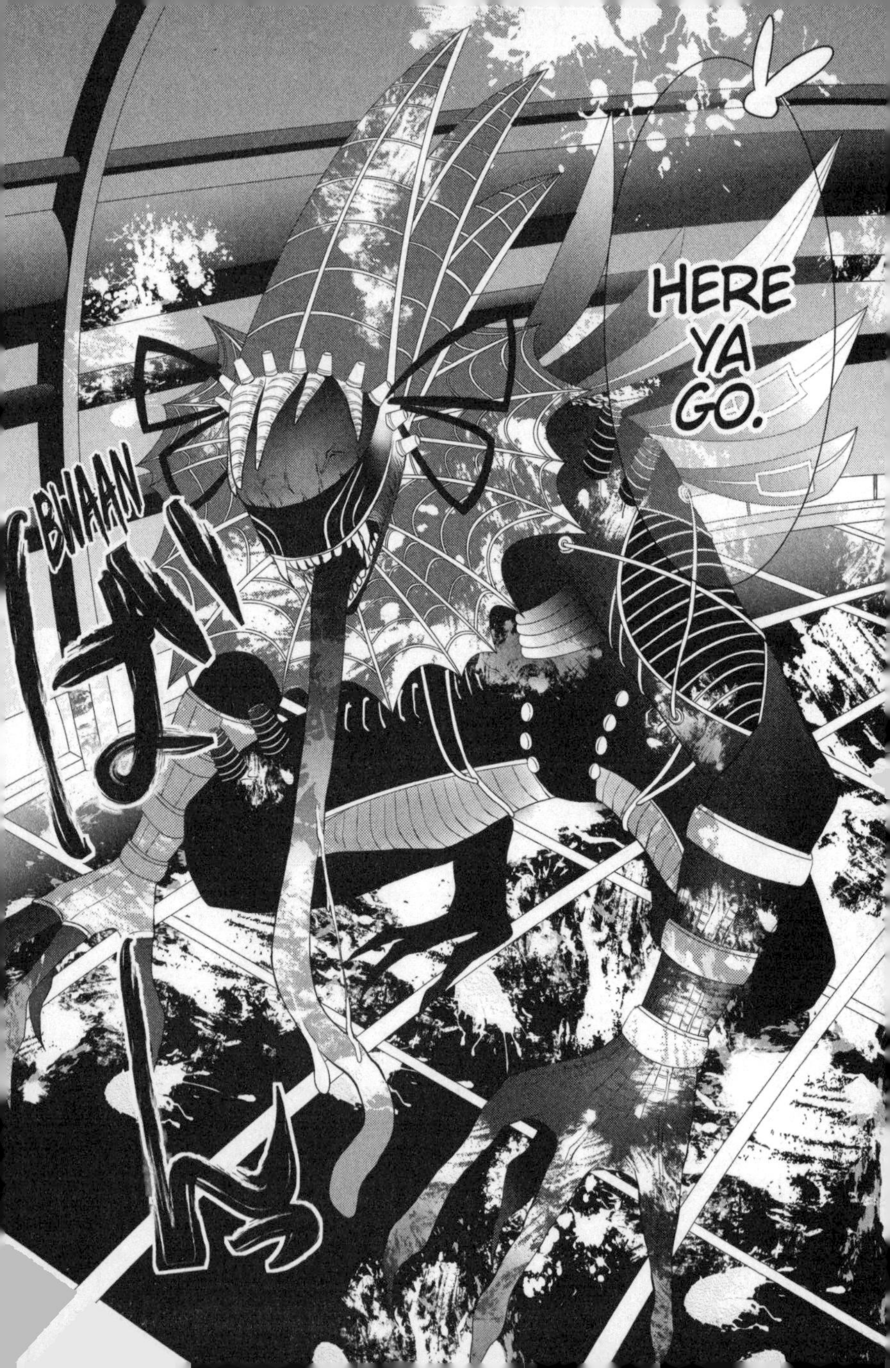
HERE YA GO.
BWAAN

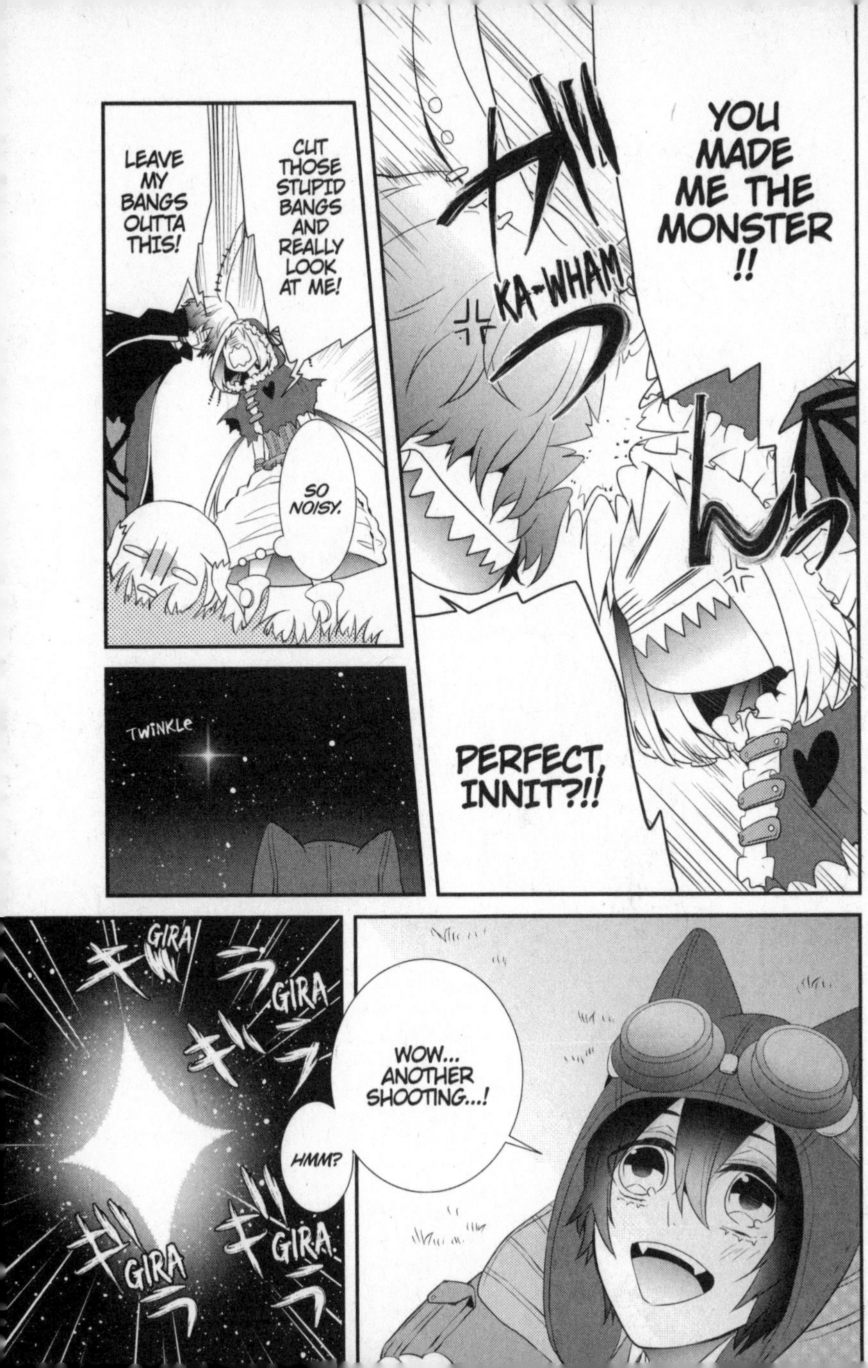
YOU MADE ME THE MONSTER!!
KA-WHAM
PERFECT, INNIT?!!
CUT THOSE STUPID BANGS AND REALLY LOOK AT ME!
LEAVE MY BANGS OUTTA THIS!
SO NOISY.
TWINKLE
WOW... ANOTHER SHOOTING...!
HMM?
GIRA
GIRA
GIRA
GIRA

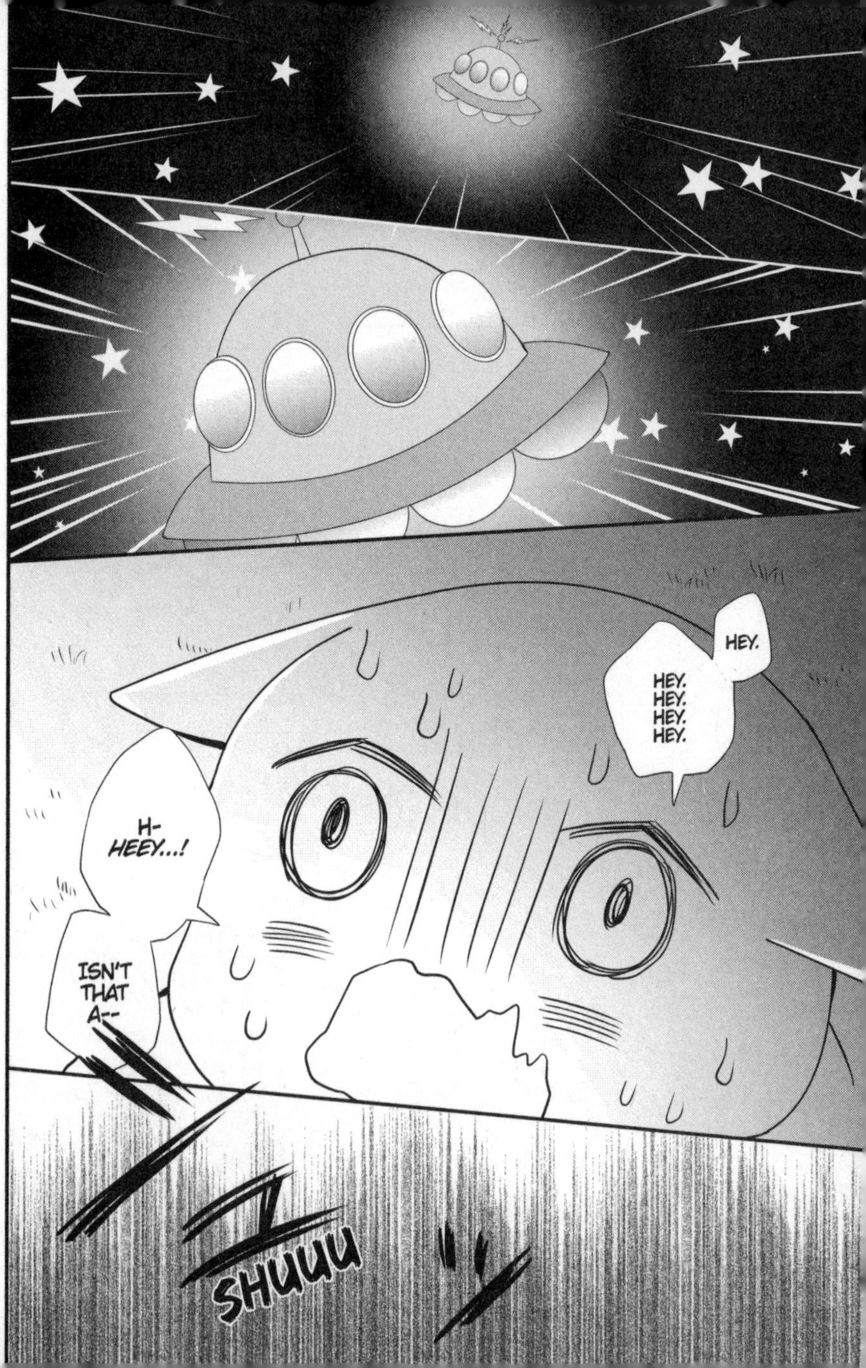
HEY.
HEY. HEY. HEY. HEY.
H- HEEY...!
ISN'T THAT A--
SHUUU

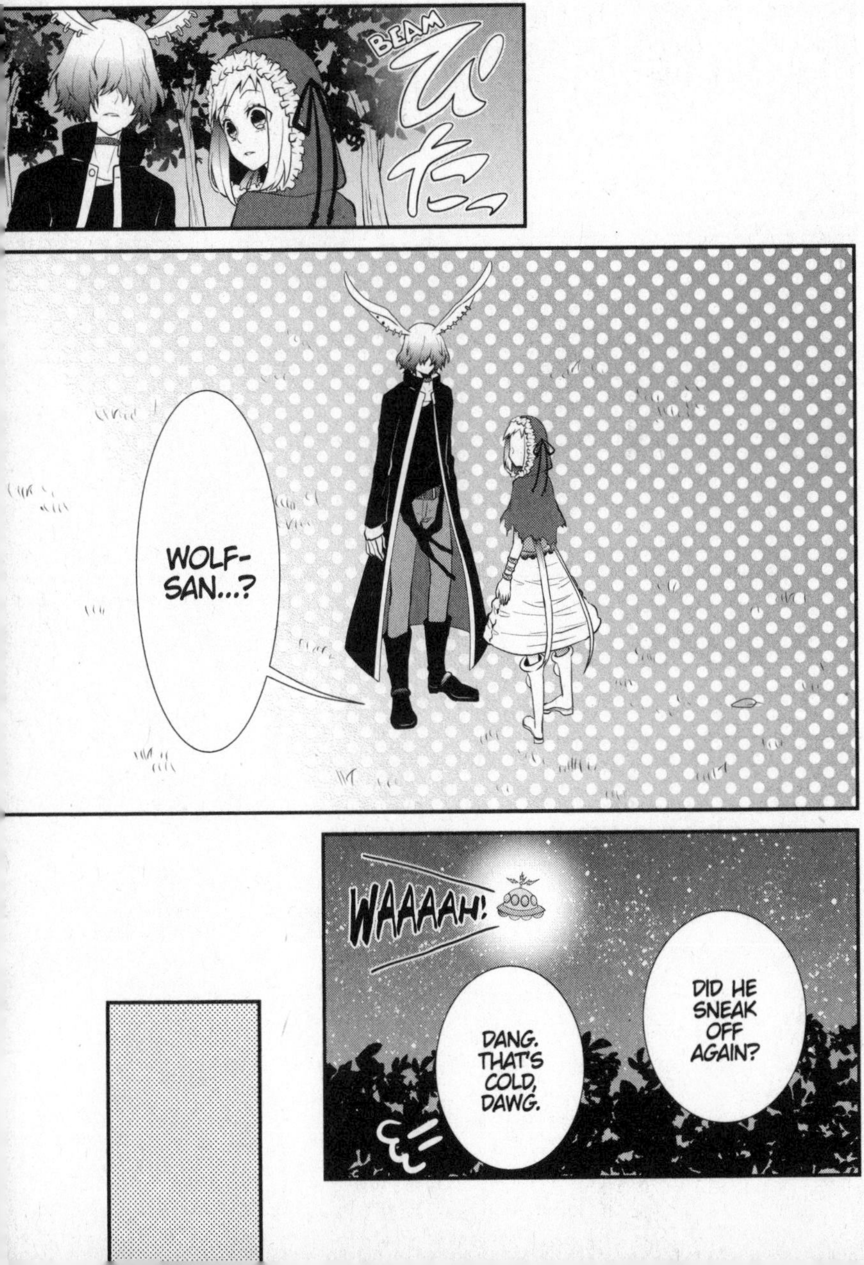
BEAM
WOLF-SAN...?
DID HE SNEAK OFF AGAIN?
DANG. THAT'S COLD, DAWG.
WAAAAH!

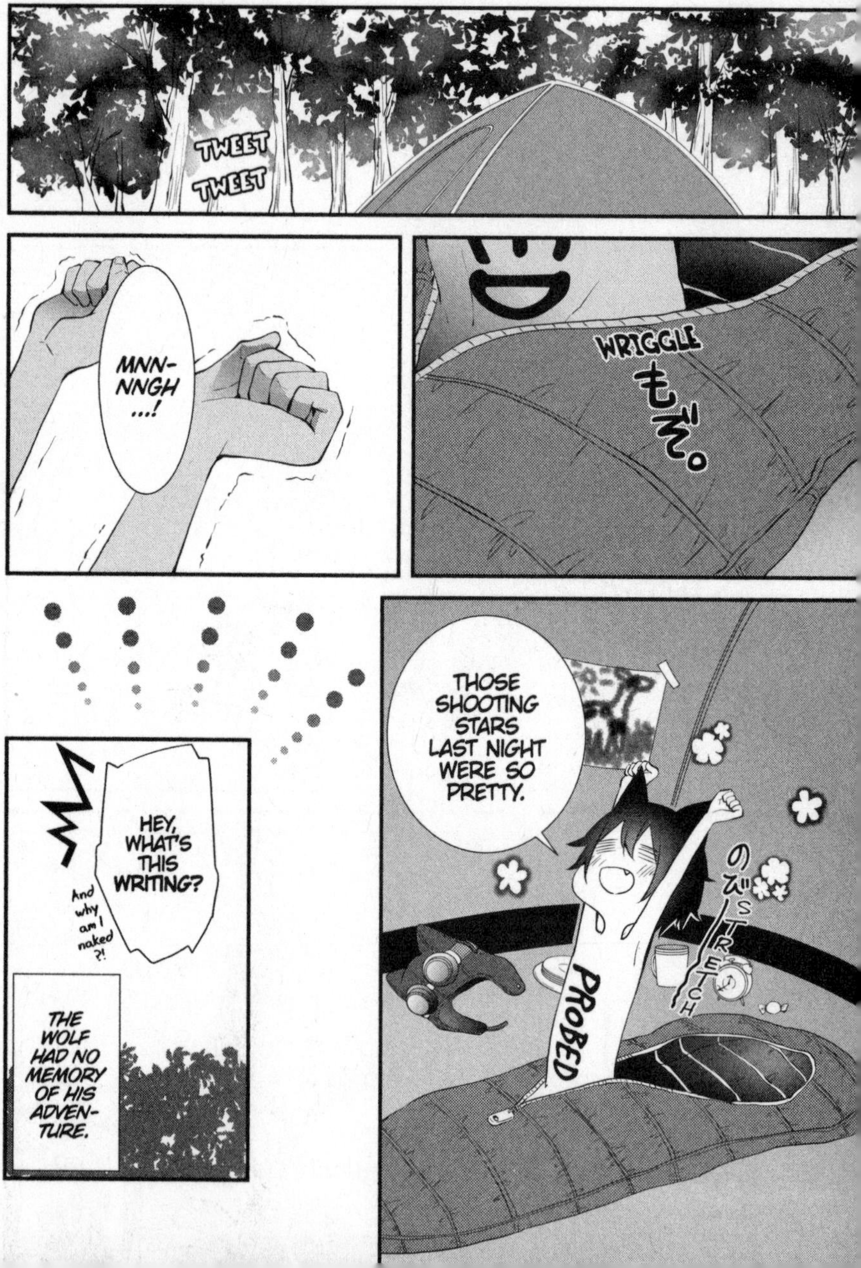
TWEET
TWEET
WRIGGLE
もぞ。
MNN-NNGH...!
THOSE SHOOTING STARS LAST NIGHT WERE SO PRETTY.
のび
STRETCH
PROBED
HEY, WHAT'S THIS WRITING?
And why am I naked?!
THE WOLF HAD NO MEMORY OF HIS ADVENTURE.

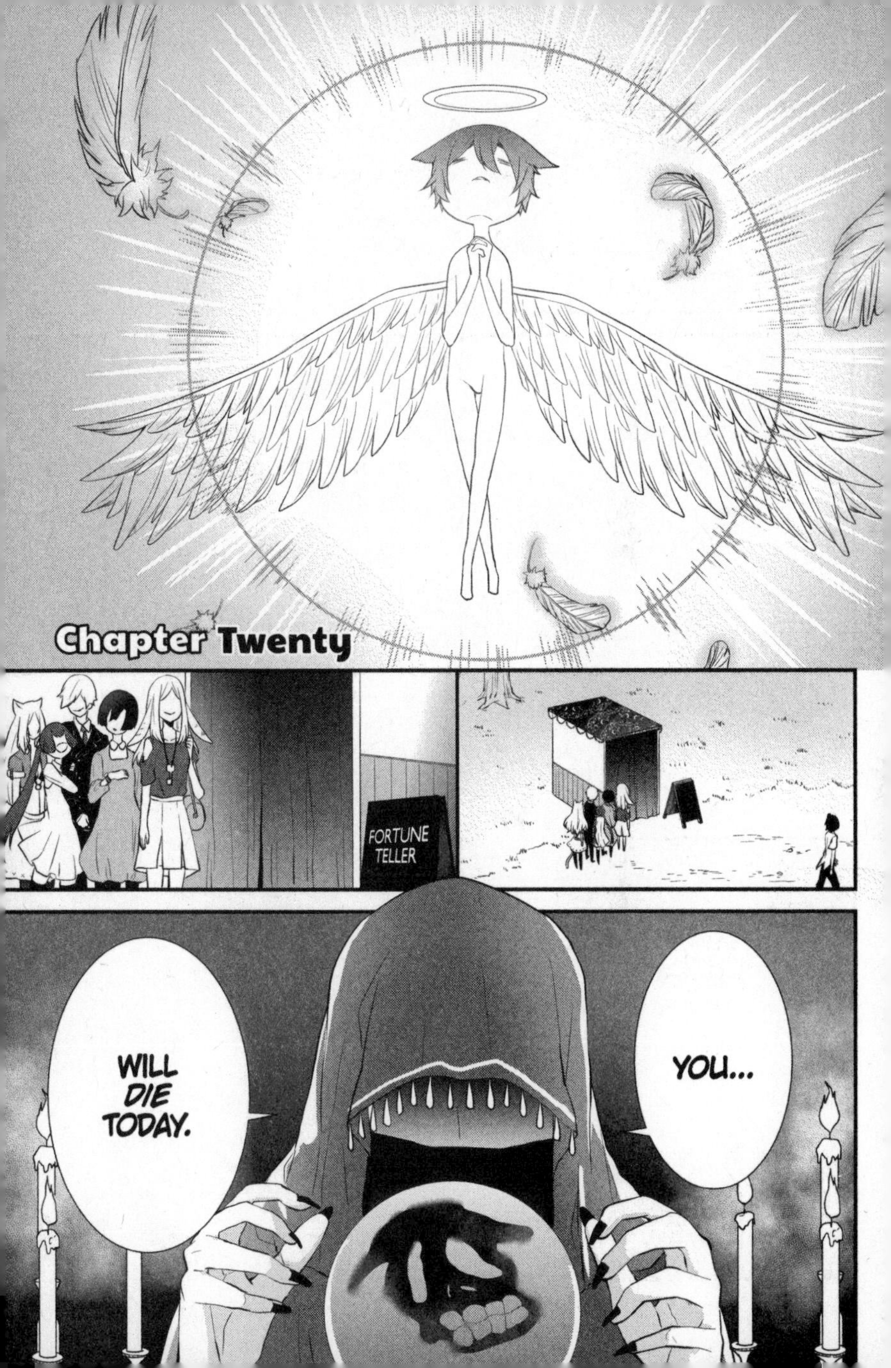
Chapter Twenty
FORTUNE TELLER
YOU...
WILL DIE TODAY.

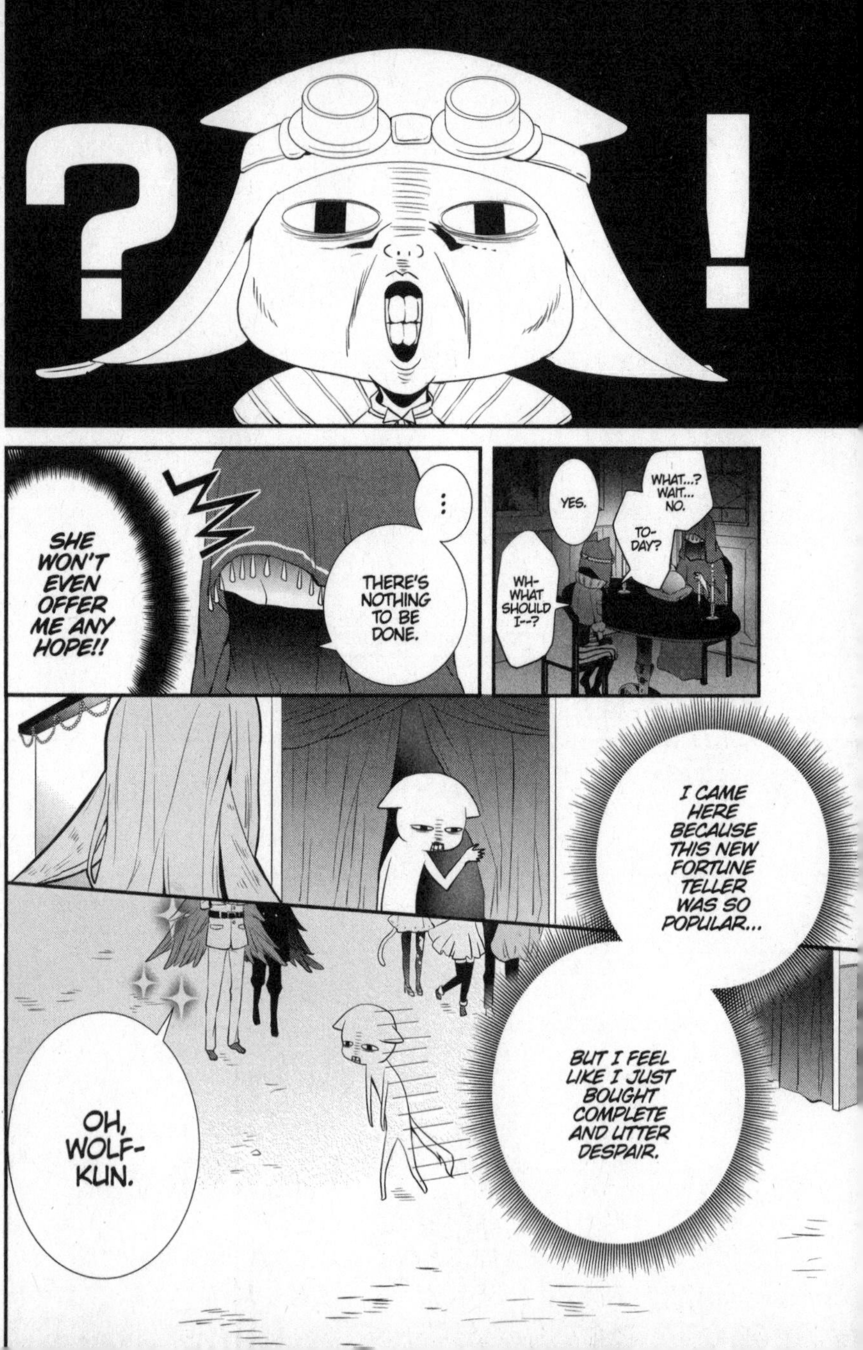
?!
WHAT...? WAIT... NO.
YES.
TO-DAY?
WH-WHAT SHOULD I--?
...
THERE'S NOTHING TO BE DONE.
SHE WON'T EVEN OFFER ME ANY HOPE!!
I CAME HERE BECAUSE THIS NEW FORTUNE TELLER WAS SO POPULAR...
BUT I FEEL LIKE I JUST BOUGHT COMPLETE AND UTTER DESPAIR.
OH, WOLF-KUN.

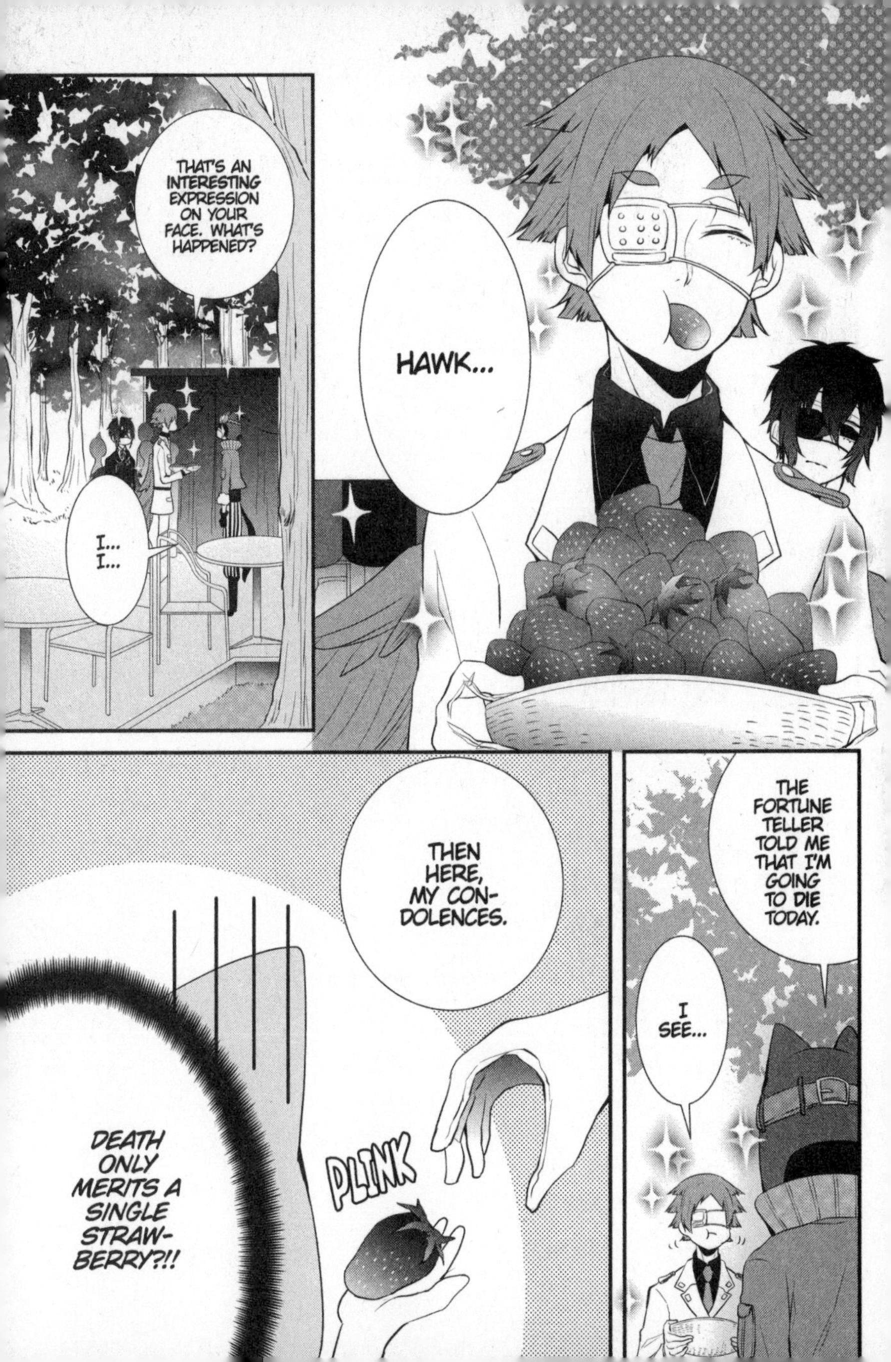
HAWK...
THAT'S AN INTERESTING EXPRESSION ON YOUR FACE. WHAT'S HAPPENED?
I... I...
THE FORTUNE TELLER TOLD ME THAT I'M GOING TO DIE TODAY.
I SEE...
THEN HERE, MY CON-DOLENCES.
PLINK
DEATH ONLY MERITS A SINGLE STRAW-BERRY?!!

THE FATEFUL DAY: PART 1

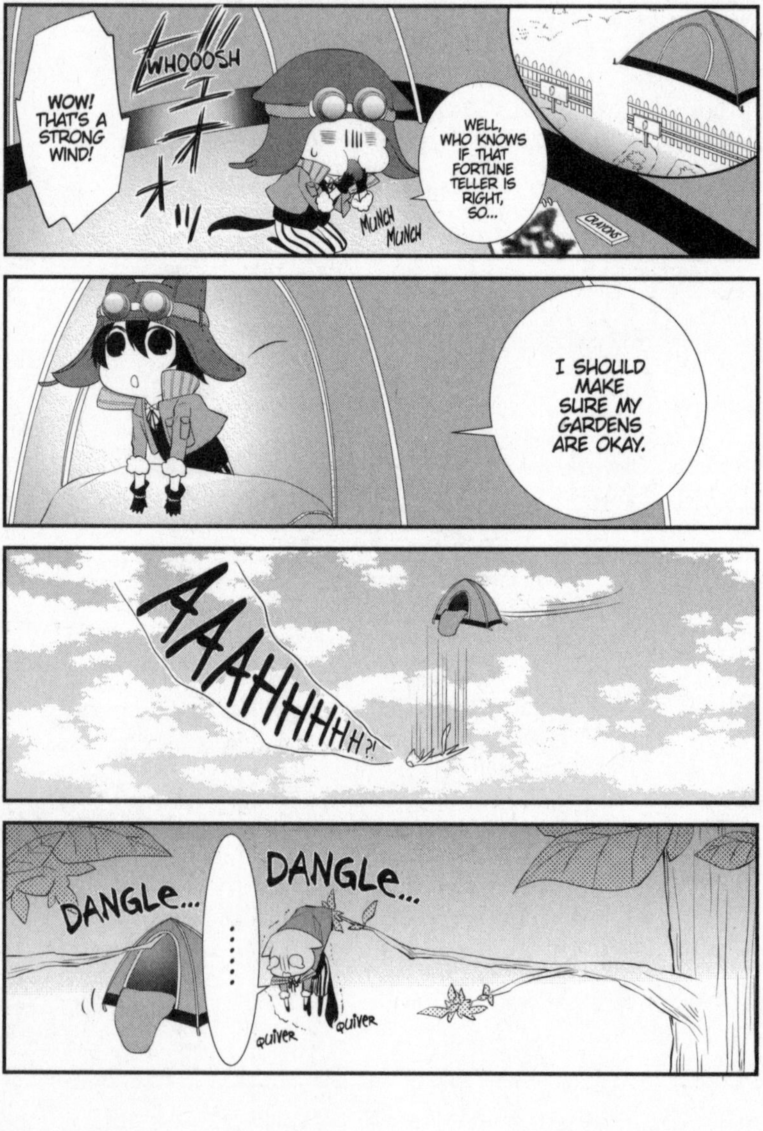
CRAYONS
WELL, WHO KNOWS IF THAT FORTUNE TELLER IS RIGHT, SO...
MUNCH MUNCH
WHOOOSH
WOW! THAT'S A STRONG WIND!
I SHOULD MAKE SURE MY GARDENS ARE OKAY.
AAAHHHHHH?!
DANGLE...
QUIVER
QUIVER
......
DANGLE...

THE FATEFUL DAY: PART 2

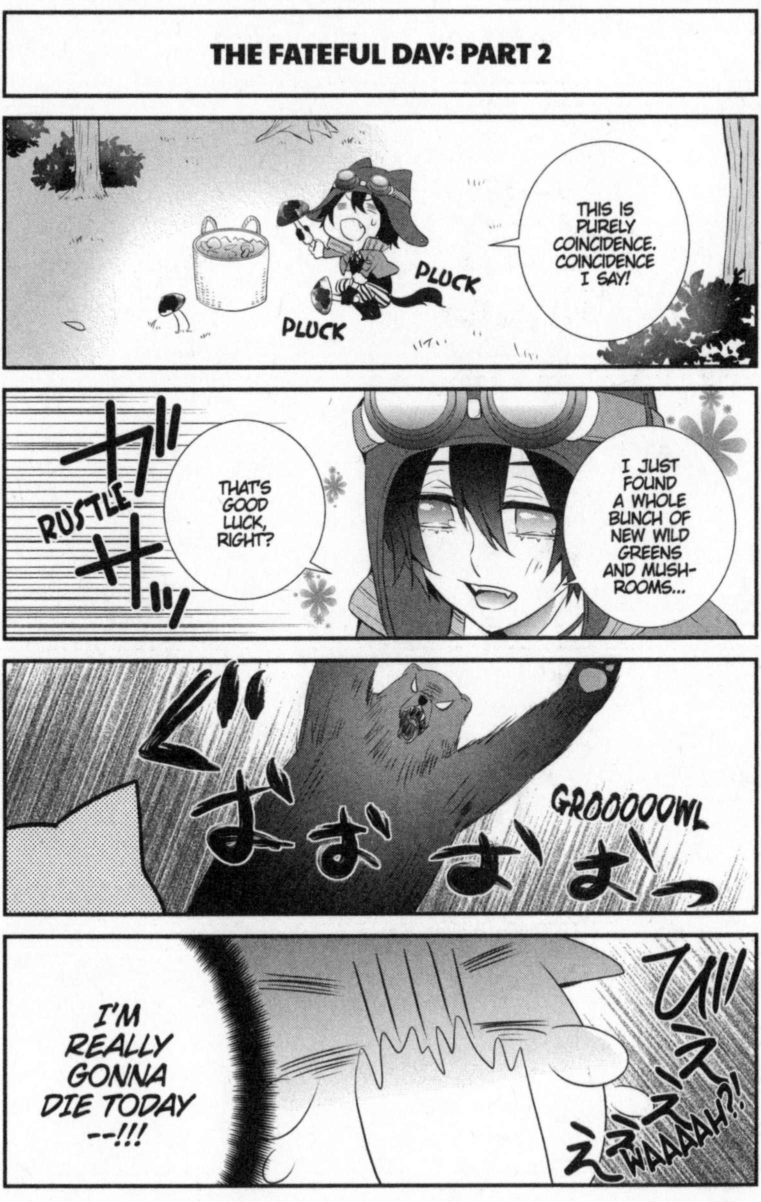
THIS IS PURELY COINCIDENCE. COINCIDENCE I SAY!
PLUCK
PLUCK
I JUST FOUND A WHOLE BUNCH OF NEW WILD GREENS AND MUSH-ROOMS...
THAT'S GOOD LUCK, RIGHT?
RUSTLE
GROOOOOWL
WAAAAH?!
I'M REALLY GONNA DIE TODAY --!!!

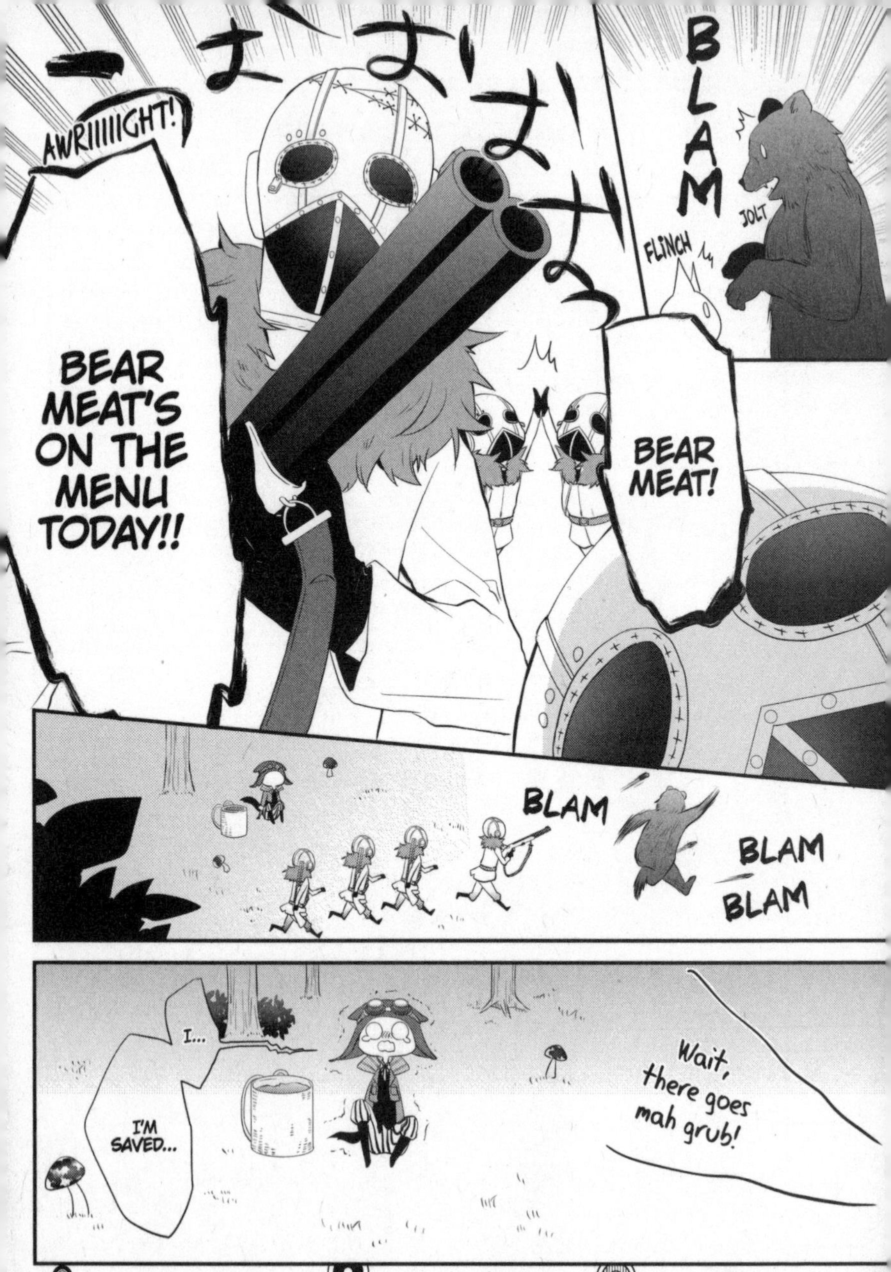
BLAM
JOLT
FLINCH
AWRIIIIGHT!
BEAR MEAT'S ON THE MENU TODAY!!
BEAR MEAT!
BLAM
BLAM
BLAM
Wait, there goes mah grub!
I...
I'M SAVED...

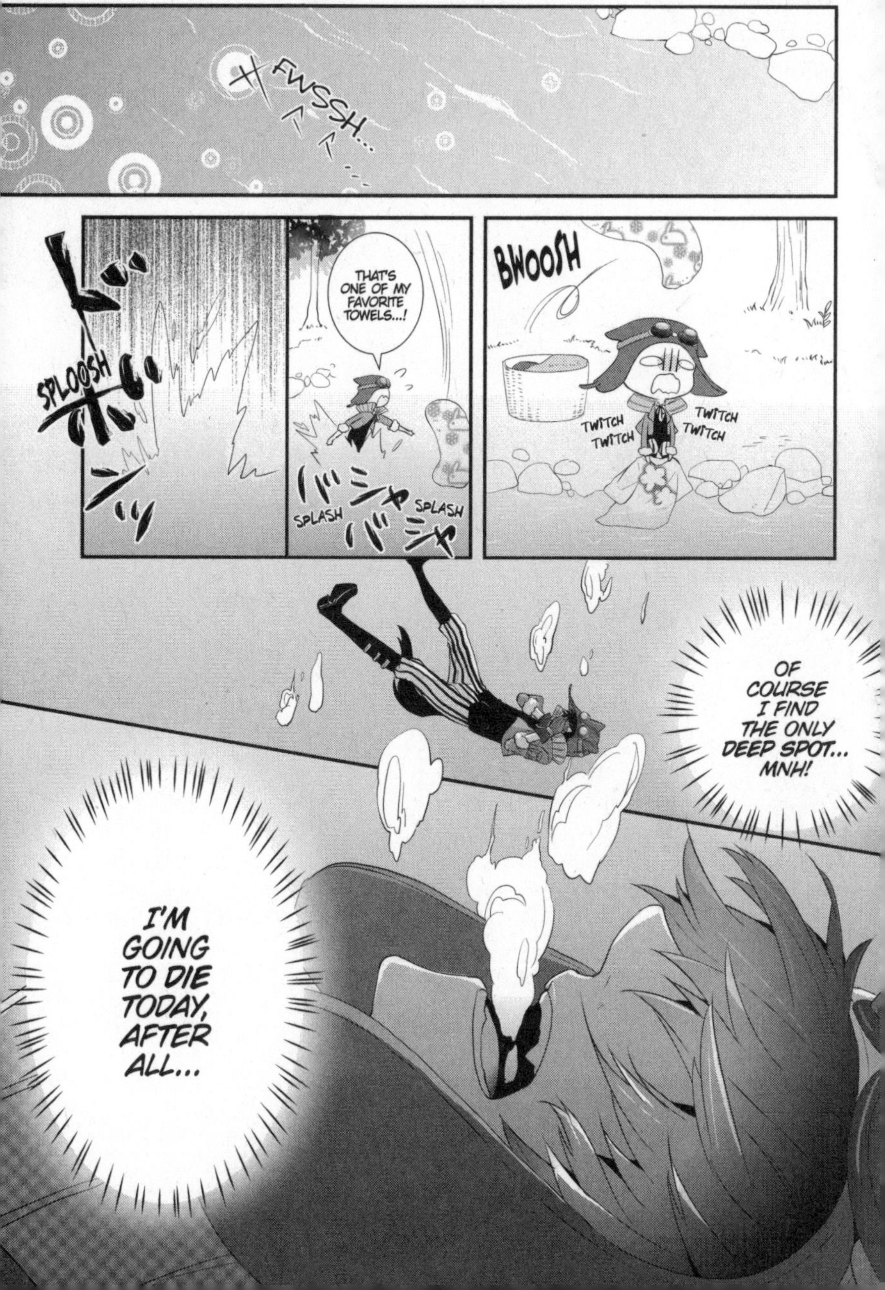
FWSSH...
BWOOSH
TWITCH TWITCH
TWITCH TWITCH
THAT'S ONE OF MY FAVORITE TOWELS...!
バシャ
SPLASH
バシャ
SPLASH
SPLOOSH
OF COURSE I FIND THE ONLY DEEP SPOT... MNH!
I'M GOING TO DIE TODAY, AFTER ALL...

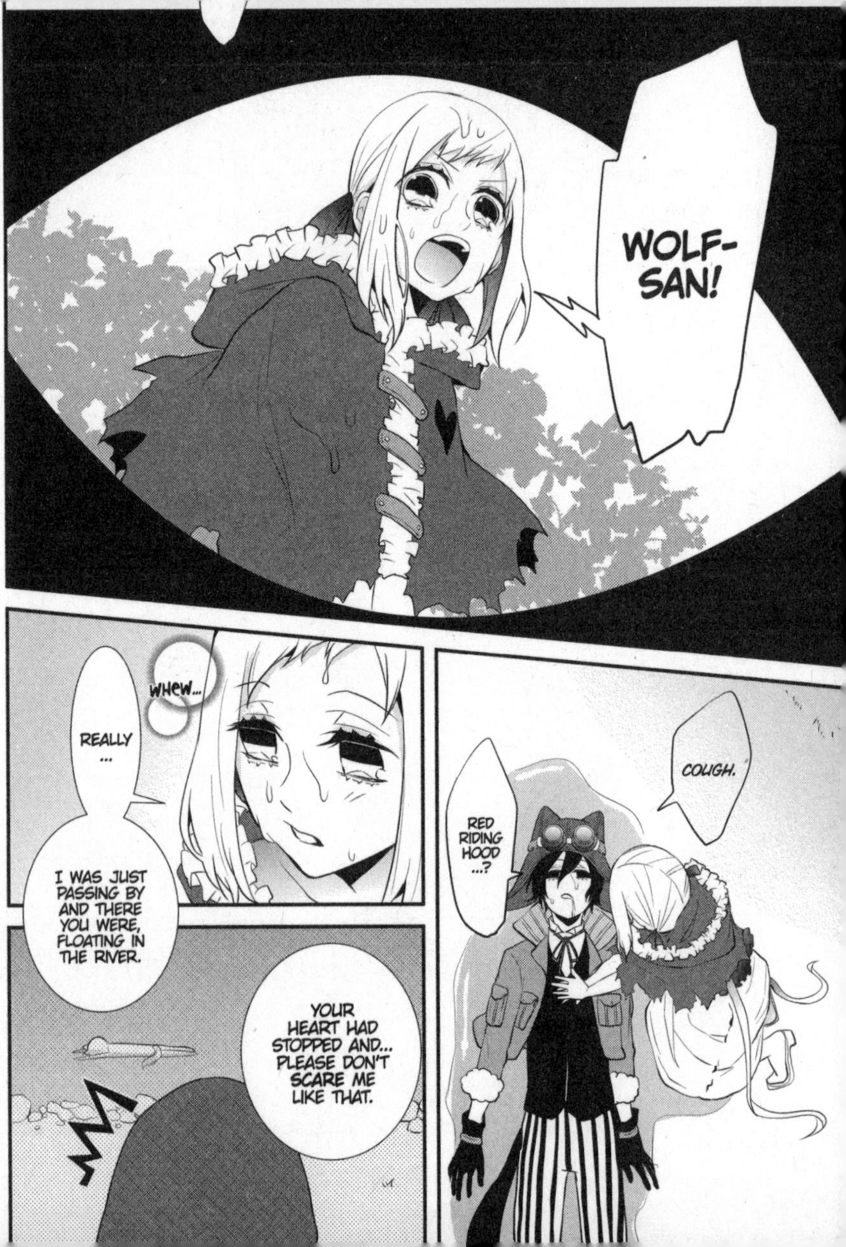
WOLF-SAN!
COUGH.
RED RIDING HOOD ...?
whew...
REALLY ...
I WAS JUST PASSING BY AND THERE YOU WERE, FLOATING IN THE RIVER.
YOUR HEART HAD STOPPED AND... PLEASE DON'T SCARE ME LIKE THAT.

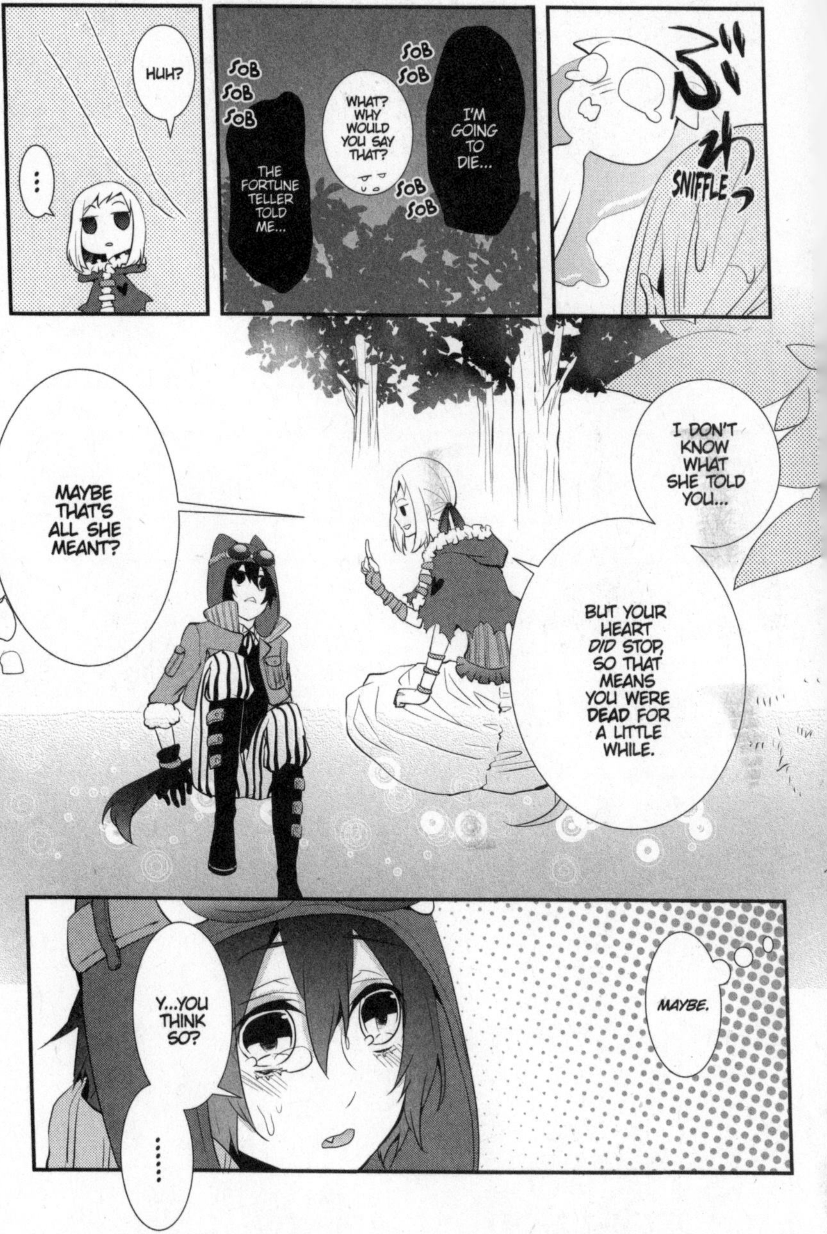
ぶわっ
SNIFFLE
SOB SOB
I'M GOING TO DIE...
SOB SOB
WHAT? WHY WOULD YOU SAY THAT?
SOB SOB SOB
THE FORTUNE TELLER TOLD ME...
HUH?
...
I DON'T KNOW WHAT SHE TOLD YOU...
BUT YOUR HEART *DID* STOP, SO THAT MEANS YOU WERE DEAD FOR A LITTLE WHILE.
MAYBE THAT'S ALL SHE MEANT?
MAYBE.
Y...YOU THINK SO?
......

WHEEW! ふねーっ♥

THAT'S GOTTA BE IT!

HE'S SO SIMPLE IT'S ADOR-ABLE.

THANK YOU, RED RIDING HOOD!

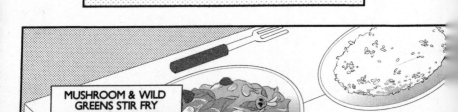

MUSHROOM & WILD GREENS STIR FRY

THUD... ぱた…

POISON

MUSHROOM & WILD GREENS STIR FRY

TOO DELICIOUS MANDARIN

CHOMP ぱく

WELL, LOOKS LIKE I MADE IT THROUGH THE DAY.

TOO DELICIOUS MANDARIN

Chapter Twenty-One

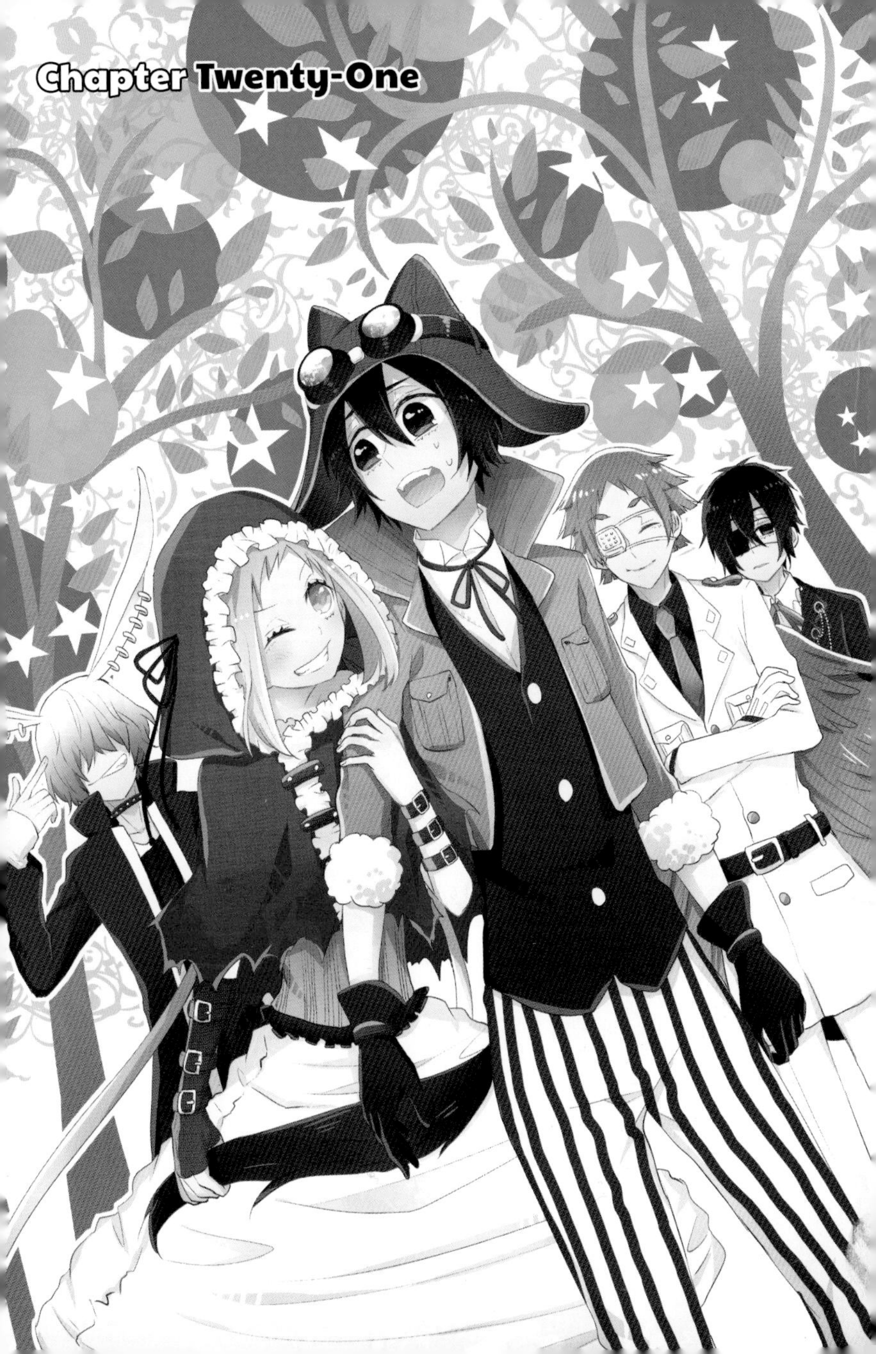

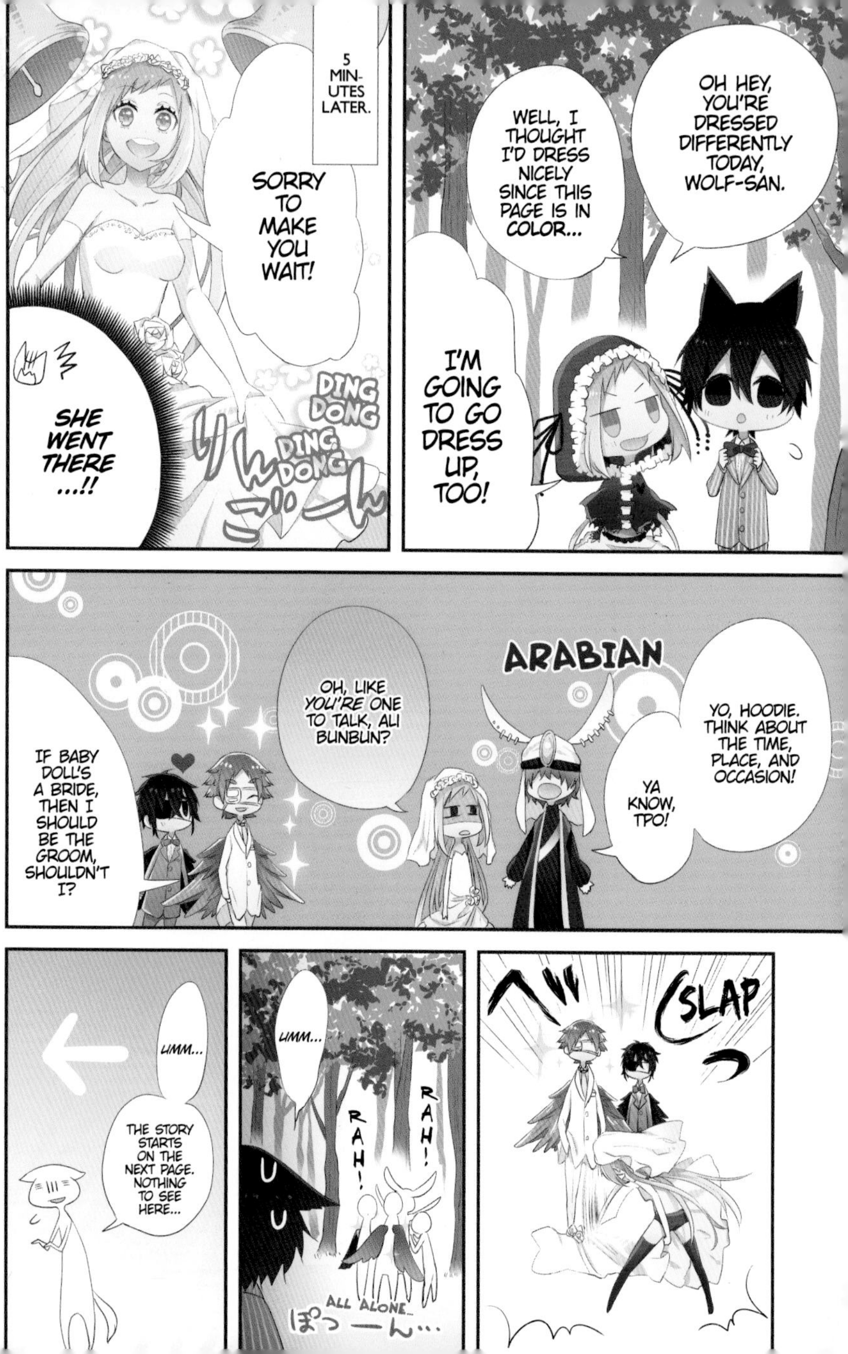
OH HEY, YOU'RE DRESSED DIFFERENTLY TODAY, WOLF-SAN.
WELL, I THOUGHT I'D DRESS NICELY SINCE THIS PAGE IS IN COLOR...
I'M GOING TO GO DRESS UP, TOO!
5 MIN-UTES LATER.
SORRY TO MAKE YOU WAIT!
DING DONG
DING DONG
SHE WENT THERE ...!!
ARABIAN
YO, HOODIE. THINK ABOUT THE TIME, PLACE, AND OCCASION!
YA KNOW, TPO!
OH, LIKE *YOU'RE* ONE TO TALK, ALI BUNBUN?
IF BABY DOLL'S A BRIDE, THEN I SHOULD BE THE GROOM, SHOULDN'T I?
SLAP
UMM...
RAH!
RAH!
ALL ALONE...
ぽつーん・・・
UMM...
THE STORY STARTS ON THE NEXT PAGE. NOTHING TO SEE HERE...

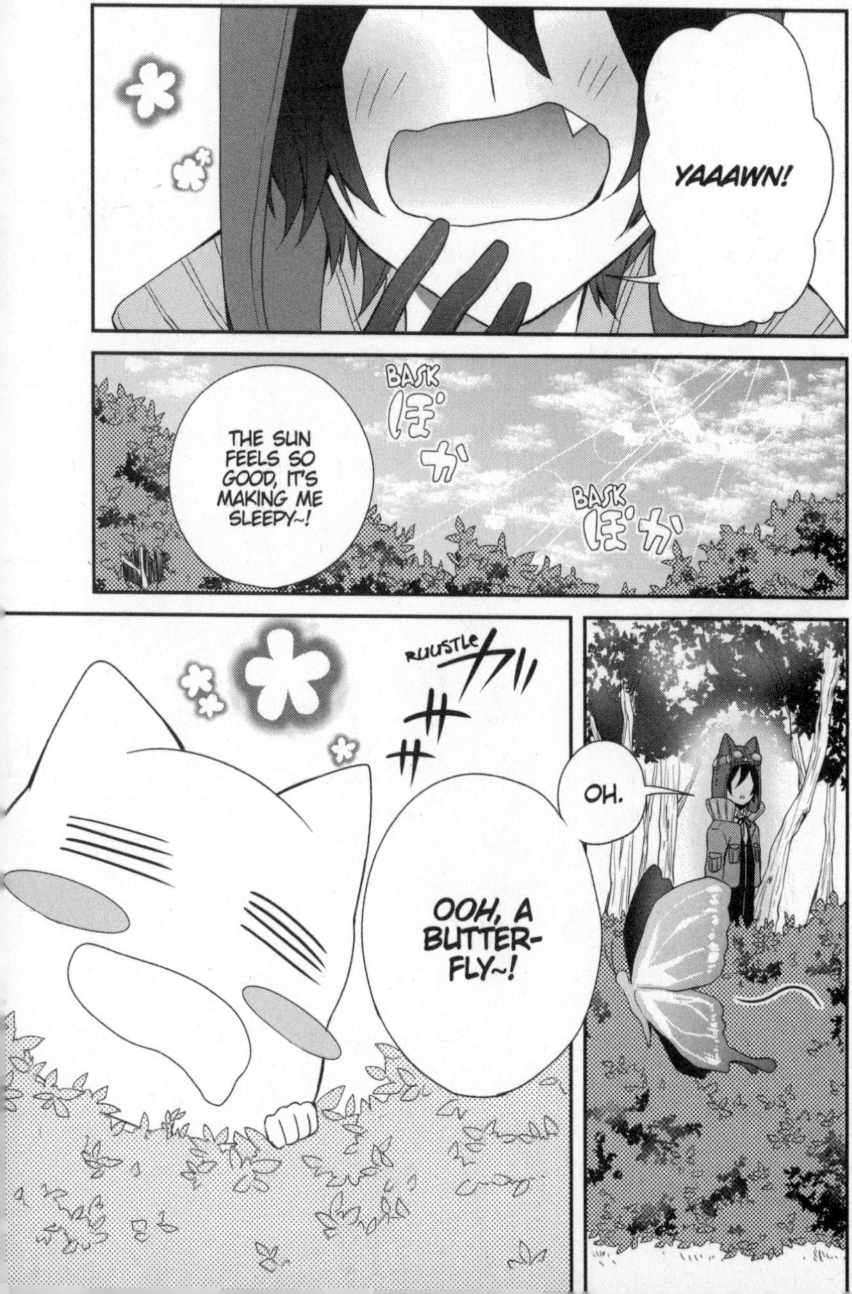
YAAAWN!
BASK
ぽか
BASK
ぽか
THE SUN FEELS SO GOOD, IT'S MAKING ME SLEEPY~!
OH.
RUUSTLE
OOH, A BUTTER-FLY~!

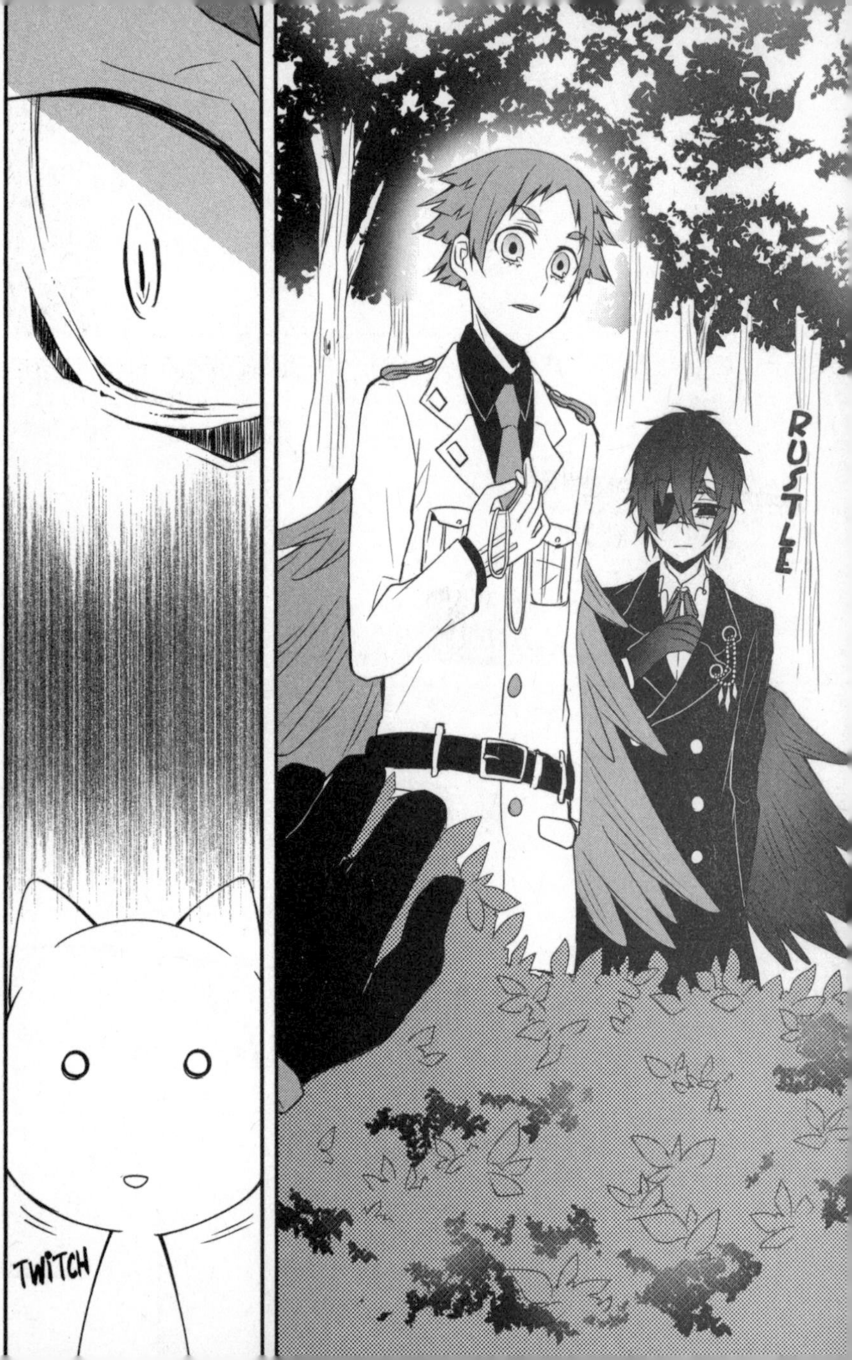
RUSTLE
TWITCH

WHEEW! ふはーっ

THAT'S GOTTA BE IT!

THANK YOU, RED RIDING HOOD!

HE'S SO SIMPLE IT'S ADORABLE.

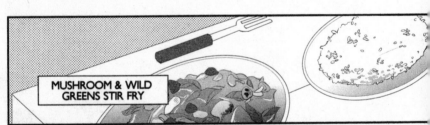

MUSHROOM & WILD GREENS STIR FRY

CHOMP ぱっ

WELL, LOOKS LIKE I MADE IT THROUGH THE DAY.

TOO DELICIOUS MANDARIN

THUD... ぱた...

POISON

MUSHROOM & WILD GREENS STIR FRY

TOO DELICIOUS MANDARIN

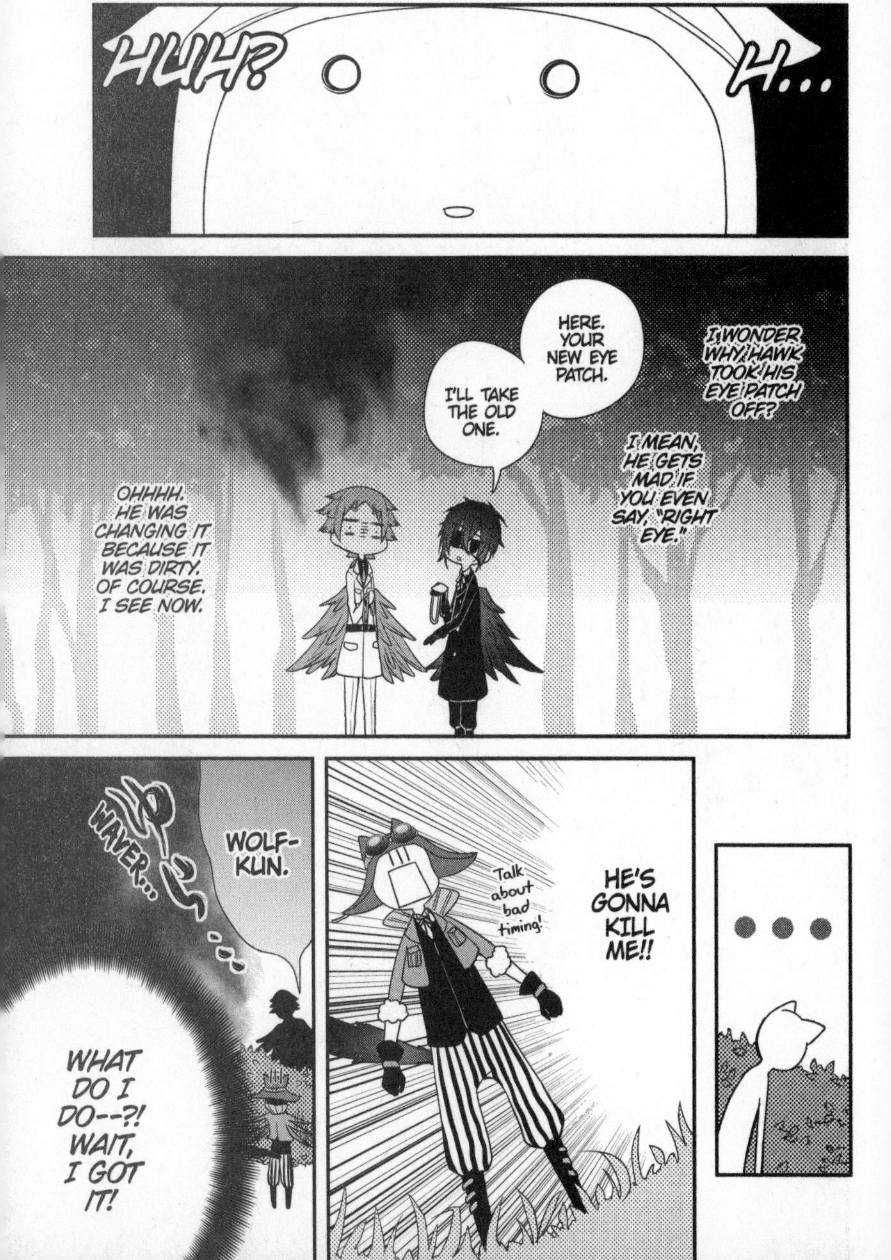
H...
HUH?
I WONDER WHY HAWK TOOK HIS EYE PATCH OFF?
I MEAN, HE GETS MAD IF YOU EVEN SAY, "RIGHT EYE."
HERE. YOUR NEW EYE PATCH.
I'LL TAKE THE OLD ONE.
OHHHH. HE WAS CHANGING IT BECAUSE IT WAS DIRTY. OF COURSE. I SEE NOW.
• • •
HE'S GONNA KILL ME!!
Talk about bad timing!
WOLF-KUN.
WAVER...
WHAT DO I DO--?! WAIT, I GOT IT!

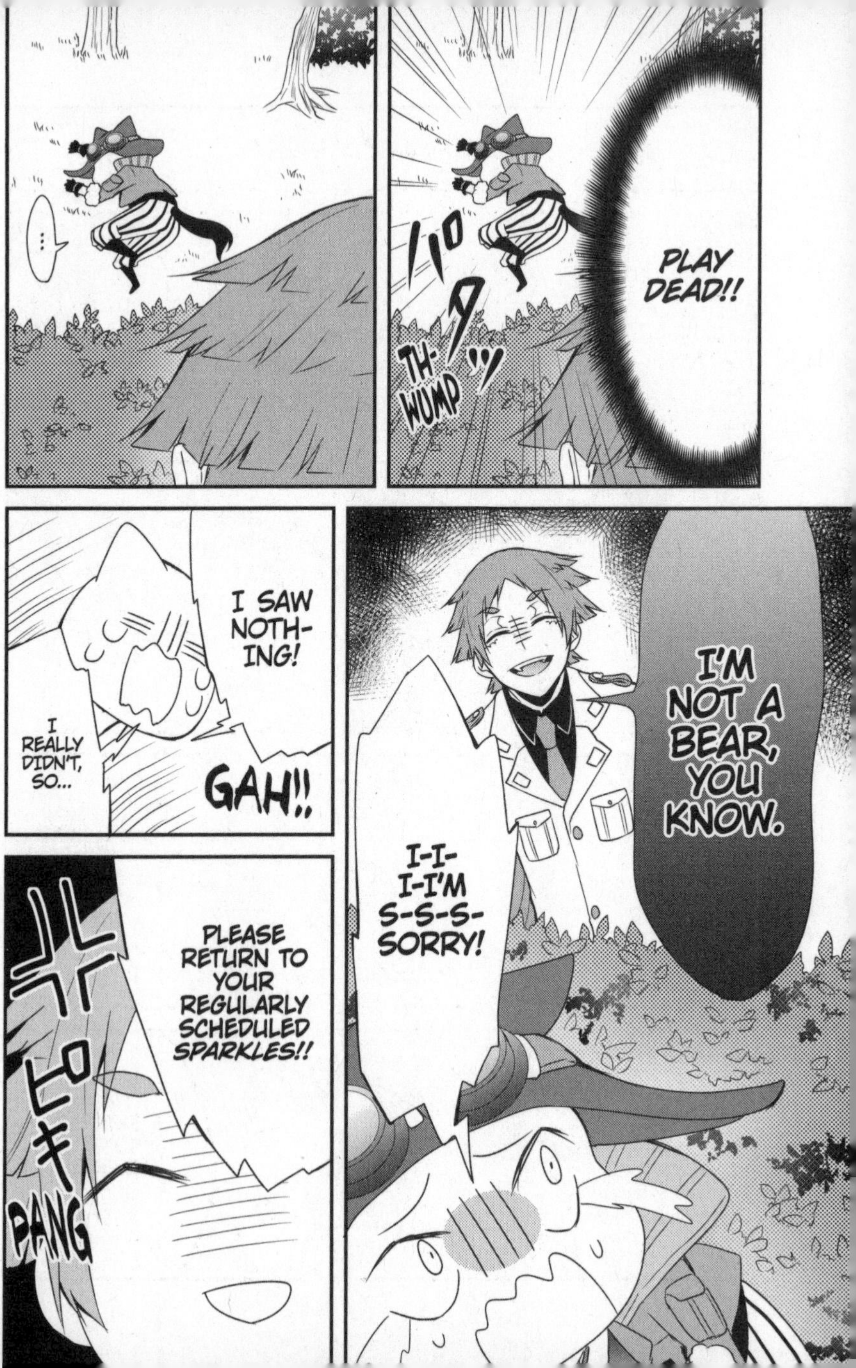
PLAY DEAD!!
TH-WUMP
...
I'M NOT A BEAR, YOU KNOW.
I-I-I-I'M S-S-S-SORRY!
I SAW NOTH-ING!
GAH!!
I REALLY DIDN'T, SO...
PLEASE RETURN TO YOUR REGULARLY SCHEDULED SPARKLES!!
PANG

CANDY AND A WHIP

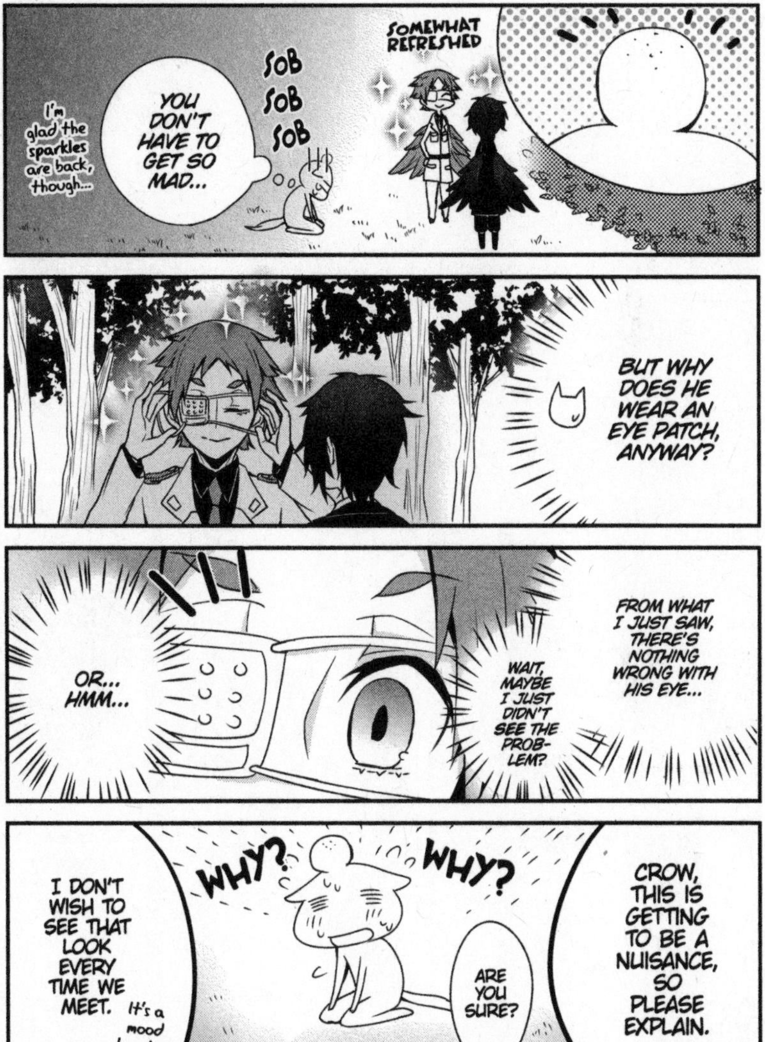
SOMEWHAT REFRESHED
SOB SOB SOB
YOU DON'T HAVE TO GET SO MAD...
I'm glad the sparkles are back, though...
BUT WHY DOES HE WEAR AN EYE PATCH, ANYWAY?
FROM WHAT I JUST SAW, THERE'S NOTHING WRONG WITH HIS EYE...
WAIT, MAYBE I JUST DIDN'T SEE THE PROB-LEM?
OR... HMM...
CROW, THIS IS GETTING TO BE A NUISANCE, SO PLEASE EXPLAIN.
WHY? WHY?
ARE YOU SURE?
I DON'T WISH TO SEE THAT LOOK EVERY TIME WE MEET.
It's a mood breaker.

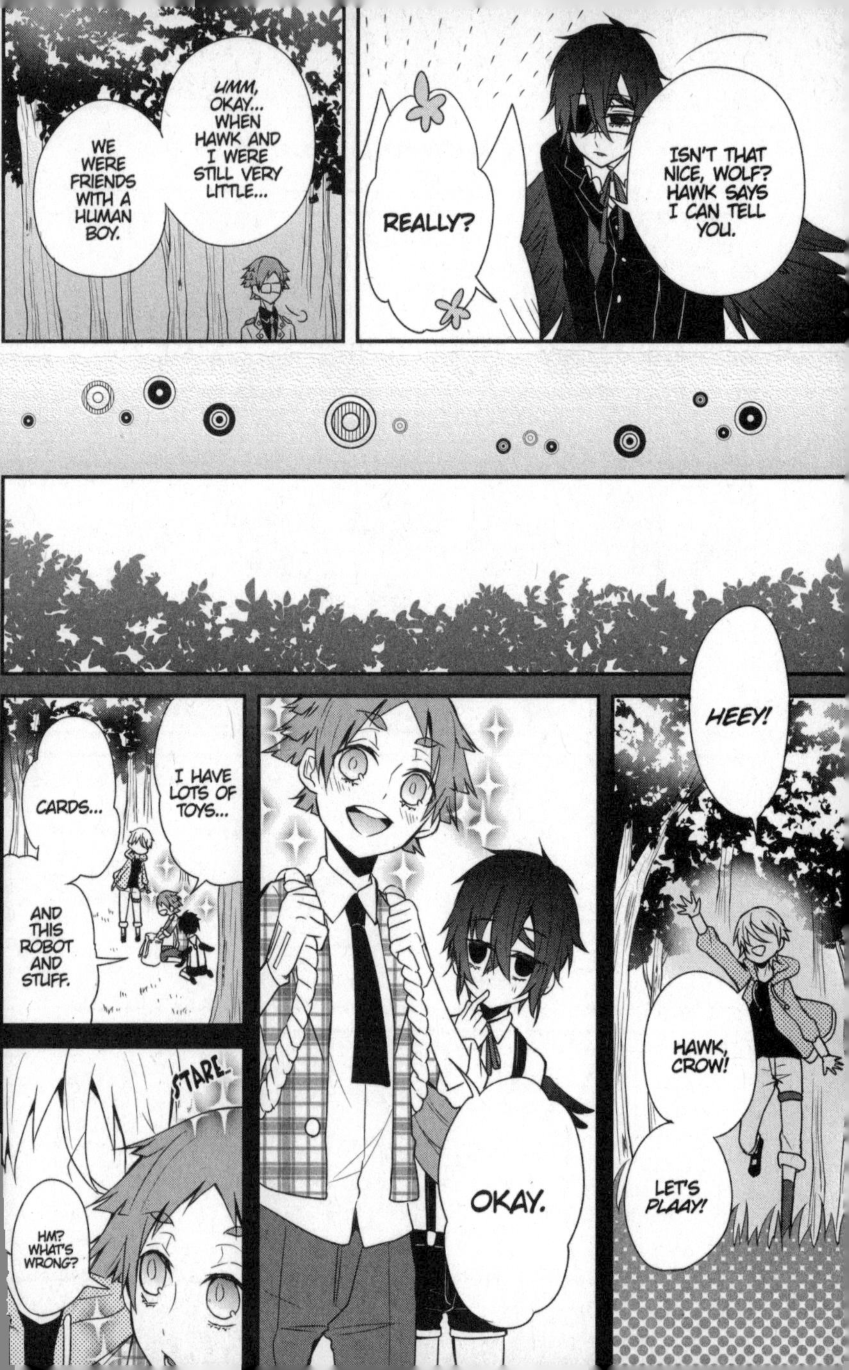

ISN'T THAT NICE, WOLF? HAWK SAYS I CAN TELL YOU.
REALLY?
UMM, OKAY... WHEN HAWK AND I WERE STILL VERY LITTLE...
WE WERE FRIENDS WITH A HUMAN BOY.
HEEY!
HAWK, CROW!
LET'S PLAAY!
OKAY.
I HAVE LOTS OF TOYS...
CARDS...
AND THIS ROBOT AND STUFF.
STARE...
HM? WHAT'S WRONG?

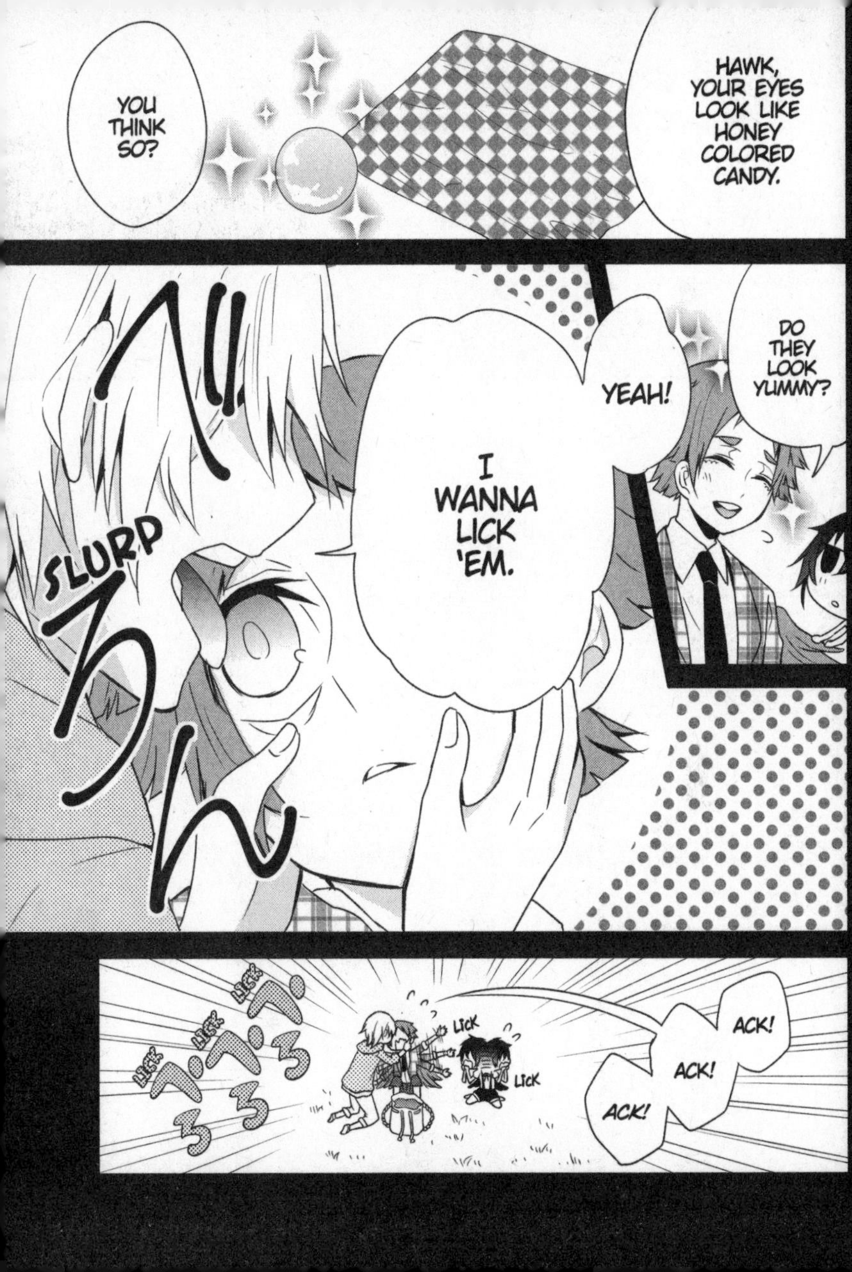
HAWK, YOUR EYES LOOK LIKE HONEY COLORED CANDY.
YOU THINK SO?
DO THEY LOOK YUMMY?
YEAH!
I WANNA LICK 'EM.
SLURP
ACK!
ACK!
ACK!
LICK
LICK
LICK
LICK
LICK

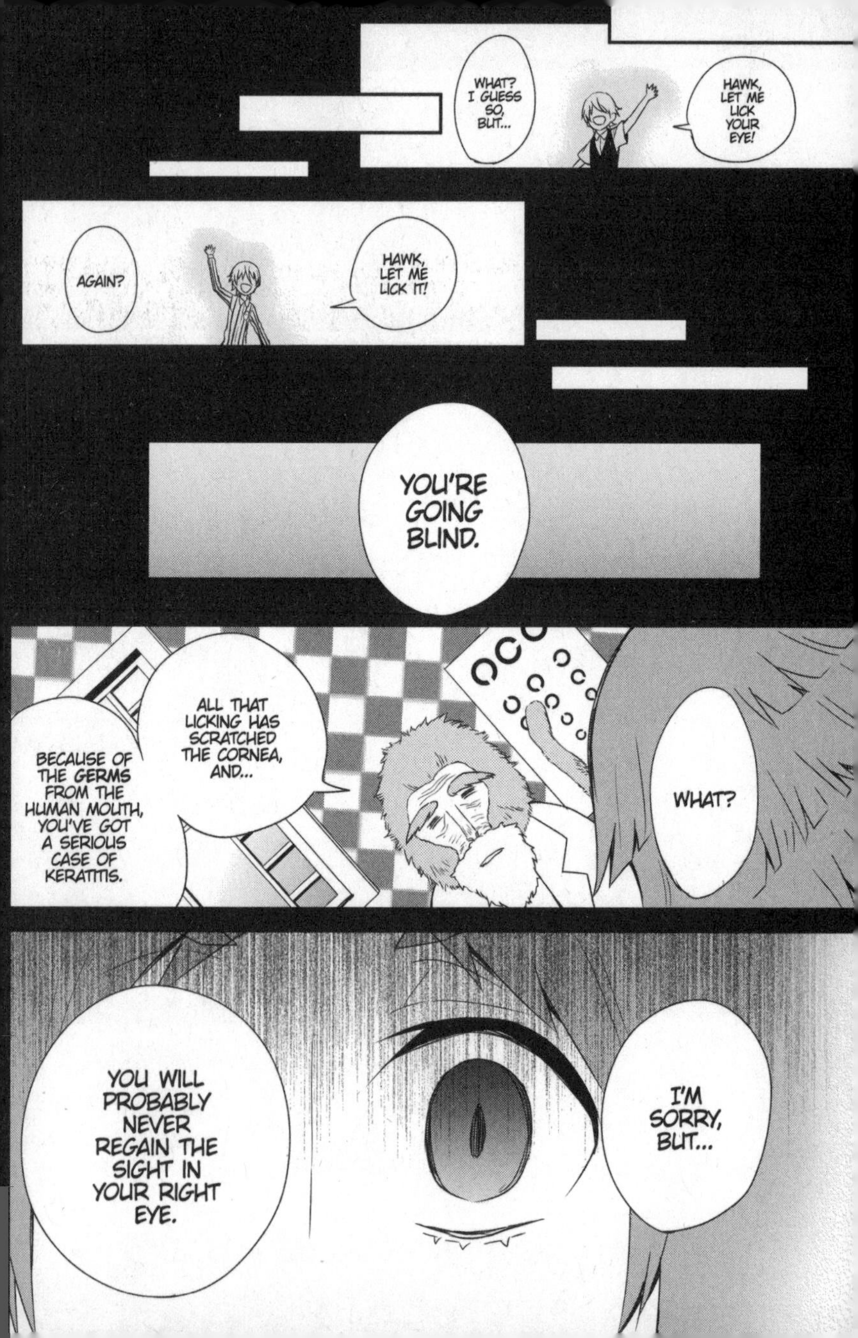
HAWK, LET ME LICK YOUR EYE!
WHAT? I GUESS SO, BUT...
HAWK, LET ME LICK IT!
AGAIN?
YOU'RE GOING BLIND.
WHAT?
ALL THAT LICKING HAS SCRATCHED THE CORNEA, AND...
BECAUSE OF THE GERMS FROM THE HUMAN MOUTH, YOU'VE GOT A SERIOUS CASE OF KERATITIS.
I'M SORRY, BUT...
YOU WILL PROBABLY NEVER REGAIN THE SIGHT IN YOUR RIGHT EYE.

LOVE → HATE

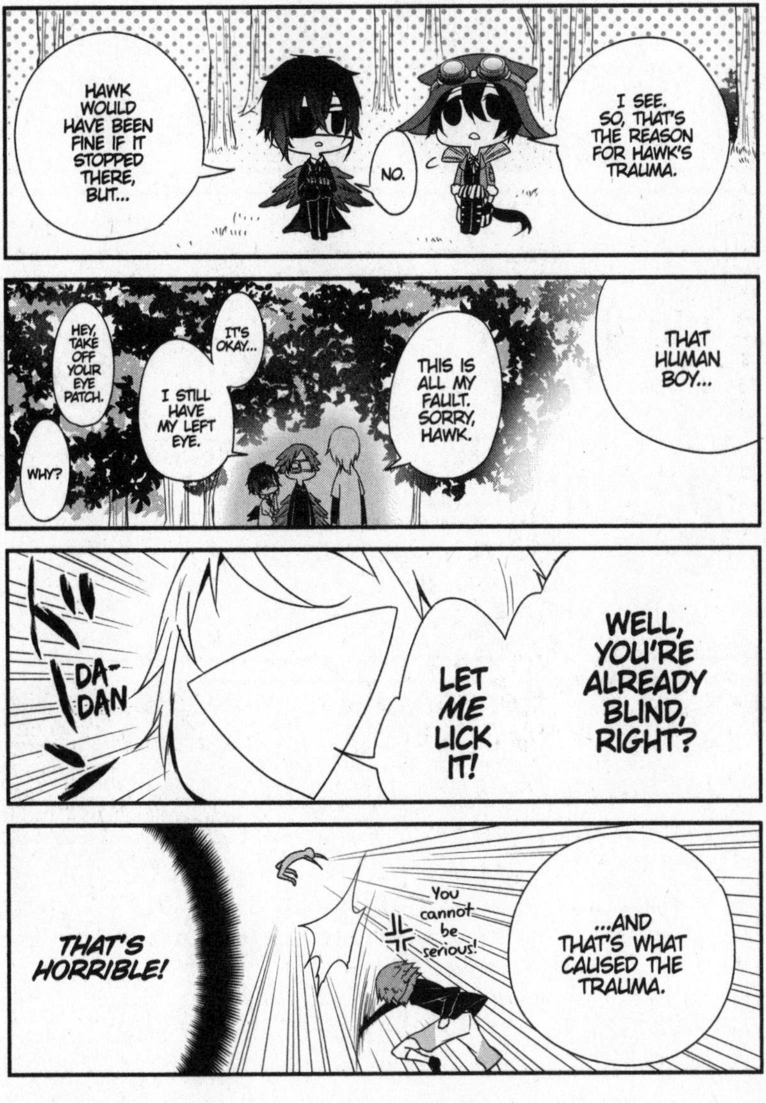
I SEE. SO, THAT'S THE REASON FOR HAWK'S TRAUMA.
NO.
HAWK WOULD HAVE BEEN FINE IF IT STOPPED THERE, BUT...
THAT HUMAN BOY...
THIS IS ALL MY FAULT. SORRY, HAWK.
IT'S OKAY...
I STILL HAVE MY LEFT EYE.
HEY, TAKE OFF YOUR EYE PATCH.
WHY?
WELL, YOU'RE ALREADY BLIND, RIGHT?
LET ME LICK IT!
DA-DAN
...AND THAT'S WHAT CAUSED THE TRAUMA.
You cannot be serious!
THAT'S HORRIBLE!

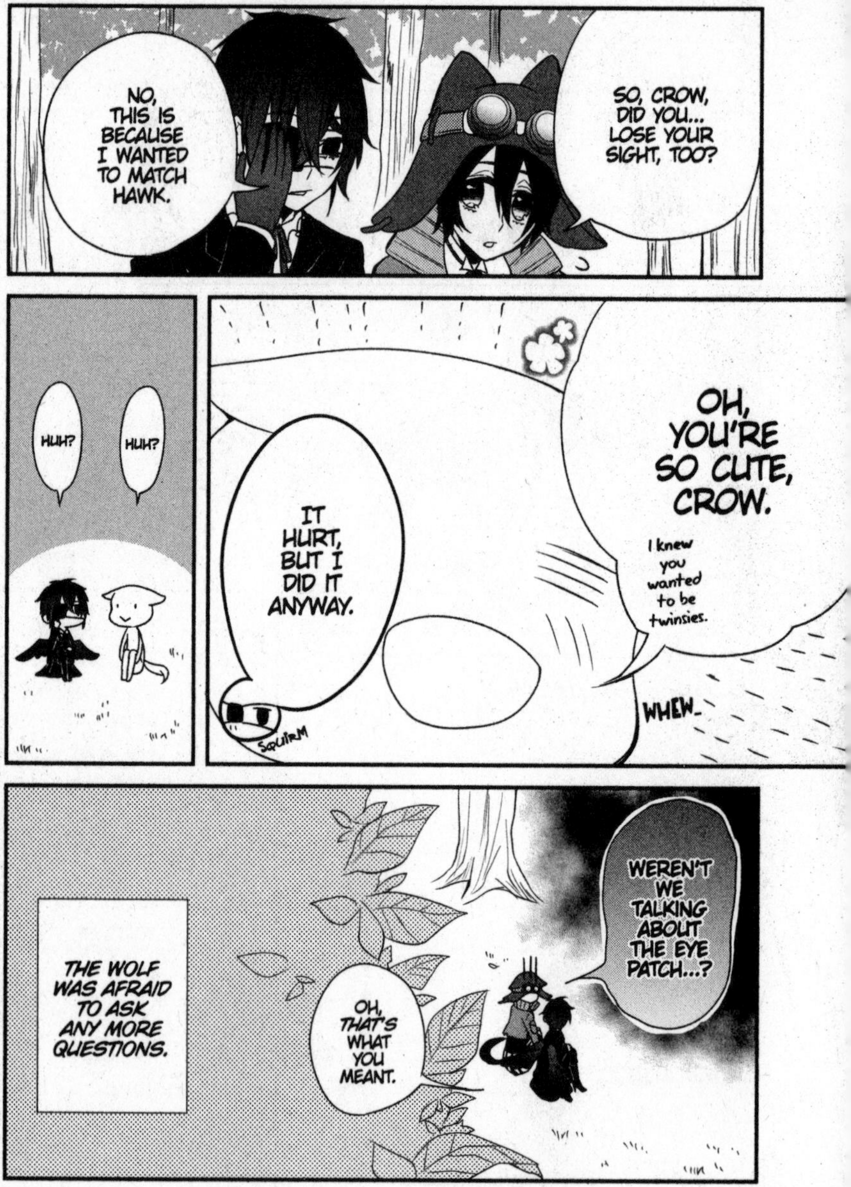
SO, CROW, DID YOU... LOSE YOUR SIGHT, TOO?
NO, THIS IS BECAUSE I WANTED TO MATCH HAWK.
OH, YOU'RE SO CUTE, CROW.
I knew you wanted to be twinsies.
WHEW_
IT HURT, BUT I DID IT ANYWAY.
SQUIRM
HUH?
HUH?
WEREN'T WE TALKING ABOUT THE EYE PATCH...?
OH, THAT'S WHAT YOU MEANT.
THE WOLF WAS AFRAID TO ASK ANY MORE QUESTIONS.

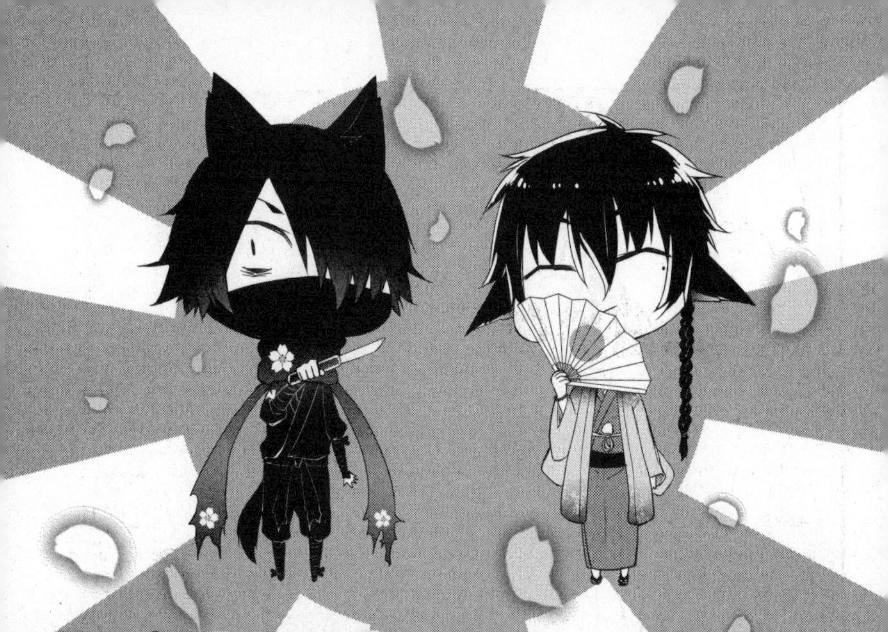

Chapter Twenty-Two

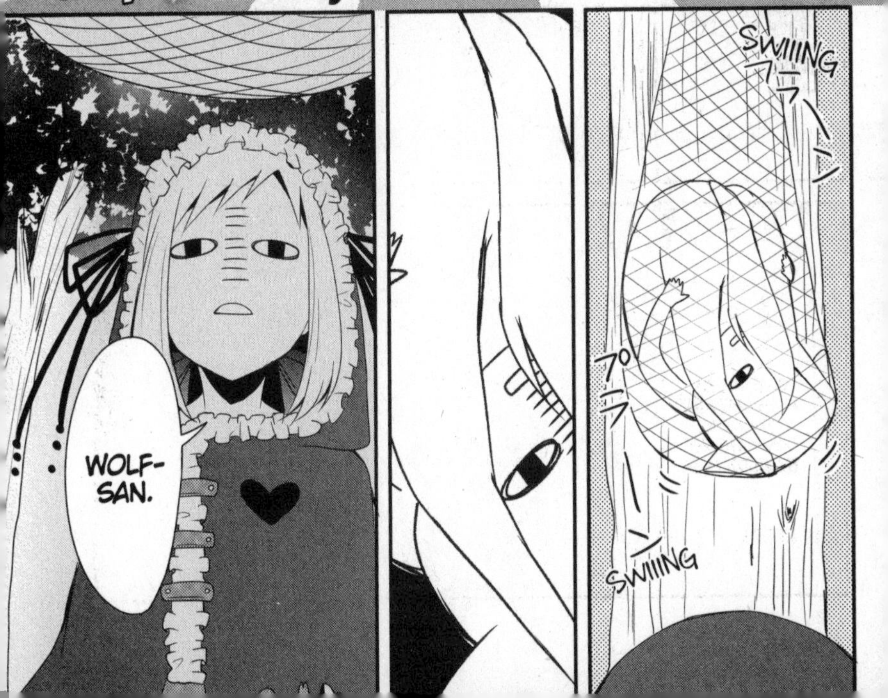
SWIIING
SWIIING
...
WOLF-SAN.

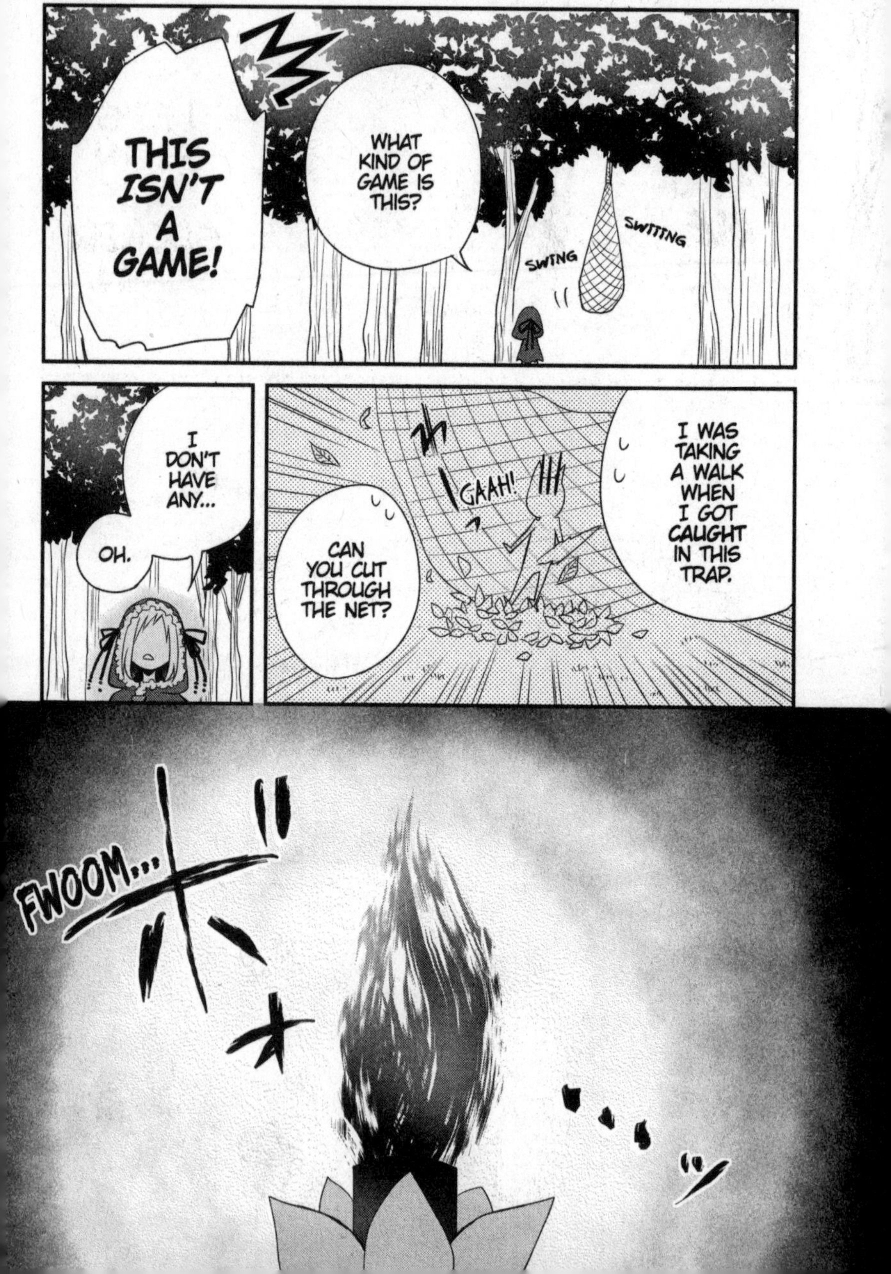
SWIIING
SWING
WHAT KIND OF GAME IS THIS?
THIS ISN'T A GAME!
I WAS TAKING A WALK WHEN I GOT CAUGHT IN THIS TRAP.
GAAH!
CAN YOU CUT THROUGH THE NET?
I DON'T HAVE ANY...
OH.
FWOOM...

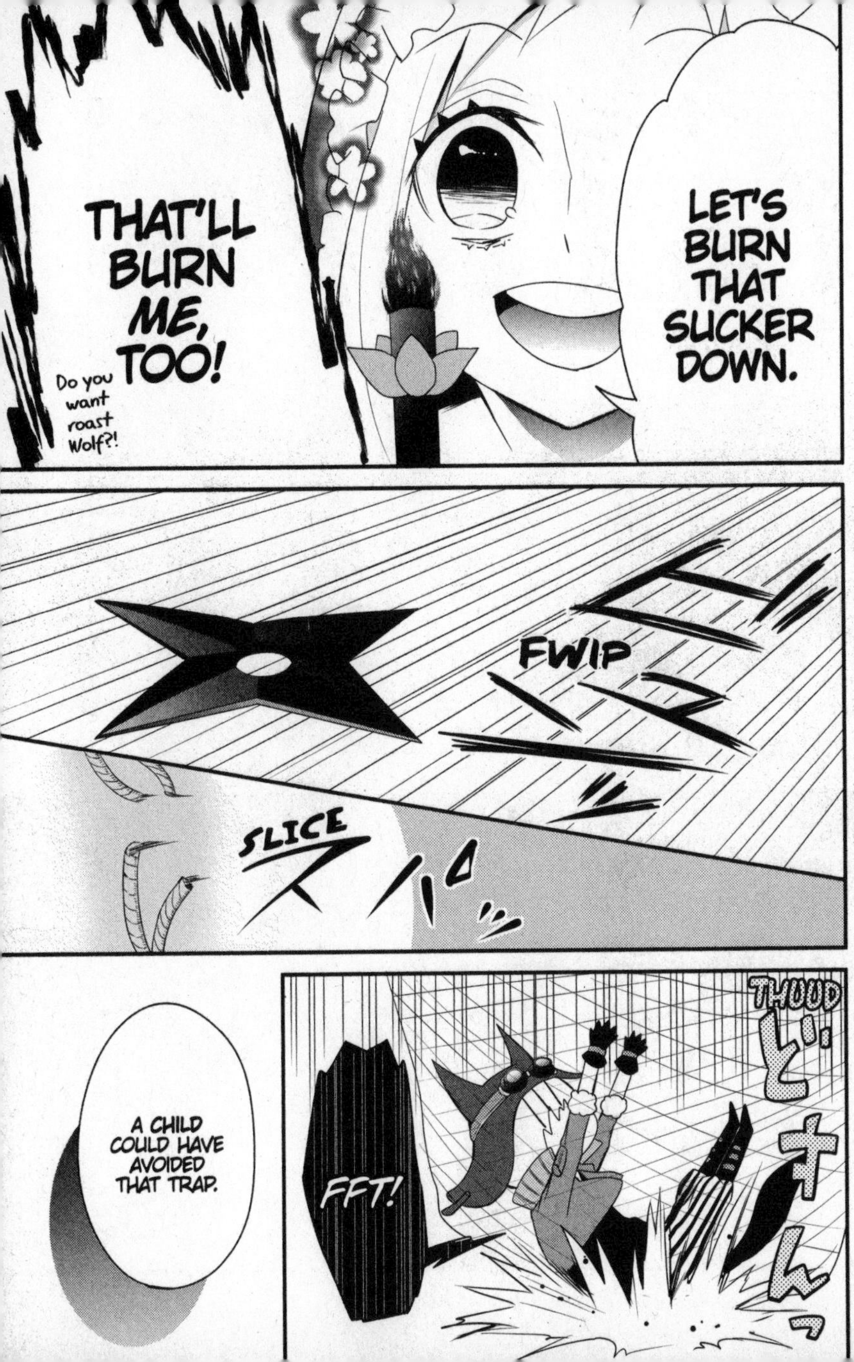
LET'S BURN THAT SUCKER DOWN.
THAT'LL BURN *ME*, TOO!
Do you want roast Wolf?!
FWIP
SLICE
THUUD
FFT!
A CHILD COULD HAVE AVOIDED THAT TRAP.

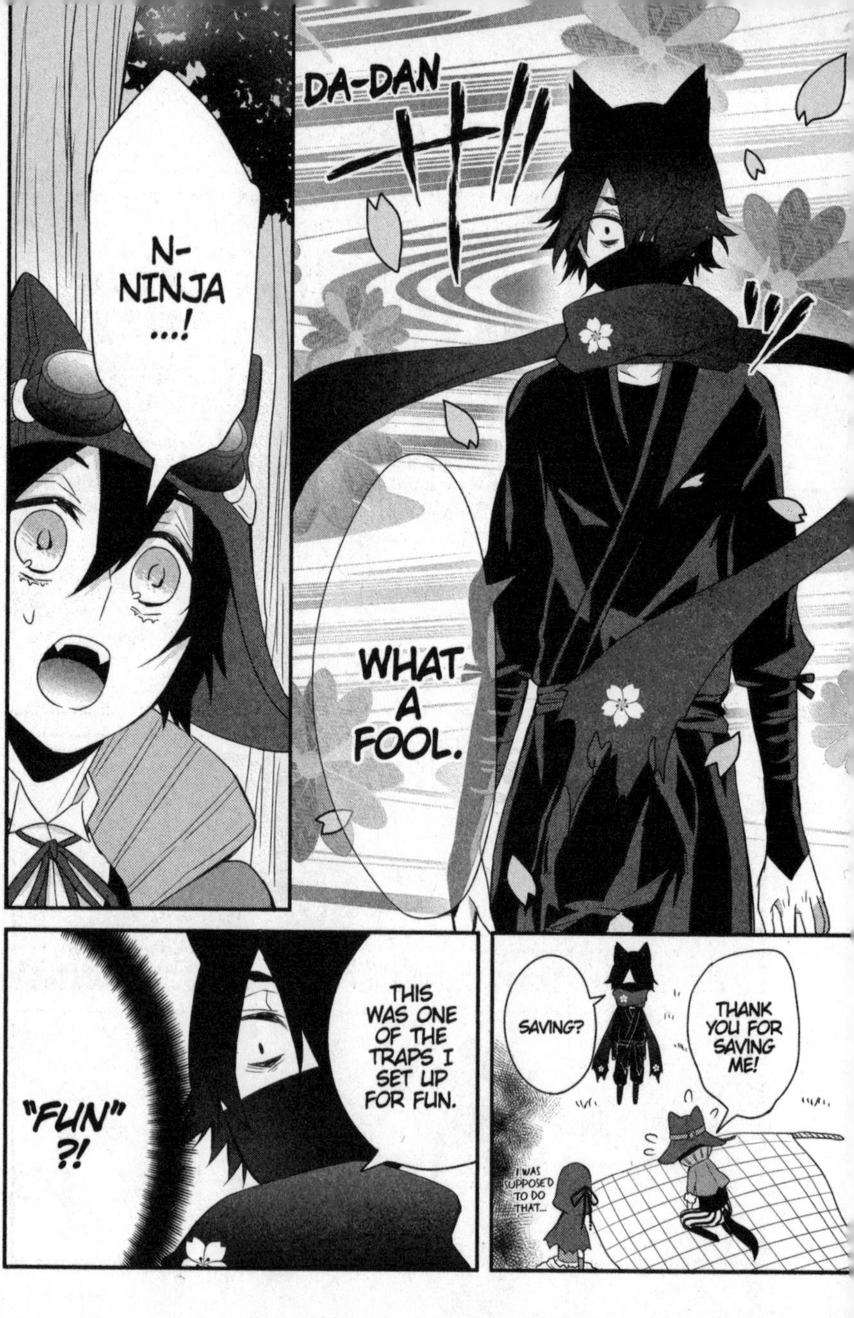
DA-DAN
WHAT A FOOL.
N-NINJA...!
THANK YOU FOR SAVING ME!
SAVING?
I WAS SUPPOSED TO DO THAT...
THIS WAS ONE OF THE TRAPS I SET UP FOR FUN.
"FUN"?!

DIFFERENT STANDARDS

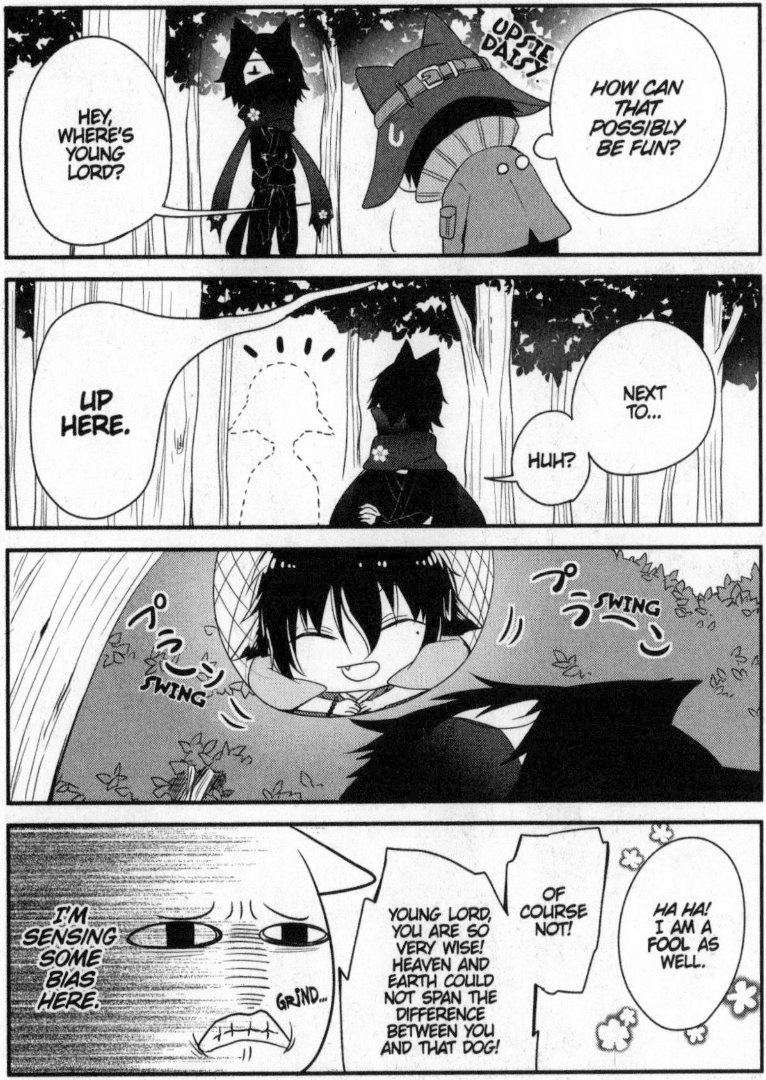
UPSIE DAISY.
HOW CAN THAT POSSIBLY BE FUN?
HEY, WHERE'S YOUNG LORD?
NEXT TO...
HUH?
UP HERE.
SWING
SWING
HA HA! I AM A FOOL AS WELL.
OF COURSE NOT!
YOUNG LORD, YOU ARE SO VERY WISE! HEAVEN AND EARTH COULD NOT SPAN THE DIFFERENCE BETWEEN YOU AND THAT DOG!
GRIND...
I'M SENSING SOME BIAS HERE.

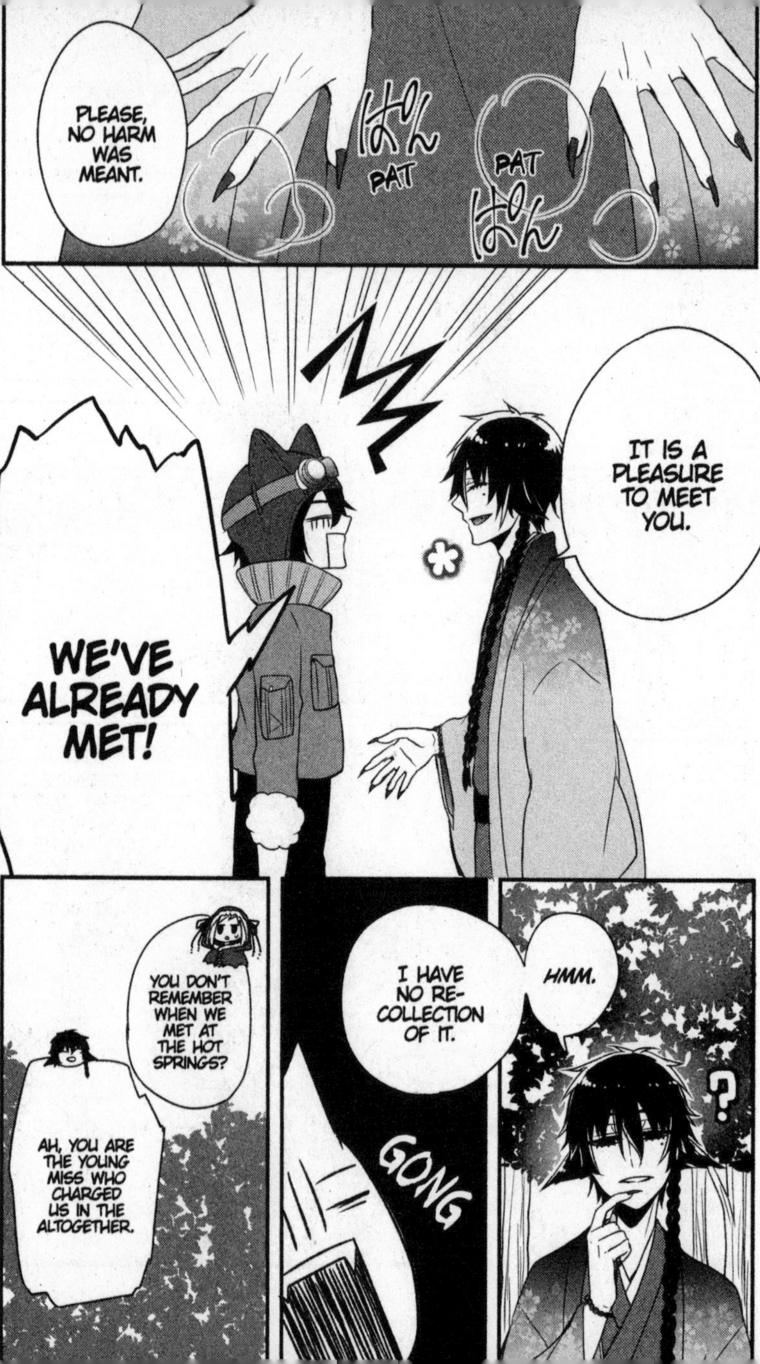
PAT
はん
はん
PAT
PLEASE, NO HARM WAS MEANT.
IT IS A PLEASURE TO MEET YOU.
WE'VE ALREADY MET!
HMM.
I HAVE NO RE-COLLECTION OF IT.
GONG
YOU DON'T REMEMBER WHEN WE MET AT THE HOT SPRINGS?
AH, YOU ARE THE YOUNG MISS WHO CHARGED US IN THE ALTOGETHER.

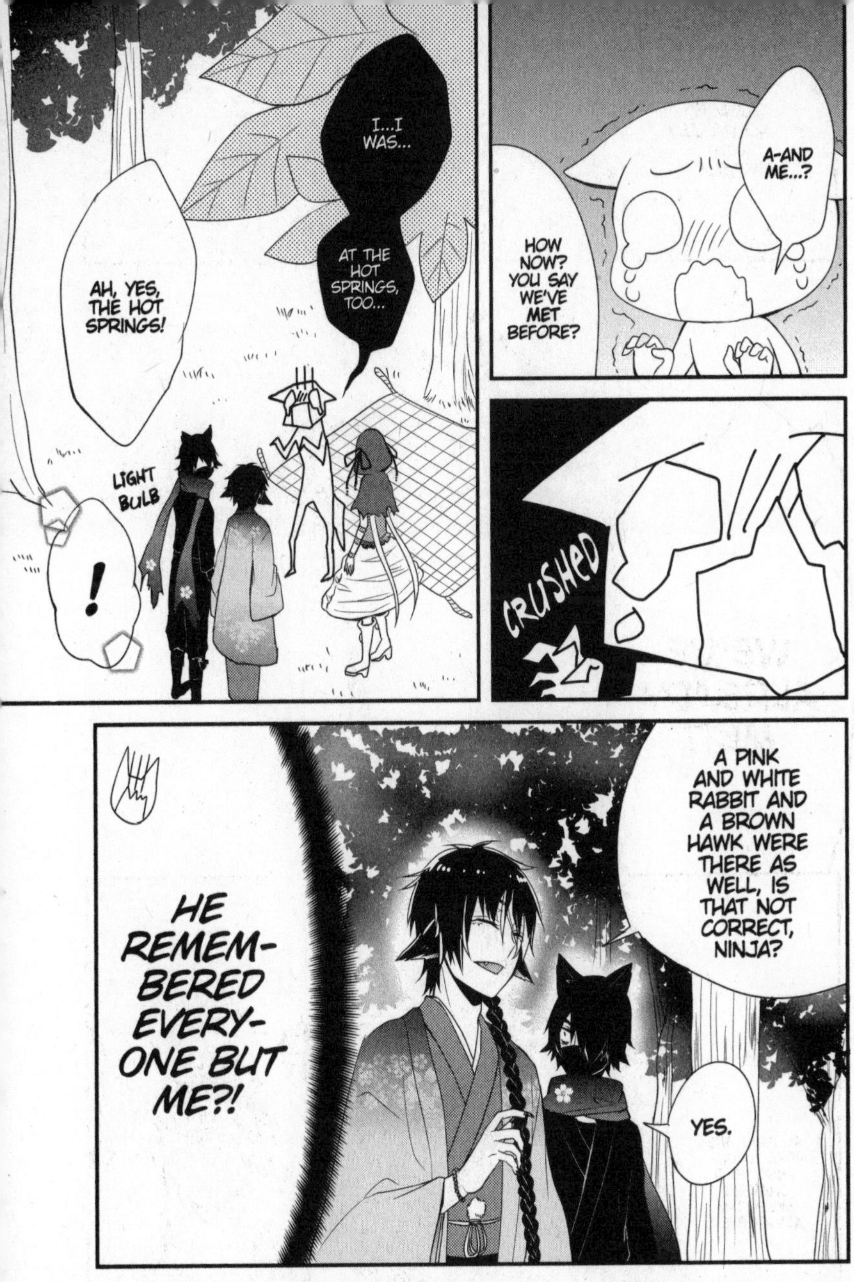
A-AND ME...?
HOW NOW? YOU SAY WE'VE MET BEFORE?
CRUSHED
I...I WAS...
AT THE HOT SPRINGS, TOO...
AH, YES, THE HOT SPRINGS!
LIGHT BULB
!
A PINK AND WHITE RABBIT AND A BROWN HAWK WERE THERE AS WELL, IS THAT NOT CORRECT, NINJA?
YES.
HE REMEMBERED EVERYONE BUT ME?!

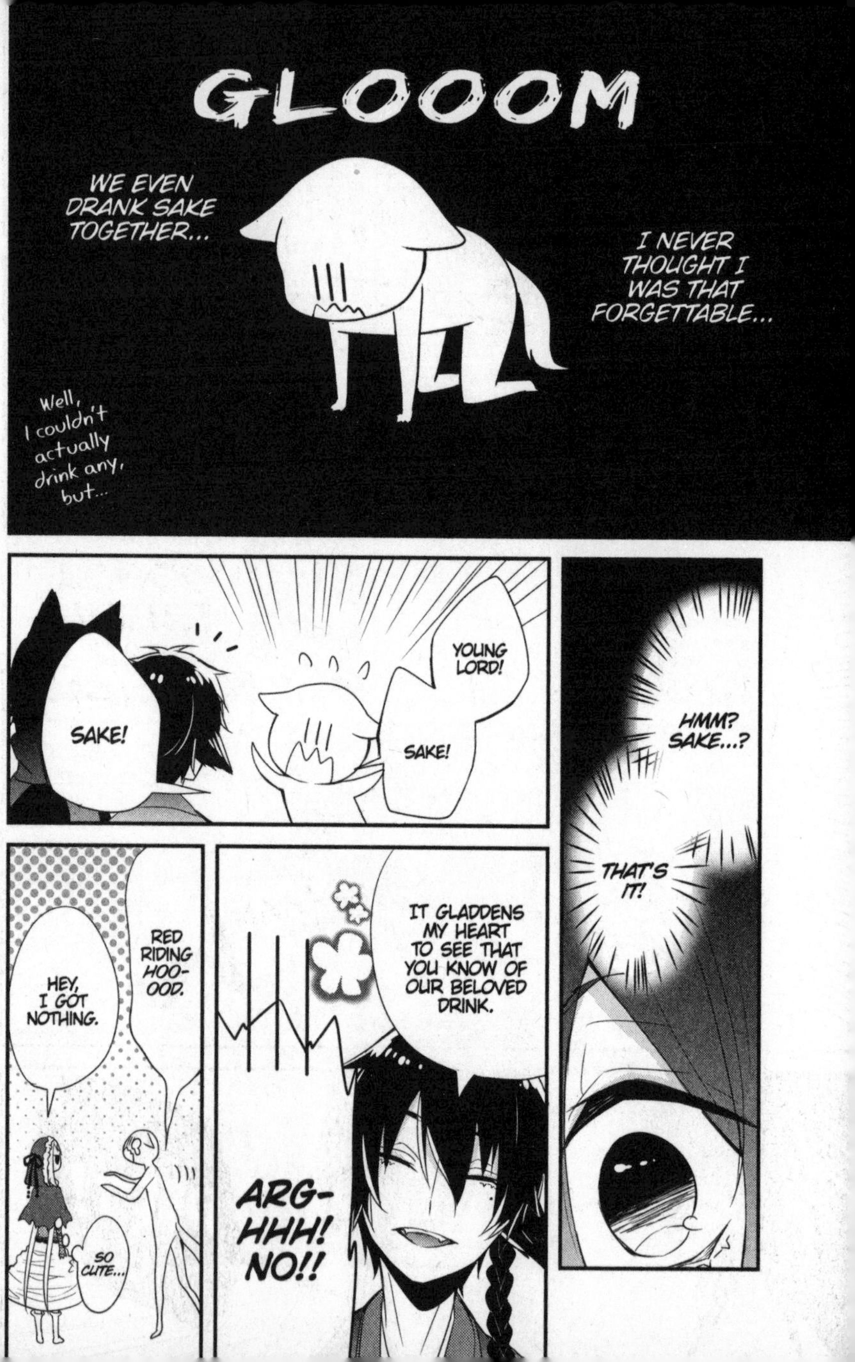
GLOOOM
I NEVER THOUGHT I WAS THAT FORGETTABLE...
WE EVEN DRANK SAKE TOGETHER...
Well, I couldn't actually drink any, but...
HMM? SAKE...?
THAT'S IT!
YOUNG LORD!
SAKE!
SAKE!
IT GLADDENS MY HEART TO SEE THAT YOU KNOW OF OUR BELOVED DRINK.
ARG-HHH! NO!!
RED RIDING HOO-OOD.
HEY, I GOT NOTHING.
SO CUTE...

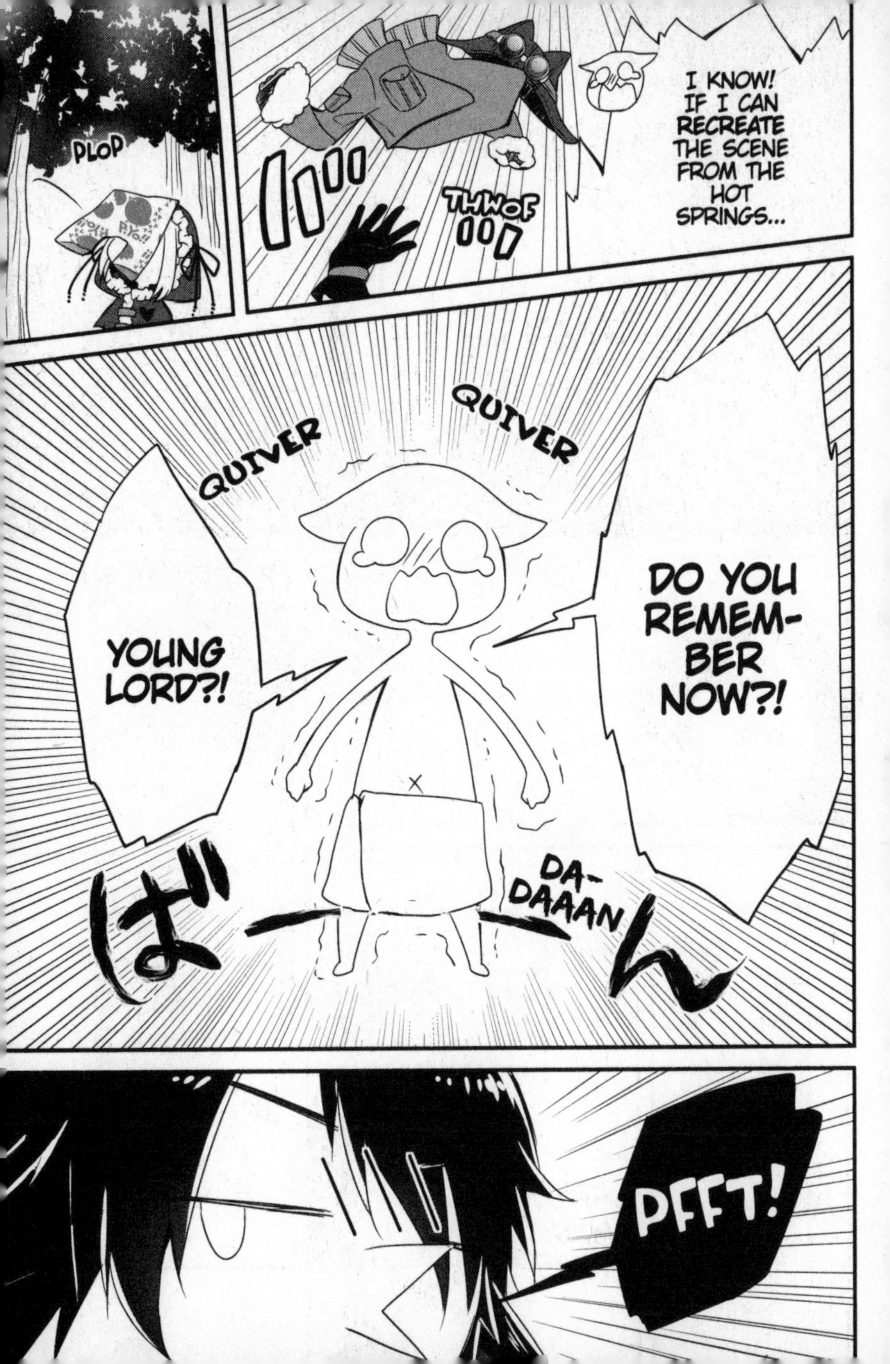
I KNOW! IF I CAN RECREATE THE SCENE FROM THE HOT SPRINGS...
THWOF
PLOP
DO YOU REMEMBER NOW?!
QUIVER
QUIVER
YOUNG LORD?!
ばん
DA-DAAAN
PFFT!

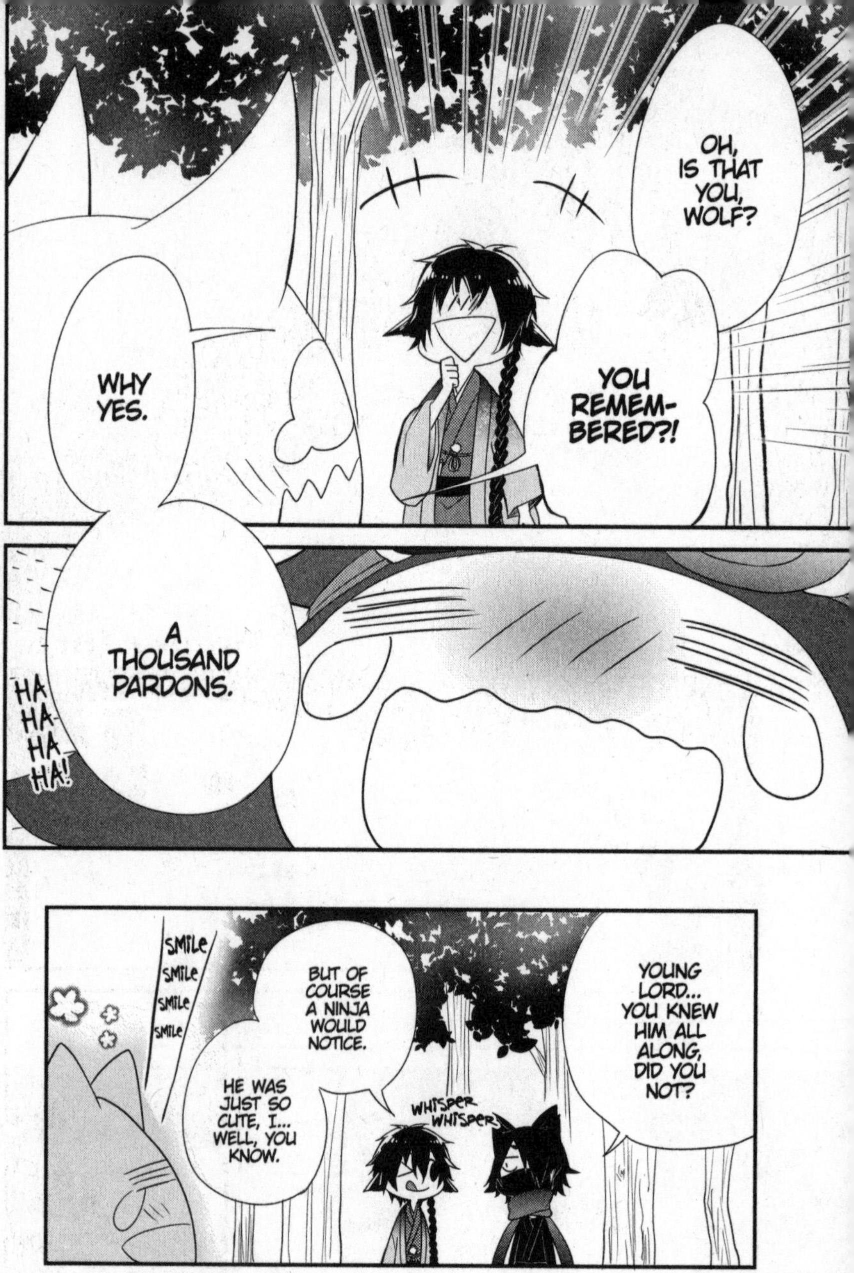
OH, IS THAT YOU, WOLF?
YOU REMEMBERED?!
WHY YES.
A THOUSAND PARDONS.
HA HA HA HA!
YOUNG LORD... YOU KNEW HIM ALL ALONG, DID YOU NOT?
WHISPER WHISPER
BUT OF COURSE A NINJA WOULD NOTICE.
HE WAS JUST SO CUTE, I... WELL, YOU KNOW.
SMILE SMILE SMILE SMILE

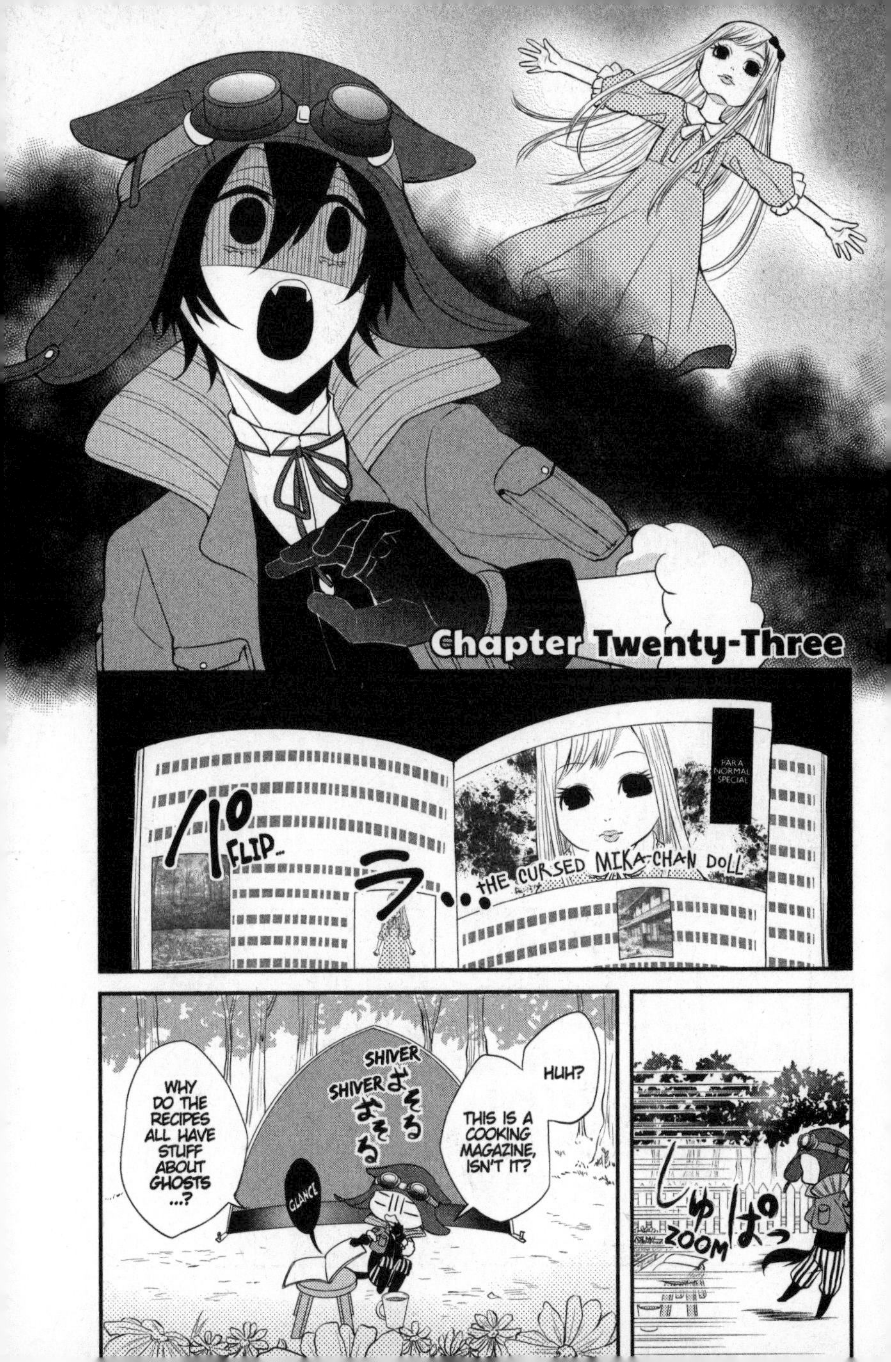
Chapter Twenty-Three
PARA NORMAL SPECIAL
THE CURSED MIKA-CHAN DOLL
パ FLIP...
ラ...
しゅぱっ ZOOM
HUH?
THIS IS A COOKING MAGAZINE, ISN'T IT?
SHIVER SHIVER
GLANCE
WHY DO THE RECIPES ALL HAVE STUFF ABOUT GHOSTS ...?

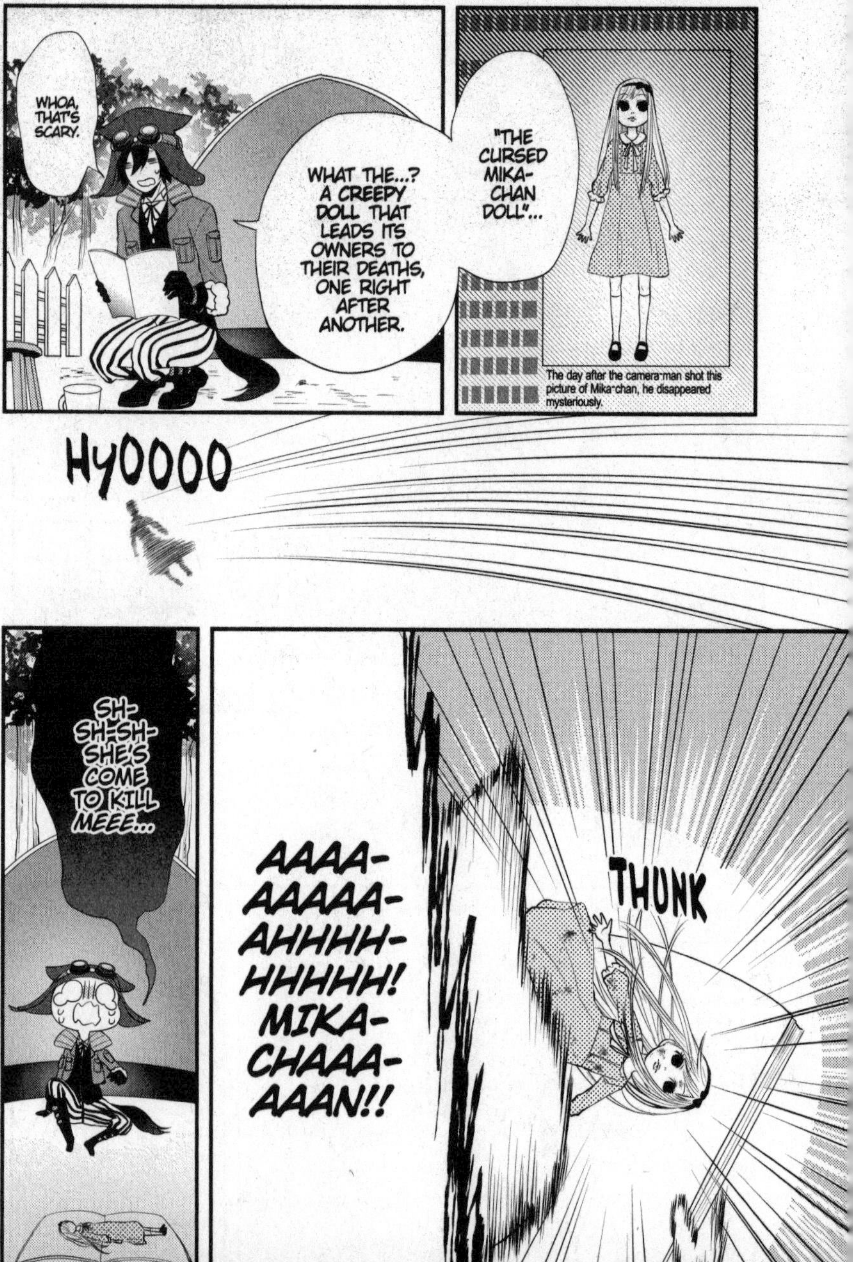
"THE CURSED MIKA-CHAN DOLL"...
The day after the camera-man shot this picture of Mika-chan, he disappeared mysteriously.
WHAT THE...? A CREEPY DOLL THAT LEADS ITS OWNERS TO THEIR DEATHS, ONE RIGHT AFTER ANOTHER.
WHOA, THAT'S SCARY.
HYOOOO
THUNK
AAAA-AAAAA-AHHHH-HHHHH! MIKA-CHAAA-AAAN!!
SH-SH-SH-SHE'S COME TO KILL MEEE...

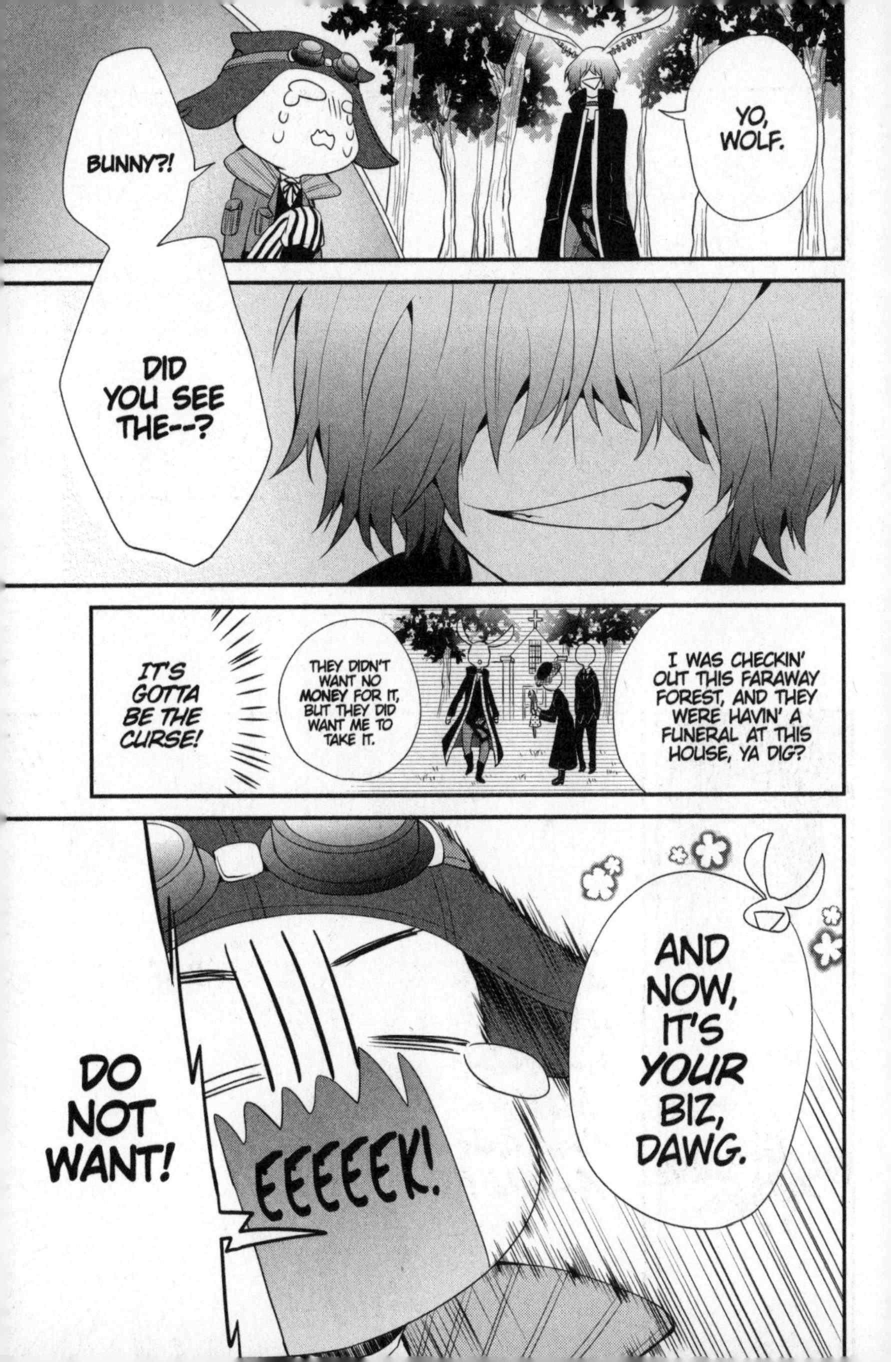
YO, WOLF.
BUNNY?!
DID YOU SEE THE--?
I WAS CHECKIN' OUT THIS FARAWAY FOREST, AND THEY WERE HAVIN' A FUNERAL AT THIS HOUSE, YA DIG?
THEY DIDN'T WANT NO MONEY FOR IT, BUT THEY DID WANT ME TO TAKE IT.
IT'S GOTTA BE THE CURSE!
AND NOW, IT'S *YOUR* BIZ, DAWG.
EEEEEEK!
DO NOT WANT!

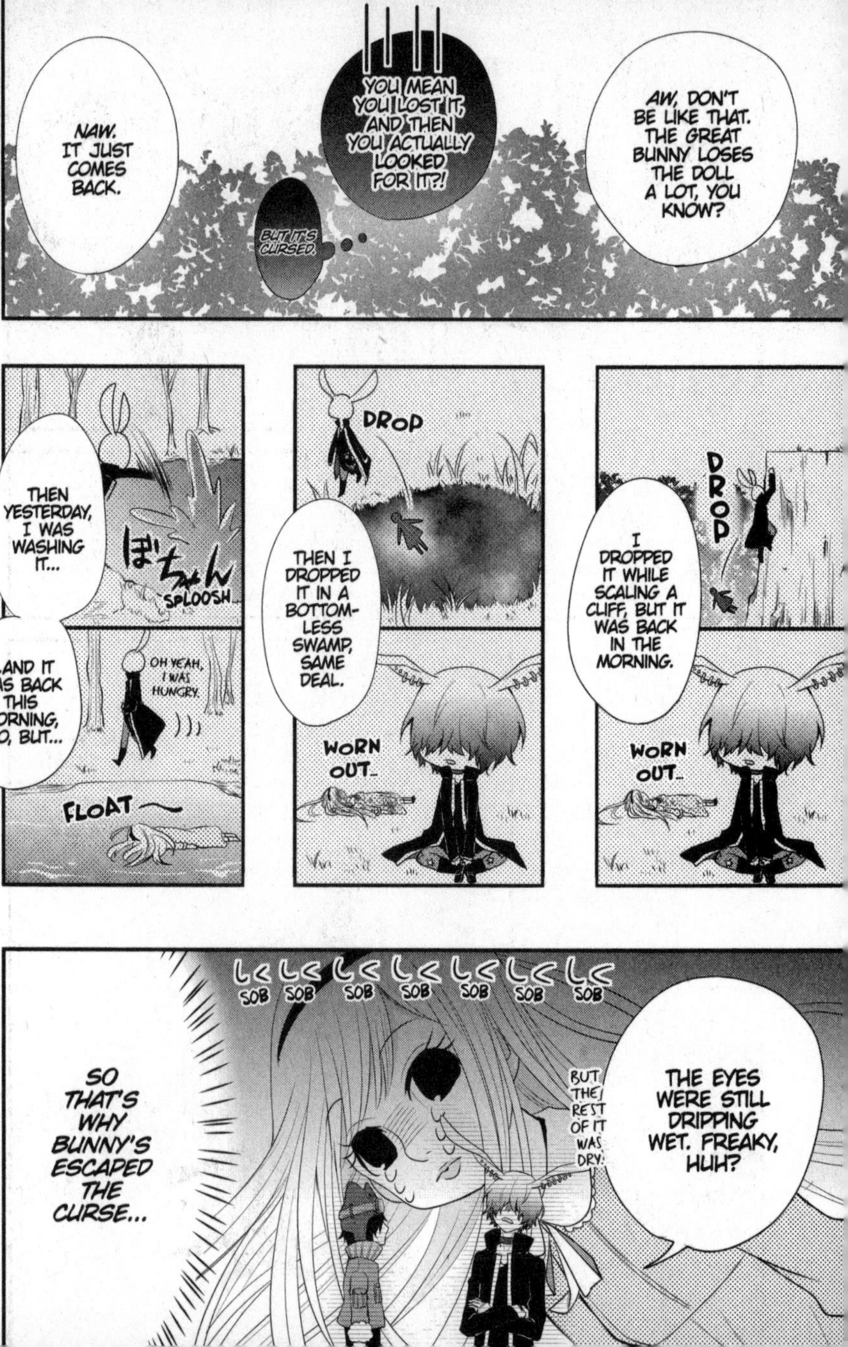
AW, DON'T BE LIKE THAT. THE GREAT BUNNY LOSES THE DOLL A LOT, YOU KNOW?
YOU MEAN YOU LOST IT, AND THEN YOU ACTUALLY LOOKED FOR IT?!
BUT IT'S CURSED.
NAW. IT JUST COMES BACK.
DROP DROP
I DROPPED IT WHILE SCALING A CLIFF, BUT IT WAS BACK IN THE MORNING.
WORN OUT...
DROP
THEN I DROPPED IT IN A BOTTOMLESS SWAMP, SAME DEAL.
WORN OUT...
THEN YESTERDAY, I WAS WASHING IT...
ぼちゃん
SPLOOSH
...AND IT WAS BACK THIS MORNING, TOO, BUT...
OH YEAH, I WAS HUNGRY.
FLOAT~
しくしくしくしくしくしくしく
SOB SOB SOB SOB SOB SOB SOB
THE EYES WERE STILL DRIPPING WET. FREAKY, HUH?
BUT THE REST OF IT WAS DRY.
SO THAT'S WHY BUNNY'S ESCAPED THE CURSE...

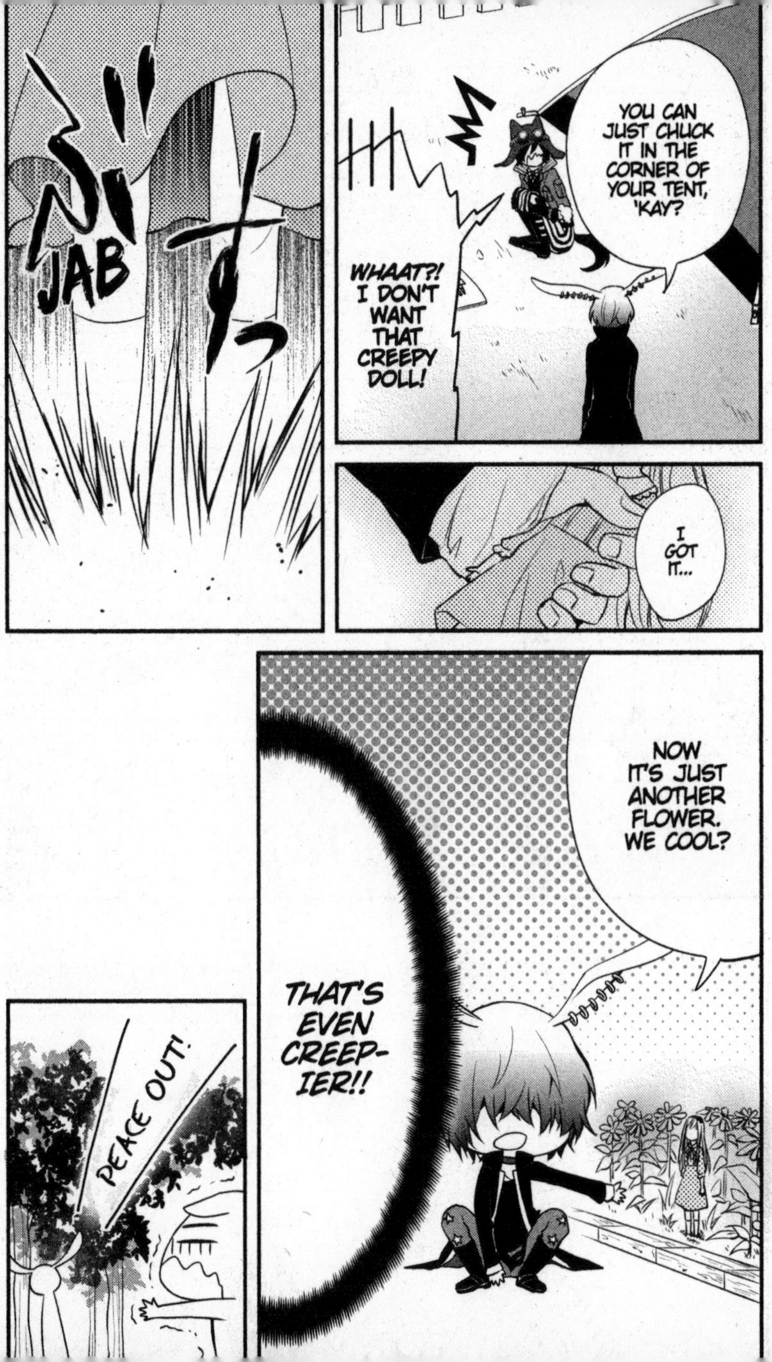
YOU CAN JUST CHUCK IT IN THE CORNER OF YOUR TENT, 'KAY?
WHAAT?! I DON'T WANT THAT CREEPY DOLL!
I GOT IT...
ぶすっ
JAB
NOW IT'S JUST ANOTHER FLOWER. WE COOL?
THAT'S EVEN CREEP-IER!!
PEACE OUT!

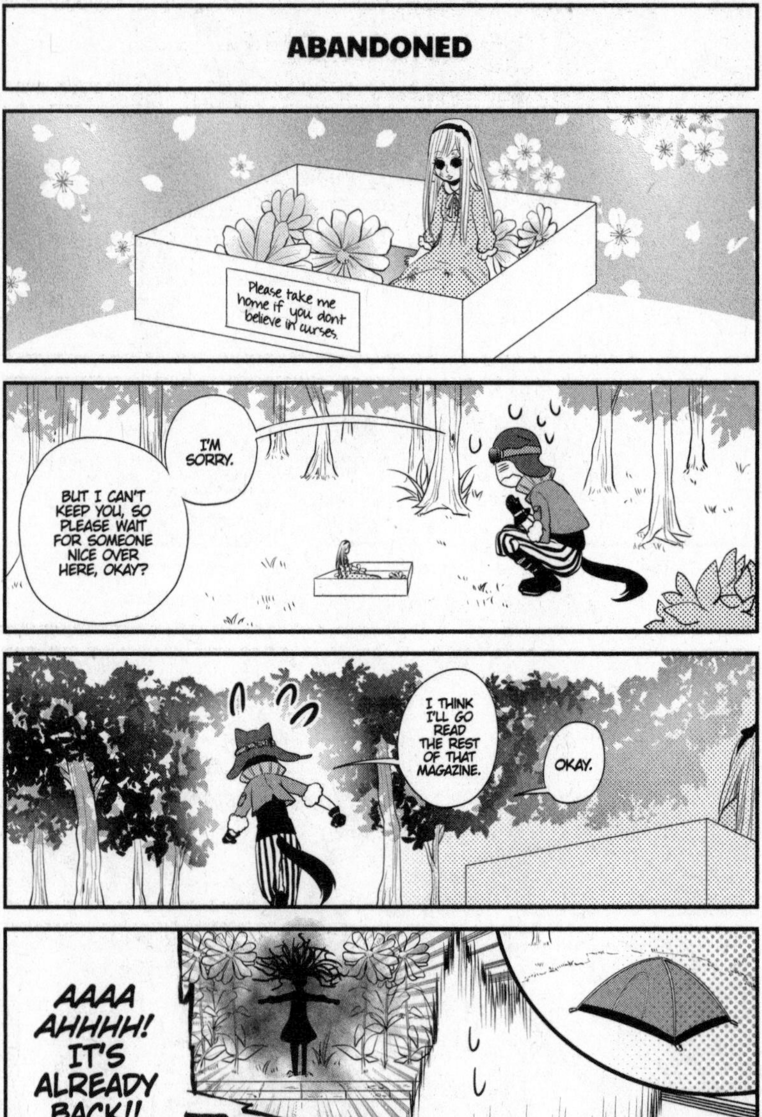
ABANDONED
Please take me home if you dont believe in curses.
I'M SORRY.
BUT I CAN'T KEEP YOU, SO PLEASE WAIT FOR SOMEONE NICE OVER HERE, OKAY?
I THINK I'LL GO READ THE REST OF THAT MAGAZINE.
OKAY.
AAAA AHHHH! IT'S ALREADY BACK!!

NO SECOND CHANCES

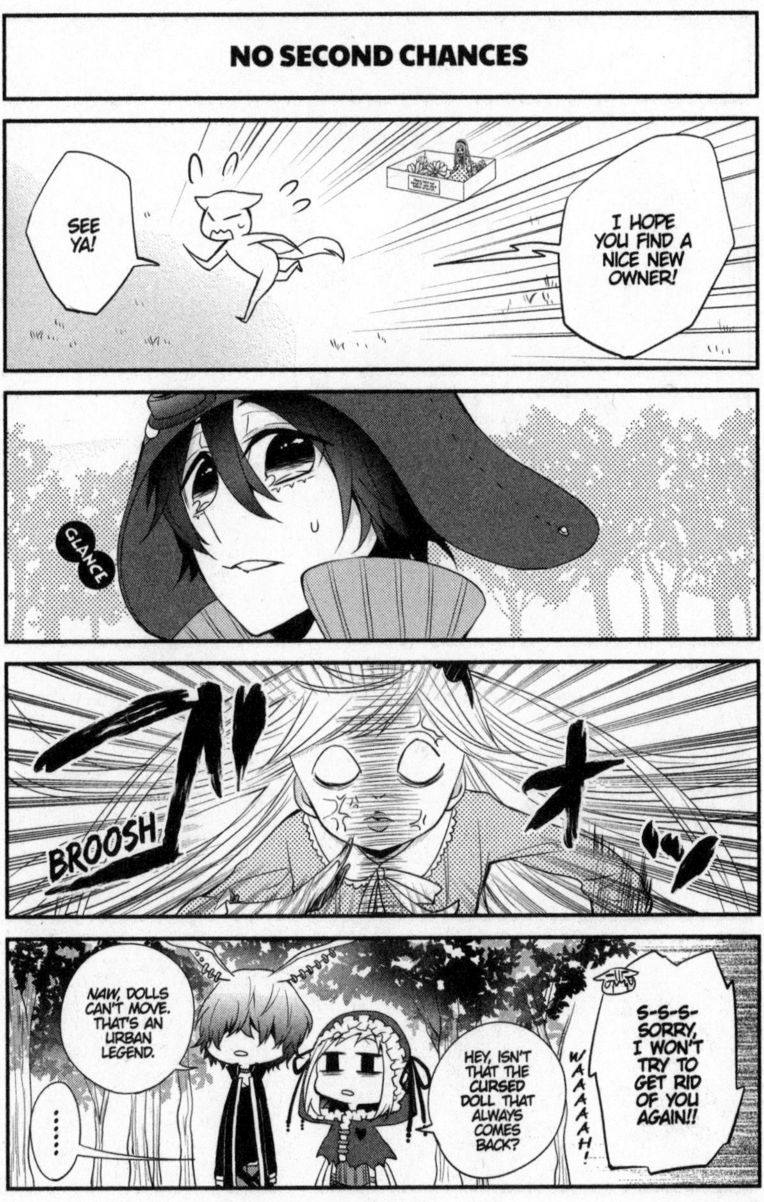
I HOPE YOU FIND A NICE NEW OWNER!
SEE YA!
GLANCE
BROOSH
S-S-S-SORRY, I WON'T TRY TO GET RID OF YOU AGAIN!!
WAAAAAAH!
HEY, ISN'T THAT THE CURSED DOLL THAT ALWAYS COMES BACK?
NAW, DOLLS CAN'T MOVE. THAT'S AN URBAN LEGEND.
......

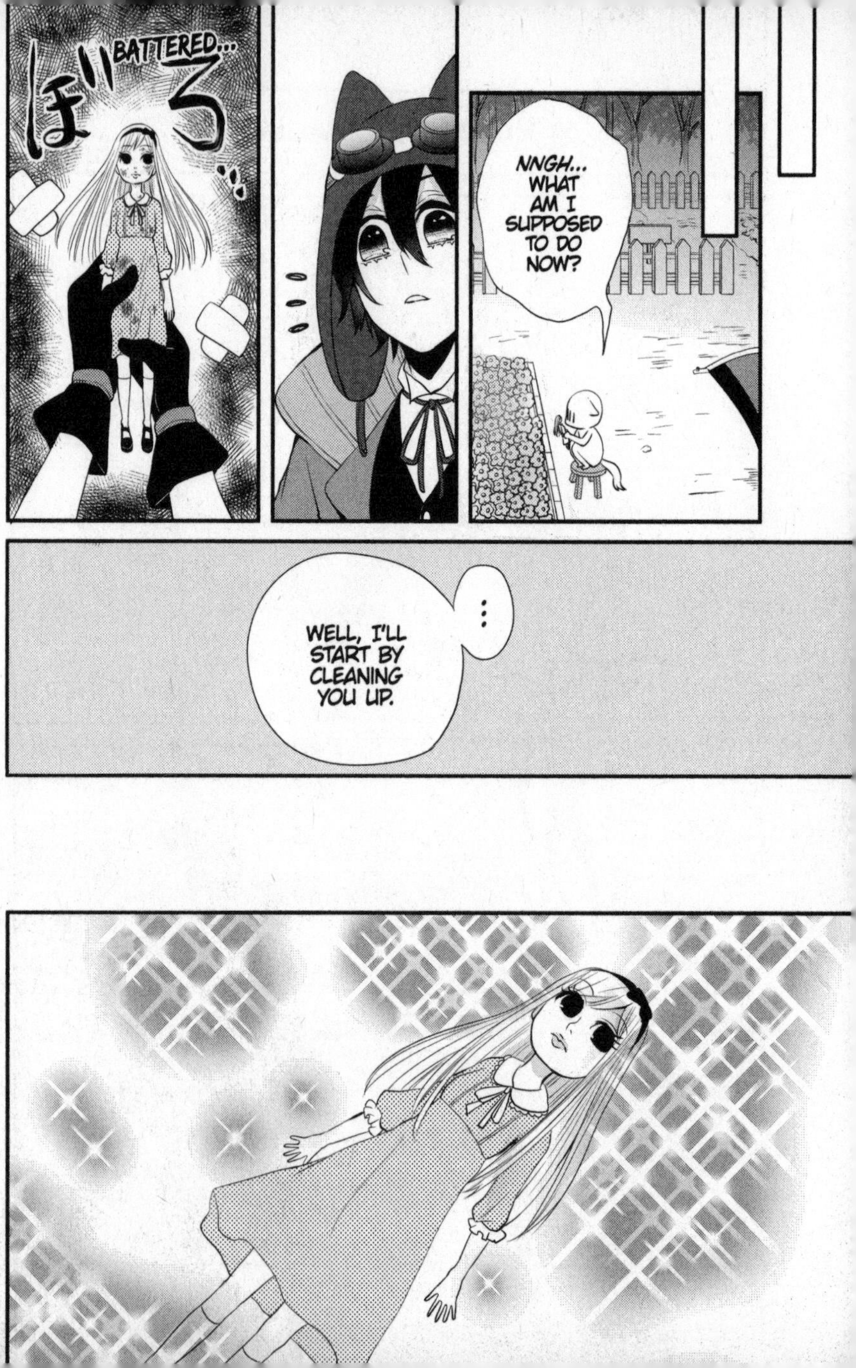
NNGH... WHAT AM I SUPPOSED TO DO NOW?
BATTERED...
...
WELL, I'LL START BY CLEANING YOU UP.

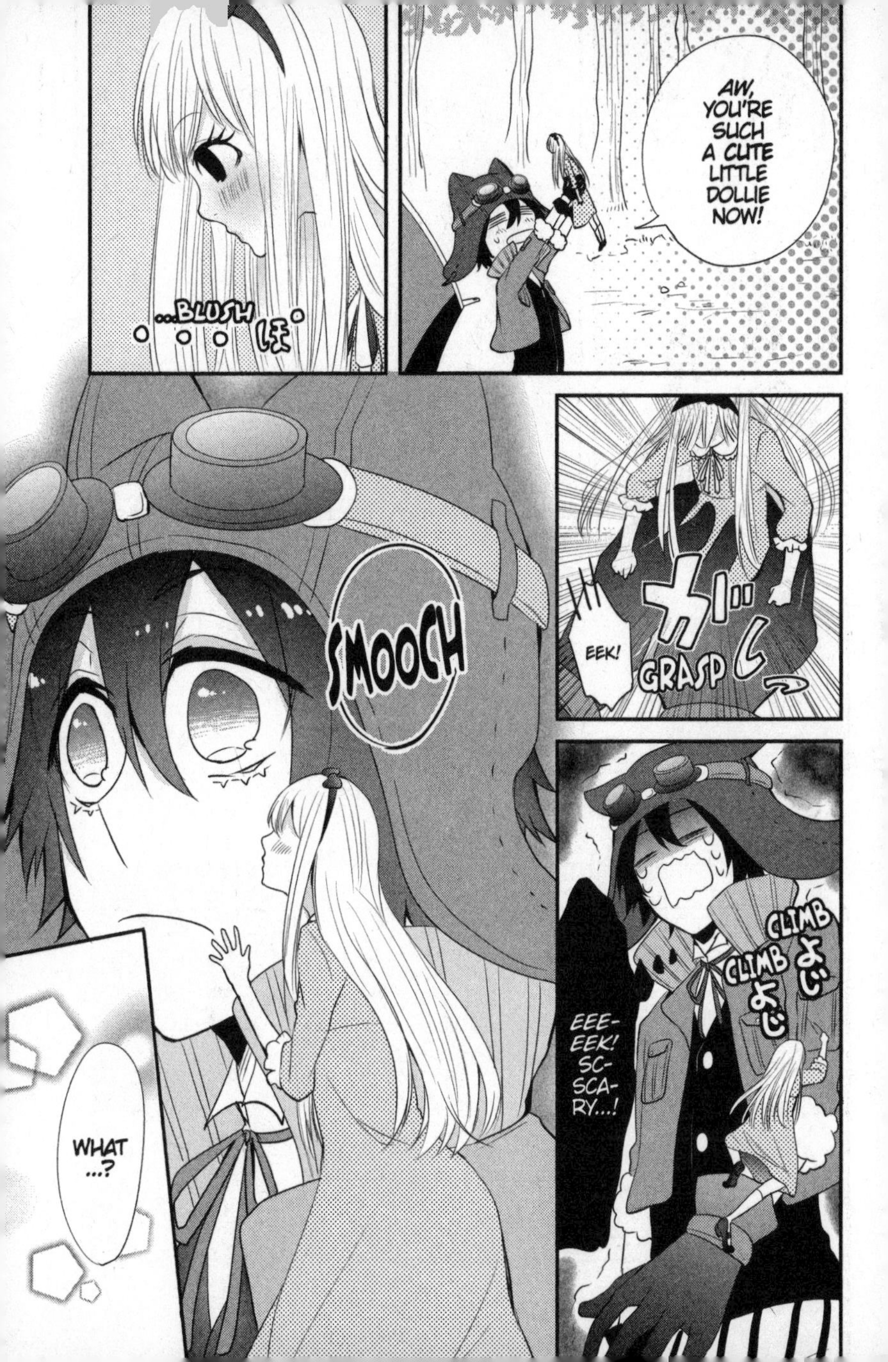
AW, YOU'RE SUCH A CUTE LITTLE DOLLIE NOW!
...BLUSH
EEK!
GRASP
CLIMB
よじ
CLIMB
よじ
EEE-EEK! SC-SCA-RY...!
SMOOCH
WHAT ...?

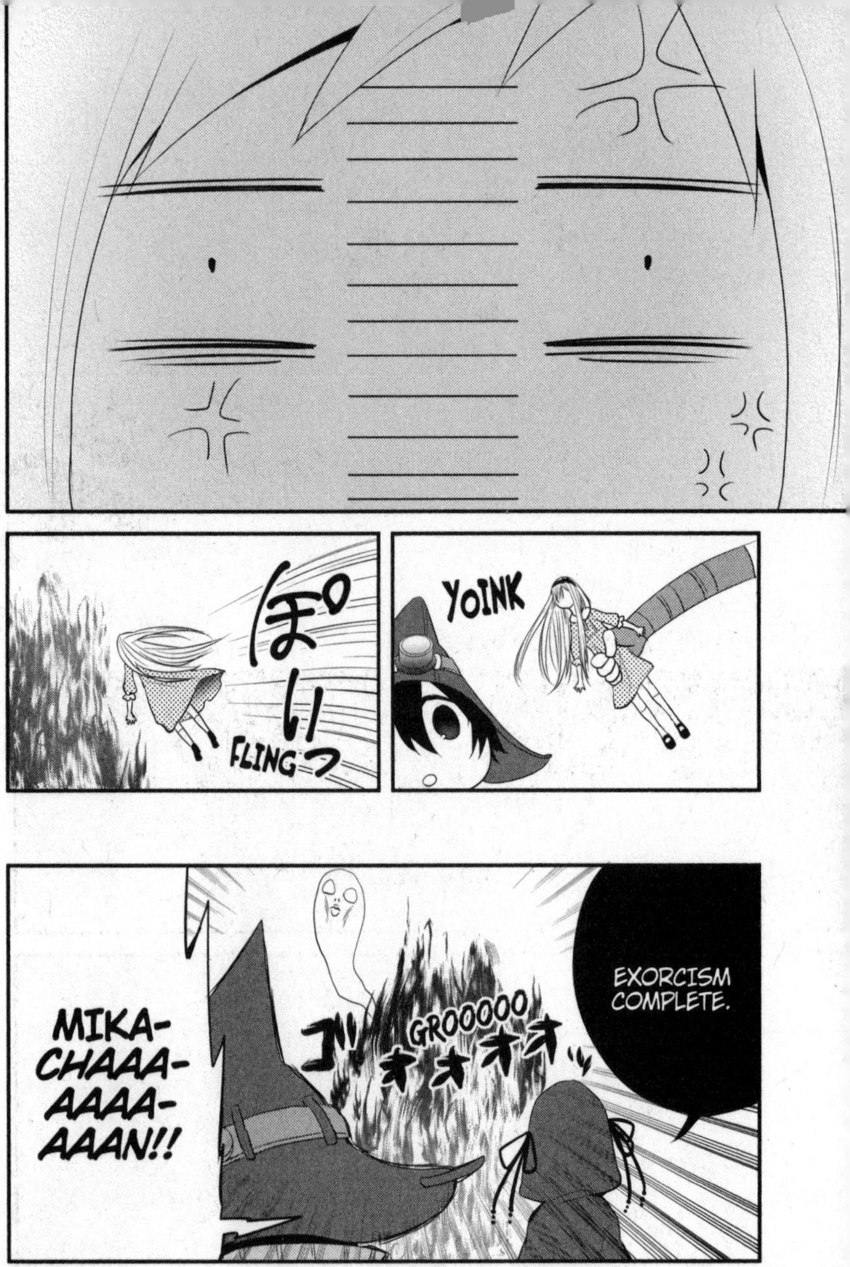
YOINK
ぽいっ
FLING
EXORCISM COMPLETE.
GROOOOO
ゴォォォォッ
MIKA-CHAAAA-AAAA-AAAN!!

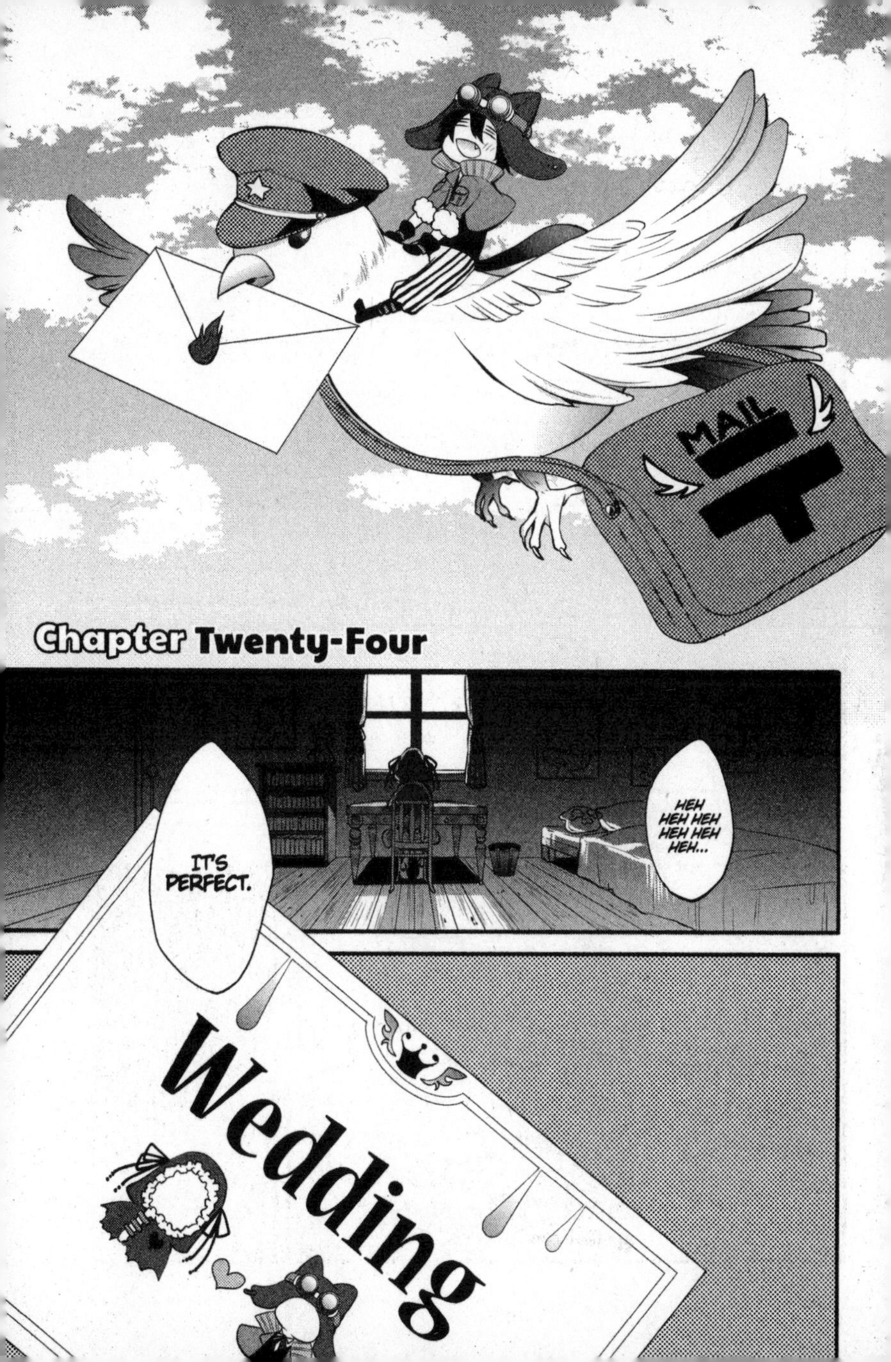
MAIL
Chapter Twenty-Four
HEH HEH HEH HEH HEH HEH...
IT'S PERFECT.
Wedding

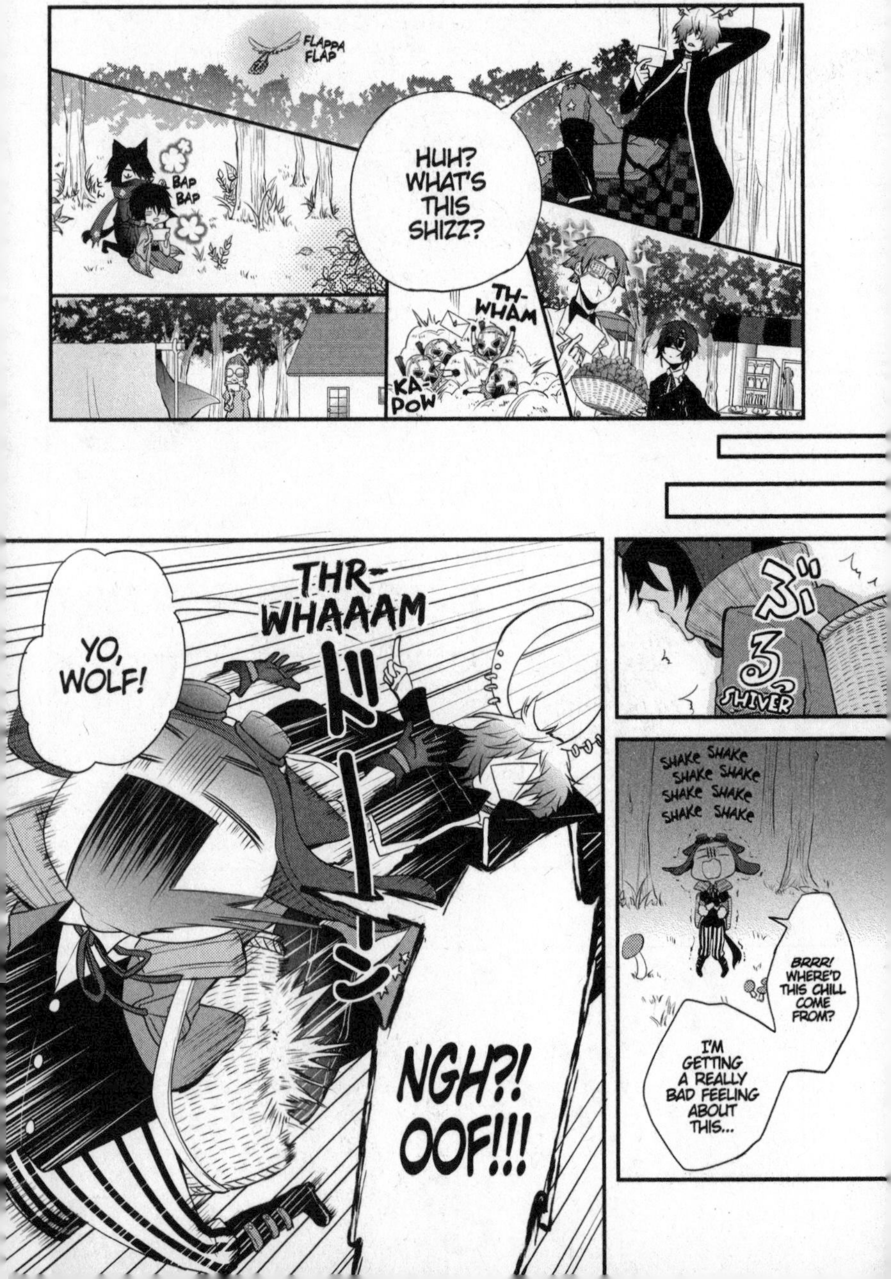
HUH? WHAT'S THIS SHIZZ?
FLAPPA FLAP
BAP BAP
TH-WHAM
KA-POW
ぶる
SHIVER
SHAKE SHAKE SHAKE SHAKE SHAKE SHAKE SHAKE SHAKE
BRRR! WHERE'D THIS CHILL COME FROM?
I'M GETTING A REALLY BAD FEELING ABOUT THIS...
YO, WOLF!
THR-WHAAAM
ドーン
NGH?! OOF!!!

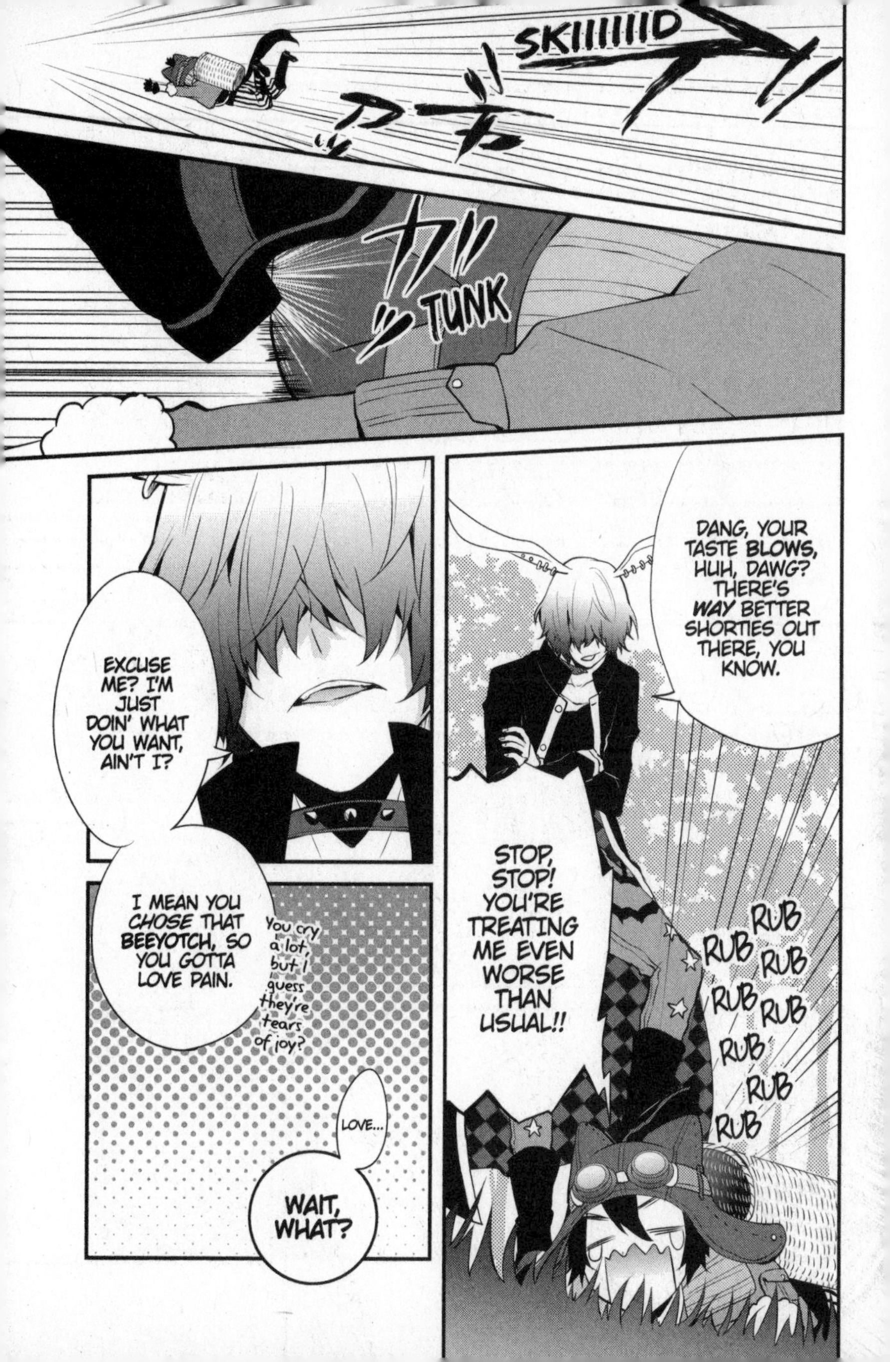
SKIIIIIID
TUNK
DANG, YOUR TASTE BLOWS, HUH, DAWG? THERE'S *WAY* BETTER SHORTIES OUT THERE, YOU KNOW.
STOP, STOP! YOU'RE TREATING ME EVEN WORSE THAN USUAL!!
RUB RUB RUB RUB RUB RUB RUB RUB RUB
EXCUSE ME? I'M JUST DOIN' WHAT YOU WANT, AIN'T I?
I MEAN YOU *CHOSE* THAT BEEYOTCH, SO YOU GOTTA LOVE PAIN.
You cry a lot, but I guess they're tears of joy?
LOVE...
WAIT, WHAT?

SENTIMENTAL

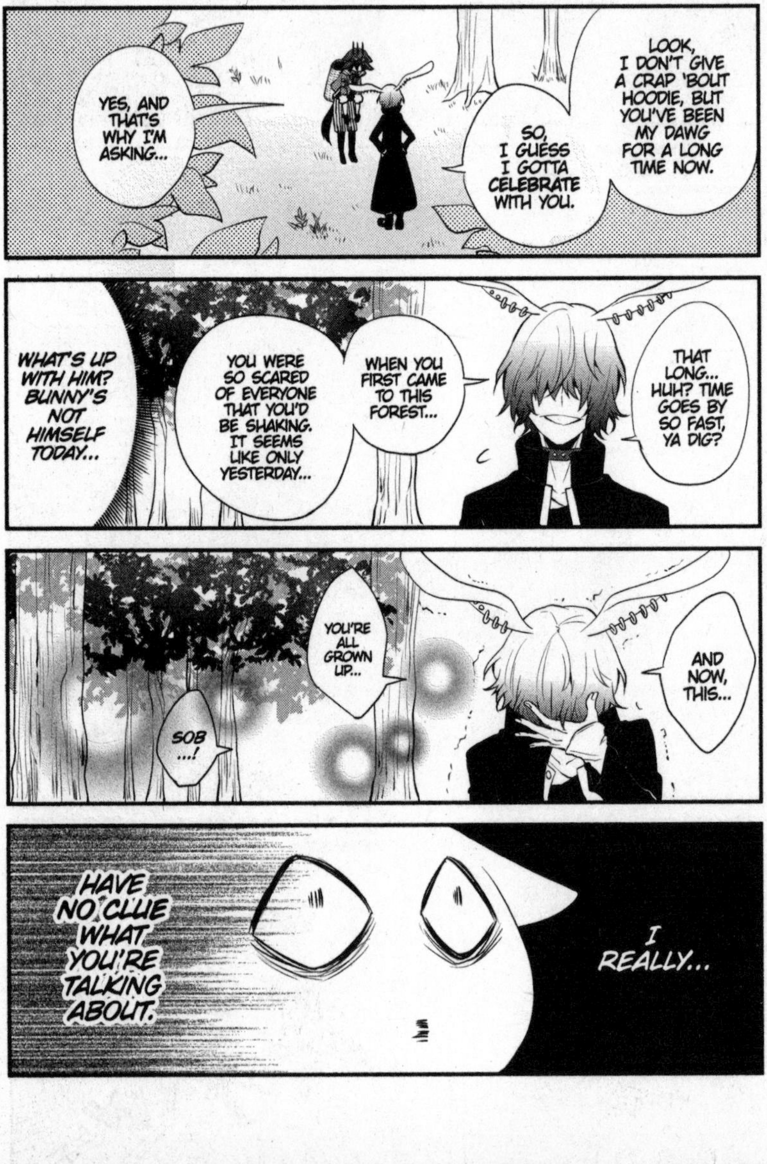
LOOK, I DON'T GIVE A CRAP 'BOUT HOODIE, BUT YOU'VE BEEN MY DAWG FOR A LONG TIME NOW.
SO, I GUESS I GOTTA CELEBRATE WITH YOU.
YES, AND THAT'S WHY I'M ASKING...
THAT LONG... HUH? TIME GOES BY SO FAST, YA DIG?
WHEN YOU FIRST CAME TO THIS FOREST...
YOU WERE SO SCARED OF EVERYONE THAT YOU'D BE SHAKING. IT SEEMS LIKE ONLY YESTERDAY...
WHAT'S UP WITH HIM? BUNNY'S NOT HIMSELF TODAY...
AND NOW, THIS...
YOU'RE ALL GROWN UP...
SOB ...!
I REALLY...
HAVE NO CLUE WHAT YOU'RE TALKING ABOUT.

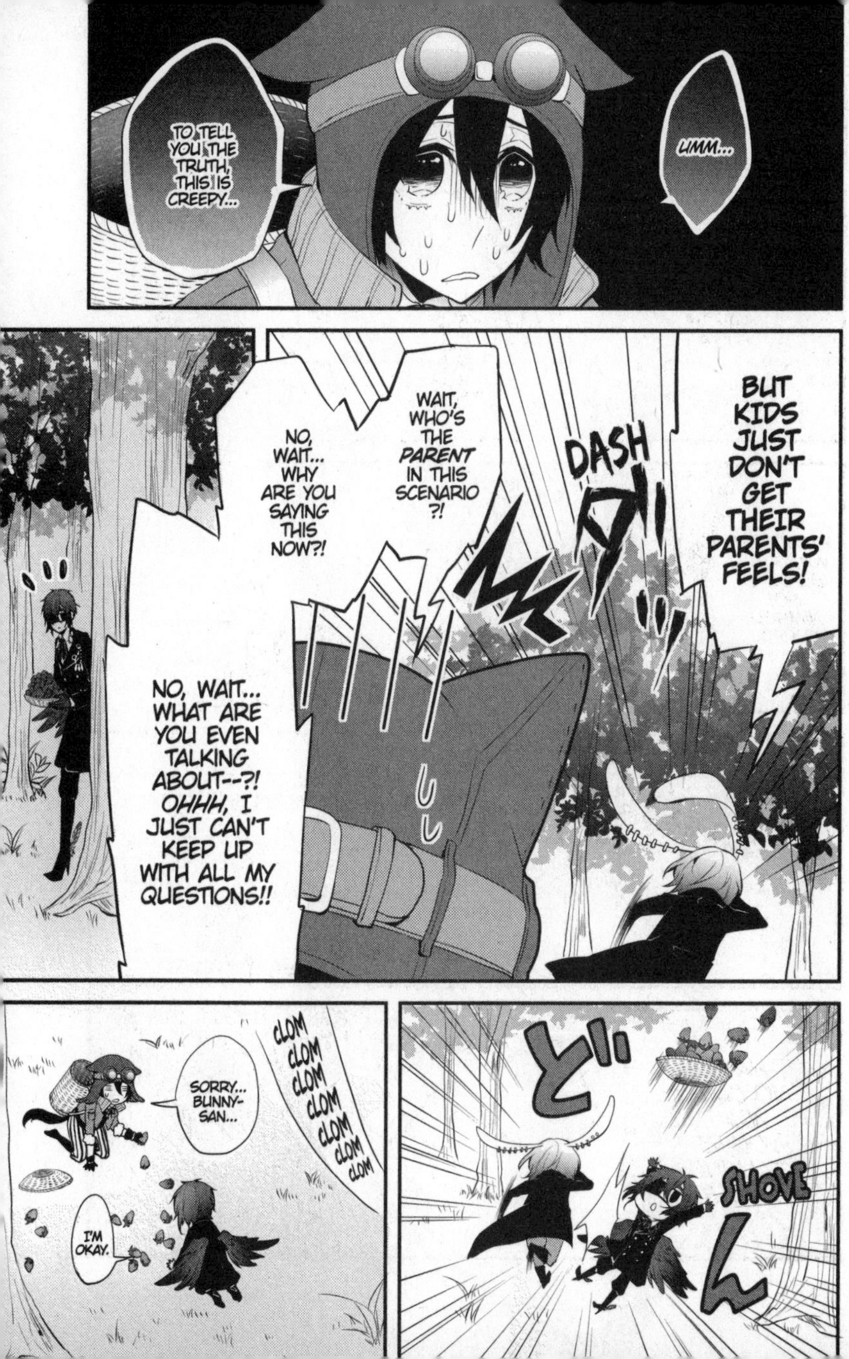
UMM...
TO TELL YOU THE TRUTH, THIS IS CREEPY...
BUT KIDS JUST DON'T GET THEIR PARENTS' FEELS!
DASH
WAIT, WHO'S THE *PARENT* IN THIS SCENARIO?!
NO, WAIT... WHY ARE YOU SAYING THIS NOW?!
NO, WAIT... WHAT ARE YOU EVEN TALKING ABOUT--?! *OHHH*, I JUST CAN'T KEEP UP WITH ALL MY QUESTIONS!!
SHOVE
CLOM CLOM CLOM CLOM CLOM CLOM CLOM CLOM
SORRY... BUNNY-SAN...
I'M OKAY.

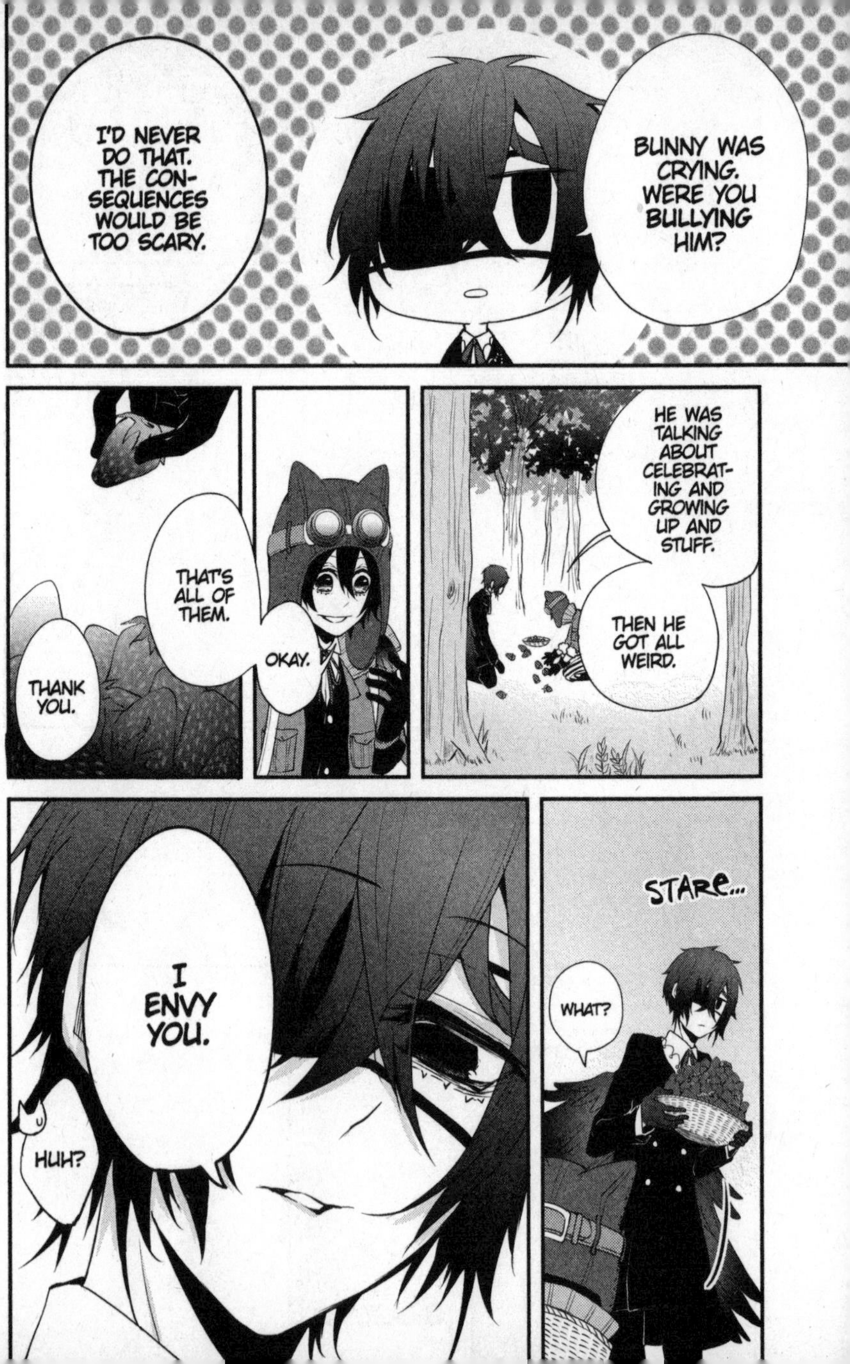
BUNNY WAS CRYING. WERE YOU BULLYING HIM?
I'D NEVER DO THAT. THE CON-SEQUENCES WOULD BE TOO SCARY.
HE WAS TALKING ABOUT CELEBRAT-ING AND GROWING UP AND STUFF.
THEN HE GOT ALL WEIRD.
THAT'S ALL OF THEM.
OKAY.
THANK YOU.
STARE...
WHAT?
I ENVY YOU.
HUH?

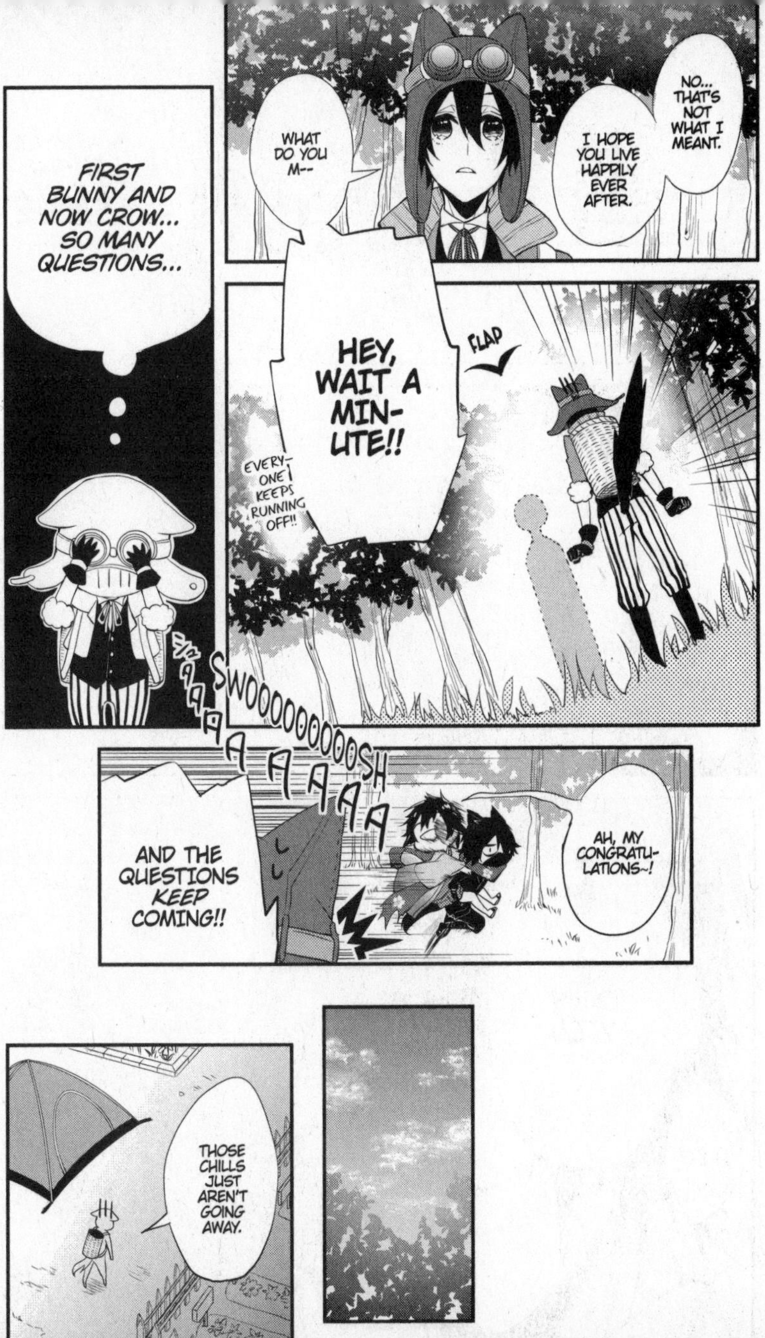
NO... THAT'S NOT WHAT I MEANT.
I HOPE YOU LIVE HAPPILY EVER AFTER.
WHAT DO YOU M--
FLAP
HEY, WAIT A MIN-UTE!!
EVERY-ONE KEEPS RUNNING OFF!!
SWOOOOOOOOOOSH
FIRST BUNNY AND NOW CROW... SO MANY QUESTIONS...
AH, MY CONGRATU-LATIONS~!
AND THE QUESTIONS KEEP COMING!!
THOSE CHILLS JUST AREN'T GOING AWAY.

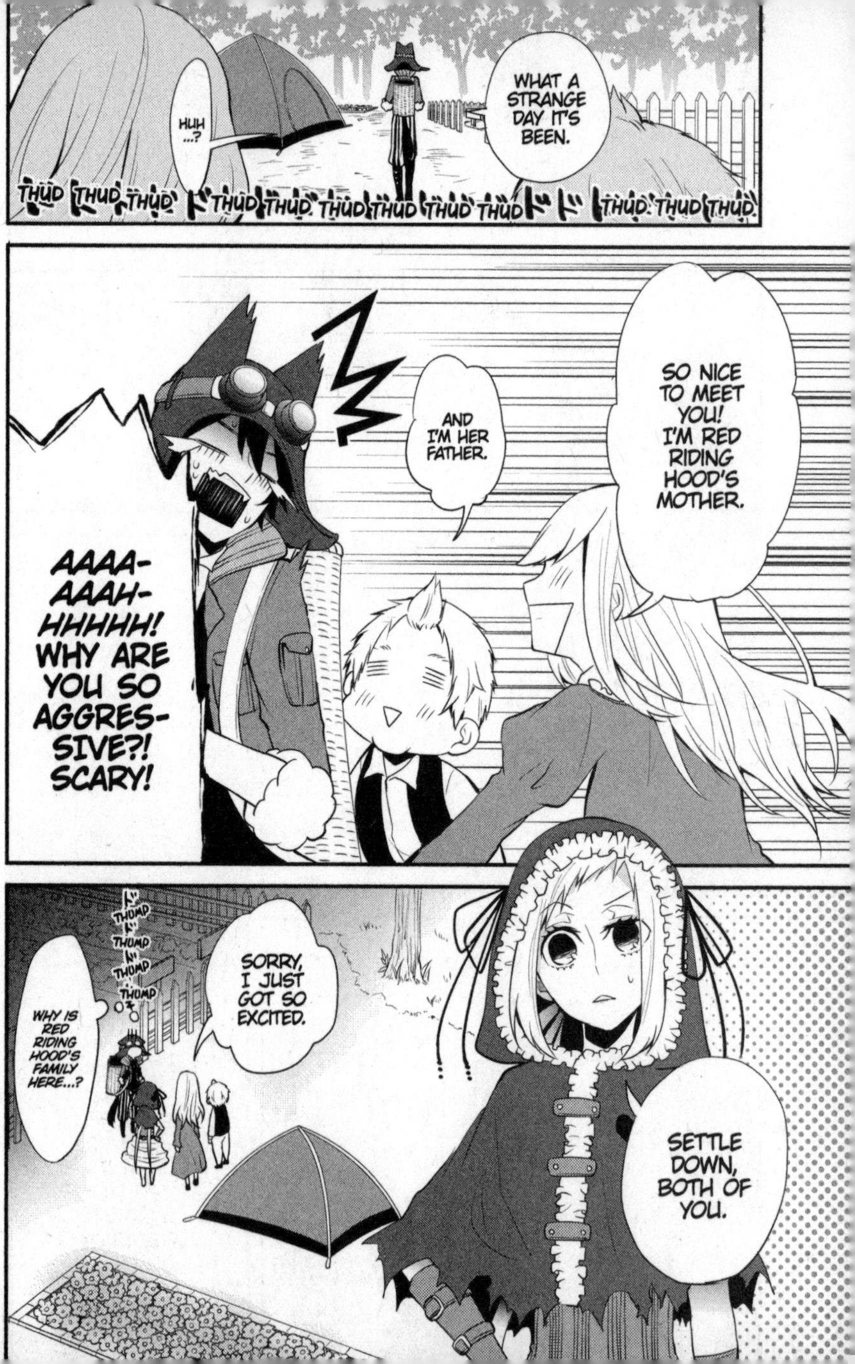
WHAT A STRANGE DAY IT'S BEEN.
HUH ...?
THUD THUD THUD THUD THUD THUD THUD THUD THUD THUD THUD THUD
SO NICE TO MEET YOU! I'M RED RIDING HOOD'S MOTHER.
AND I'M HER FATHER.
AAAA-AAAH-HHHHH! WHY ARE YOU SO AGGRES-SIVE?! SCARY!
SETTLE DOWN, BOTH OF YOU.
SORRY, I JUST GOT SO EXCITED.
THUMP THUMP THUMP THUMP
WHY IS RED RIDING HOOD'S FAMILY HERE...?

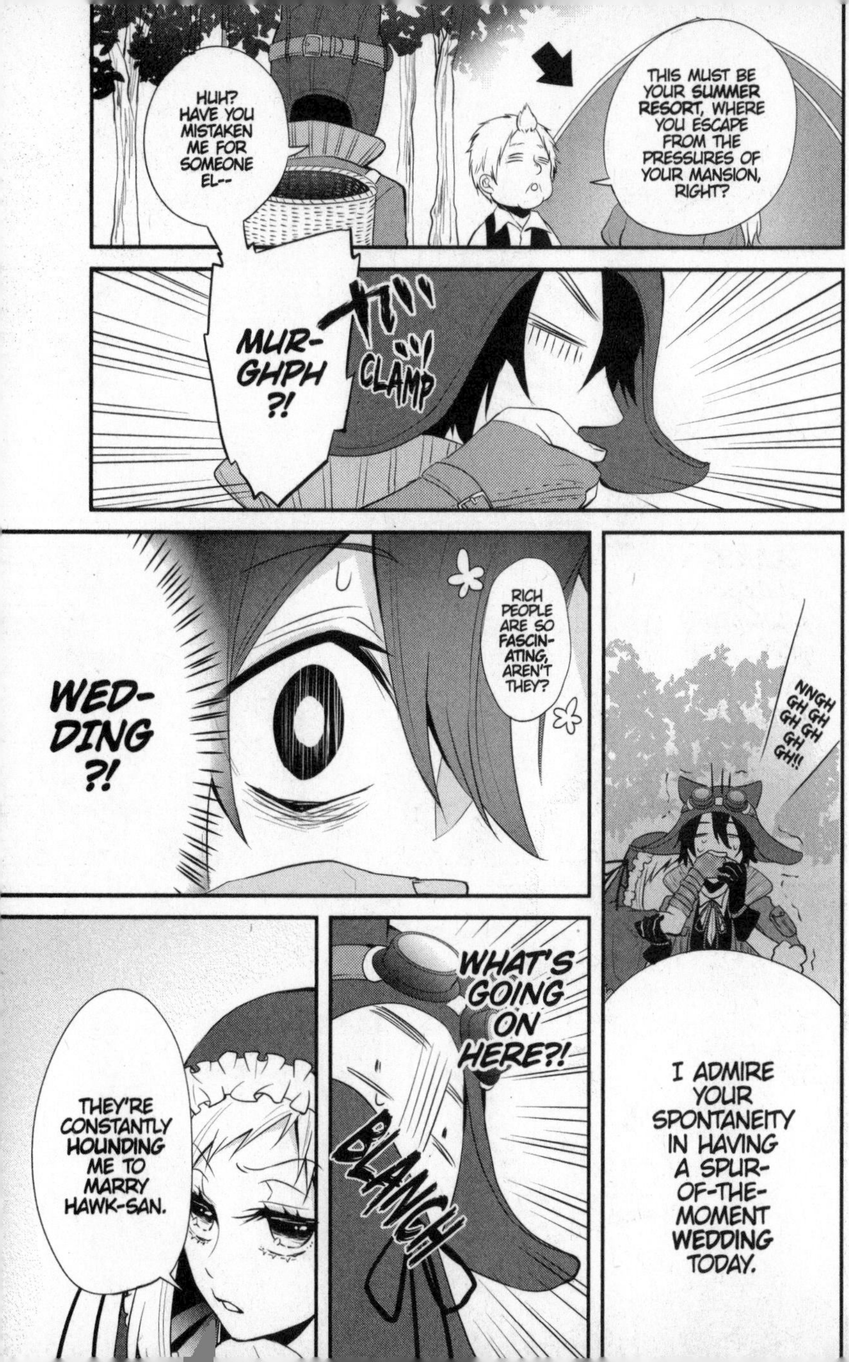
THIS MUST BE YOUR SUMMER RESORT, WHERE YOU ESCAPE FROM THE PRESSURES OF YOUR MANSION, RIGHT?
HUH? HAVE YOU MISTAKEN ME FOR SOMEONE EL--
CLAMP
MUR-GHPH ?!
NNGH GH GH GH GH GH GH!!
I ADMIRE YOUR SPONTANEITY IN HAVING A SPUR-OF-THE-MOMENT WEDDING TODAY.
RICH PEOPLE ARE SO FASCIN-ATING, AREN'T THEY?
WED-DING ?!
WHAT'S GOING ON HERE?!
BLANCH
THEY'RE CONSTANTLY HOUNDING ME TO MARRY HAWK-SAN.

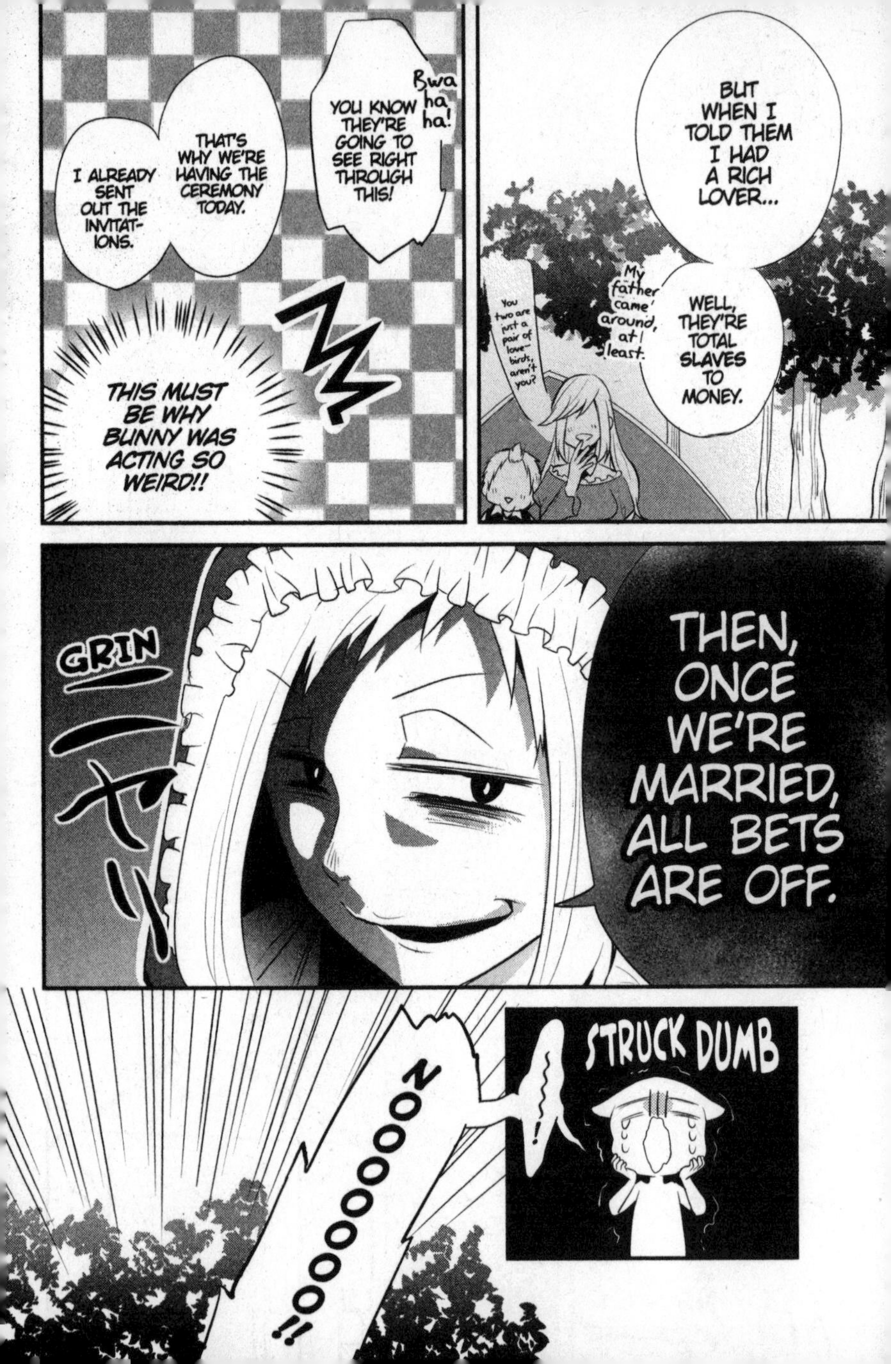

BUT WHEN I TOLD THEM I HAD A RICH LOVER...
WELL, THEY'RE TOTAL SLAVES TO MONEY.
My father came around, at least.
You two are just a pair of love-birds, aren't you?
Bwa ha ha!
YOU KNOW THEY'RE GOING TO SEE RIGHT THROUGH THIS!
THAT'S WHY WE'RE HAVING THE CEREMONY TODAY.
I ALREADY SENT OUT THE INVITAT-IONS.
THIS MUST BE WHY BUNNY WAS ACTING SO WEIRD!!
THEN, ONCE WE'RE MARRIED, ALL BETS ARE OFF.
GRIN
STRUCK DUMB
!
NOOOOOOOOOO!!

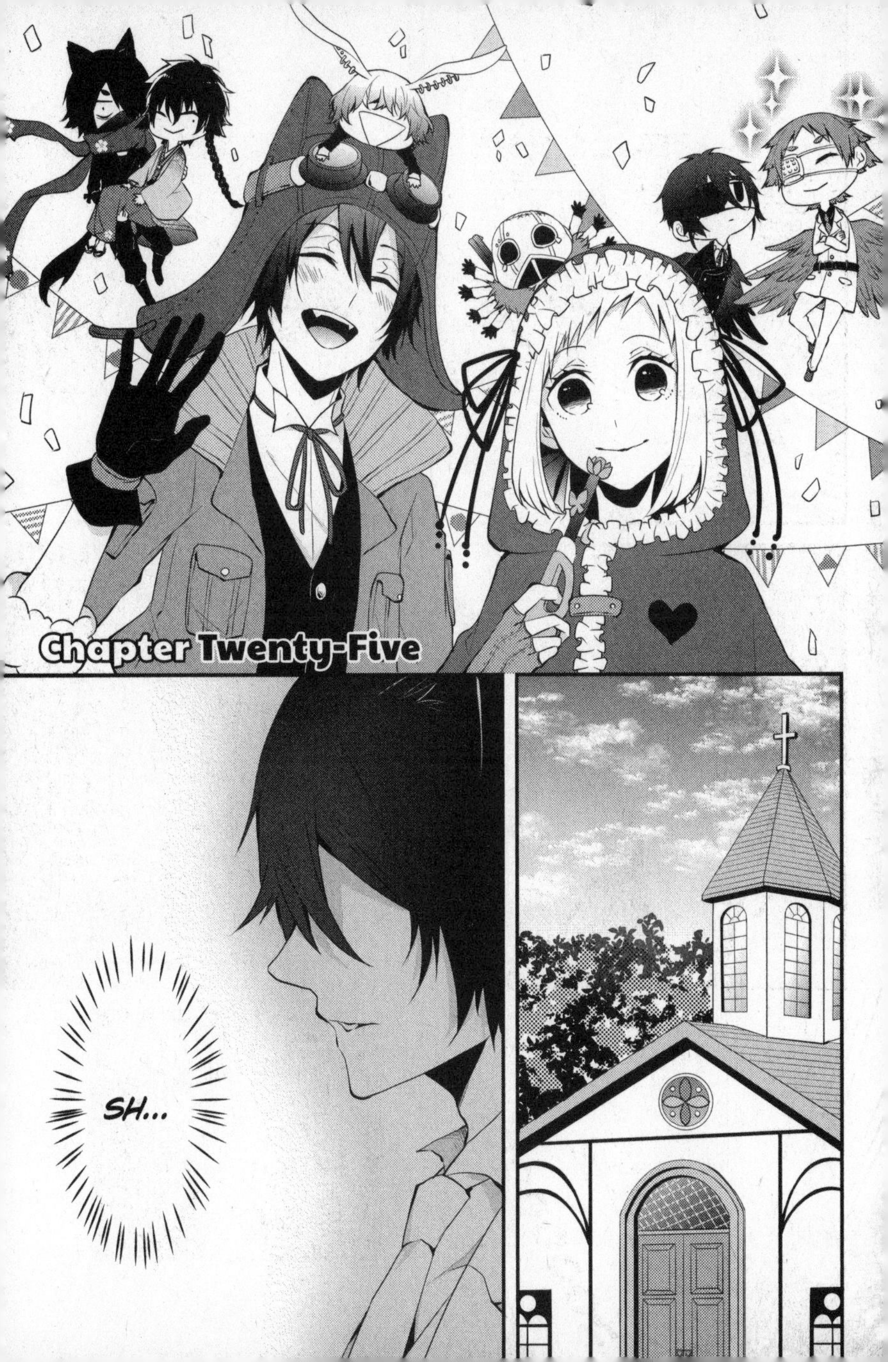
Chapter Twenty-Five
SH...

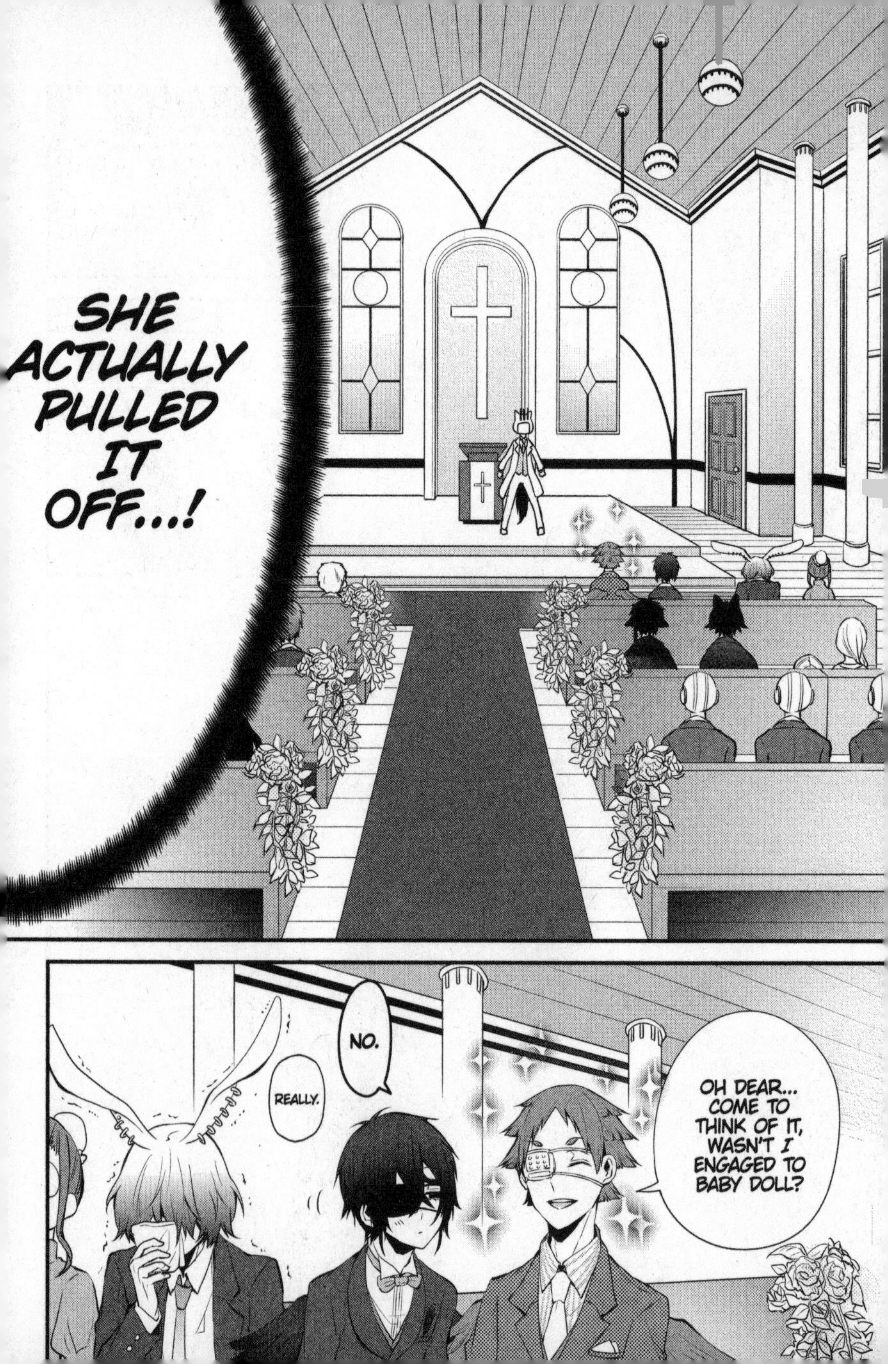
SHE ACTUALLY PULLED IT OFF...!
OH DEAR... COME TO THINK OF IT, WASN'T I ENGAGED TO BABY DOLL?
NO.
REALLY.

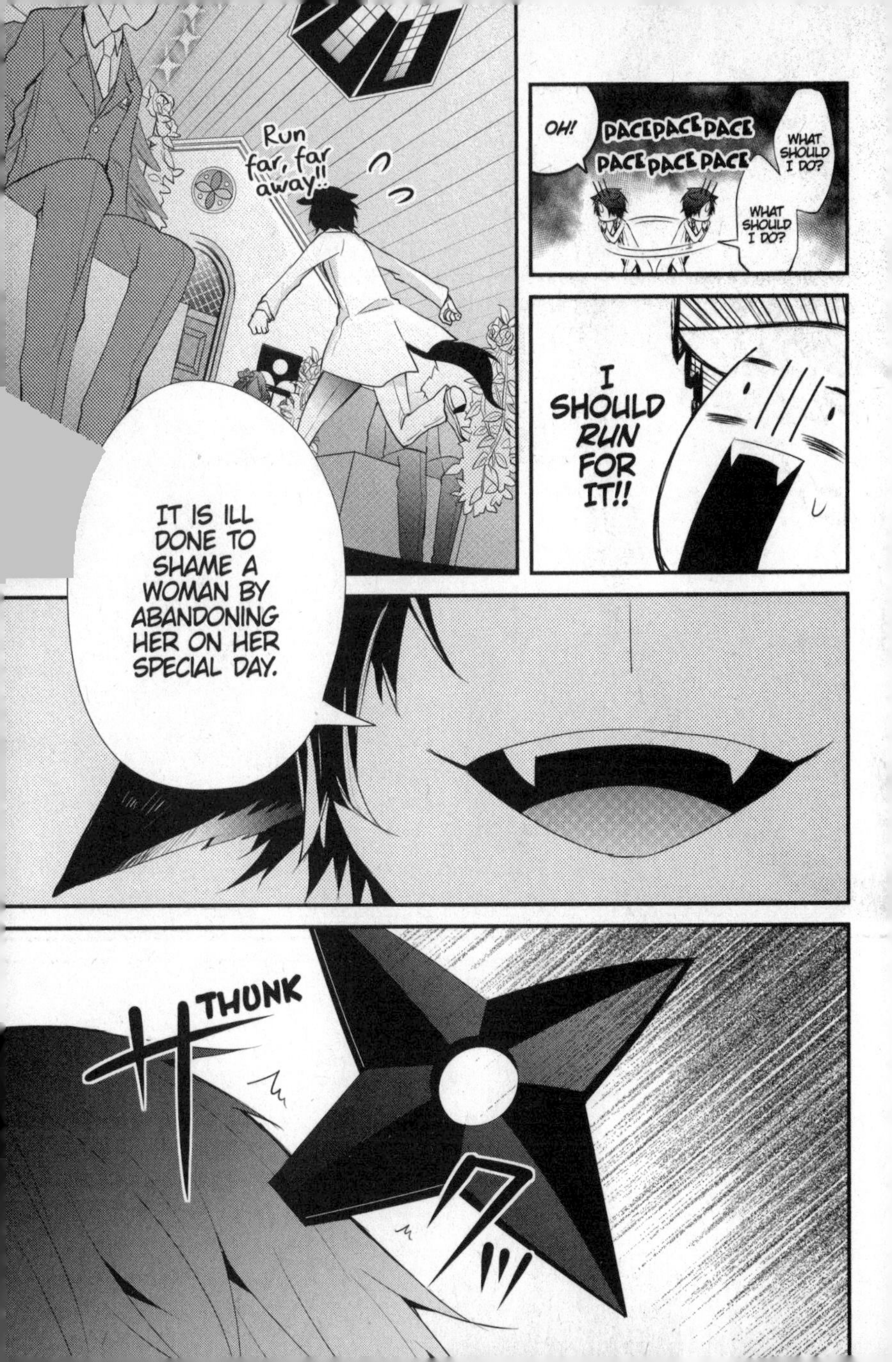
WHAT SHOULD I DO?
PACEPACEPACE PACEPACEPACE
OH!
WHAT SHOULD I DO?
I SHOULD RUN FOR IT!!
Run far, far away!!
IT IS ILL DONE TO SHAME A WOMAN BY ABANDONING HER ON HER SPECIAL DAY.
THUNK

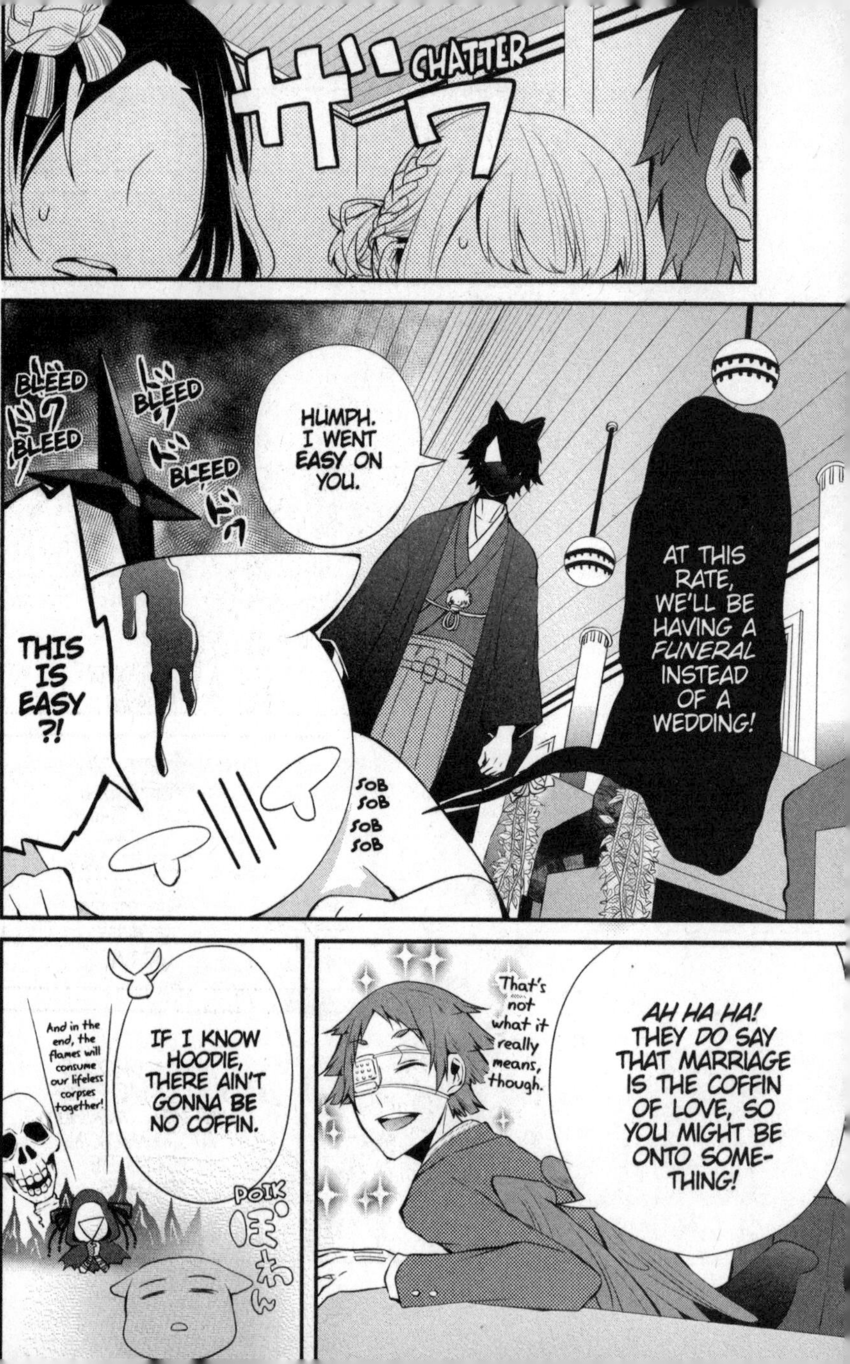
CHATTER
HUMPH. I WENT EASY ON YOU.
BLEED BLEED BLEED BLEED
THIS IS EASY?!
SOB SOB SOB SOB
AT THIS RATE, WE'LL BE HAVING A *FUNERAL* INSTEAD OF A WEDDING!
AH HA HA! THEY *DO* SAY THAT MARRIAGE IS THE COFFIN OF LOVE, SO YOU MIGHT BE ONTO SOMETHING!
That's not what it really means, though.
IF I KNOW HOODIE, THERE AIN'T GONNA BE NO COFFIN.
And in the end, the flames will consume our lifeless corpses together!
POIK

Please see Chapter 2.

WHAT IF

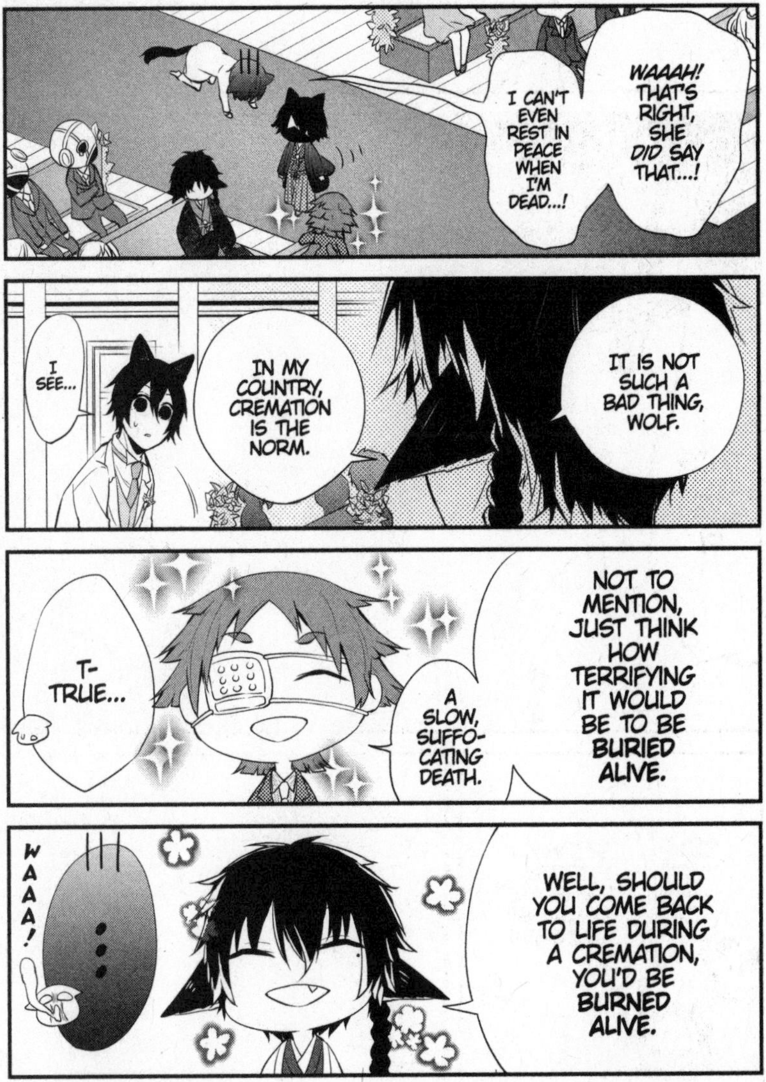
WAAAH! THAT'S RIGHT, SHE DID SAY THAT...!
I CAN'T EVEN REST IN PEACE WHEN I'M DEAD...!
IT IS NOT SUCH A BAD THING, WOLF.
IN MY COUNTRY, CREMATION IS THE NORM.
I SEE...
NOT TO MENTION, JUST THINK HOW TERRIFYING IT WOULD BE TO BE BURIED ALIVE.
A SLOW, SUFFOCATING DEATH.
T-TRUE...
WELL, SHOULD YOU COME BACK TO LIFE DURING A CREMATION, YOU'D BE BURNED ALIVE.
WAAAA!

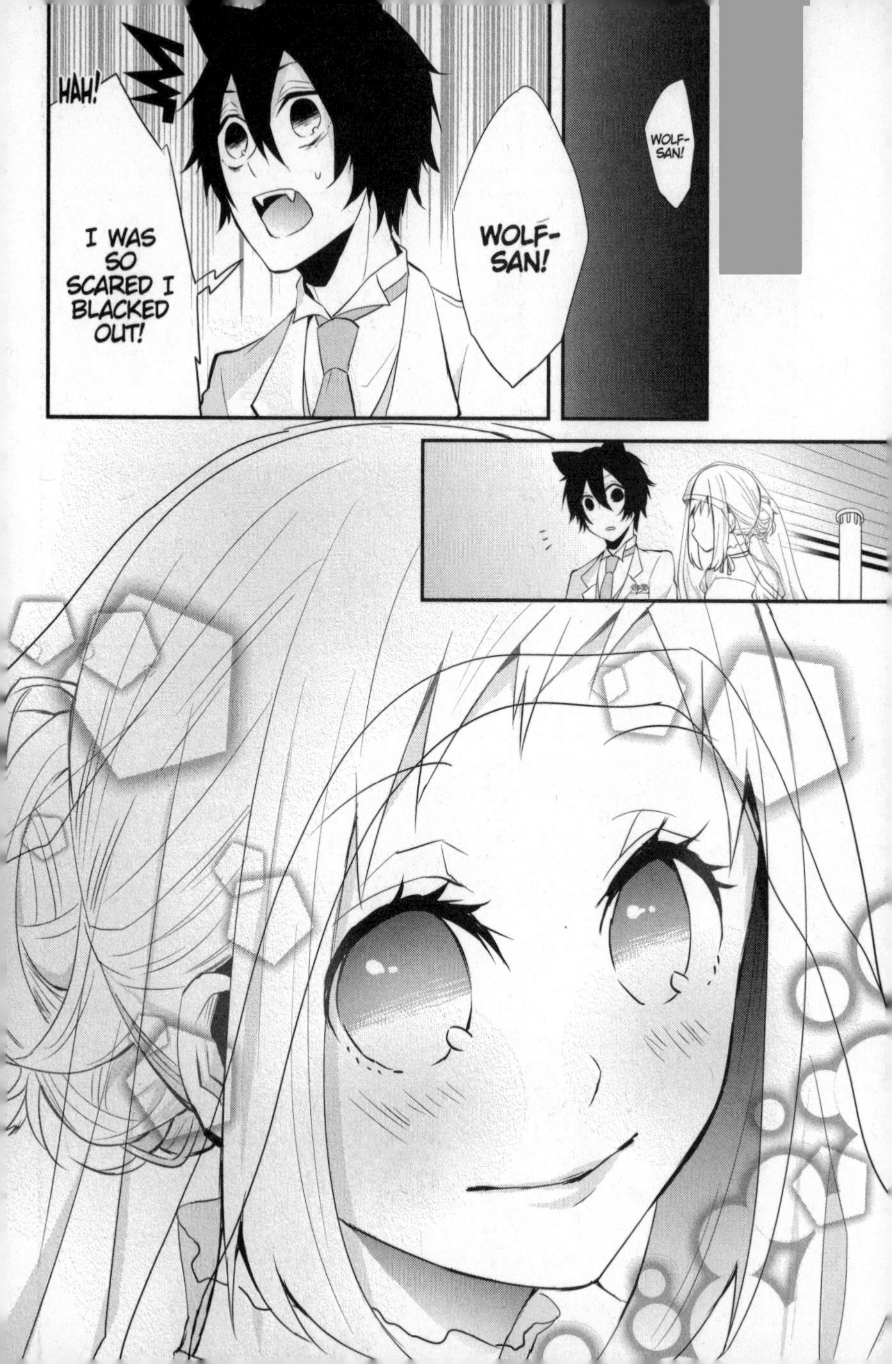
WOLF-SAN!
HAH!
WOLF-SAN!
I WAS SO SCARED I BLACKED OUT!

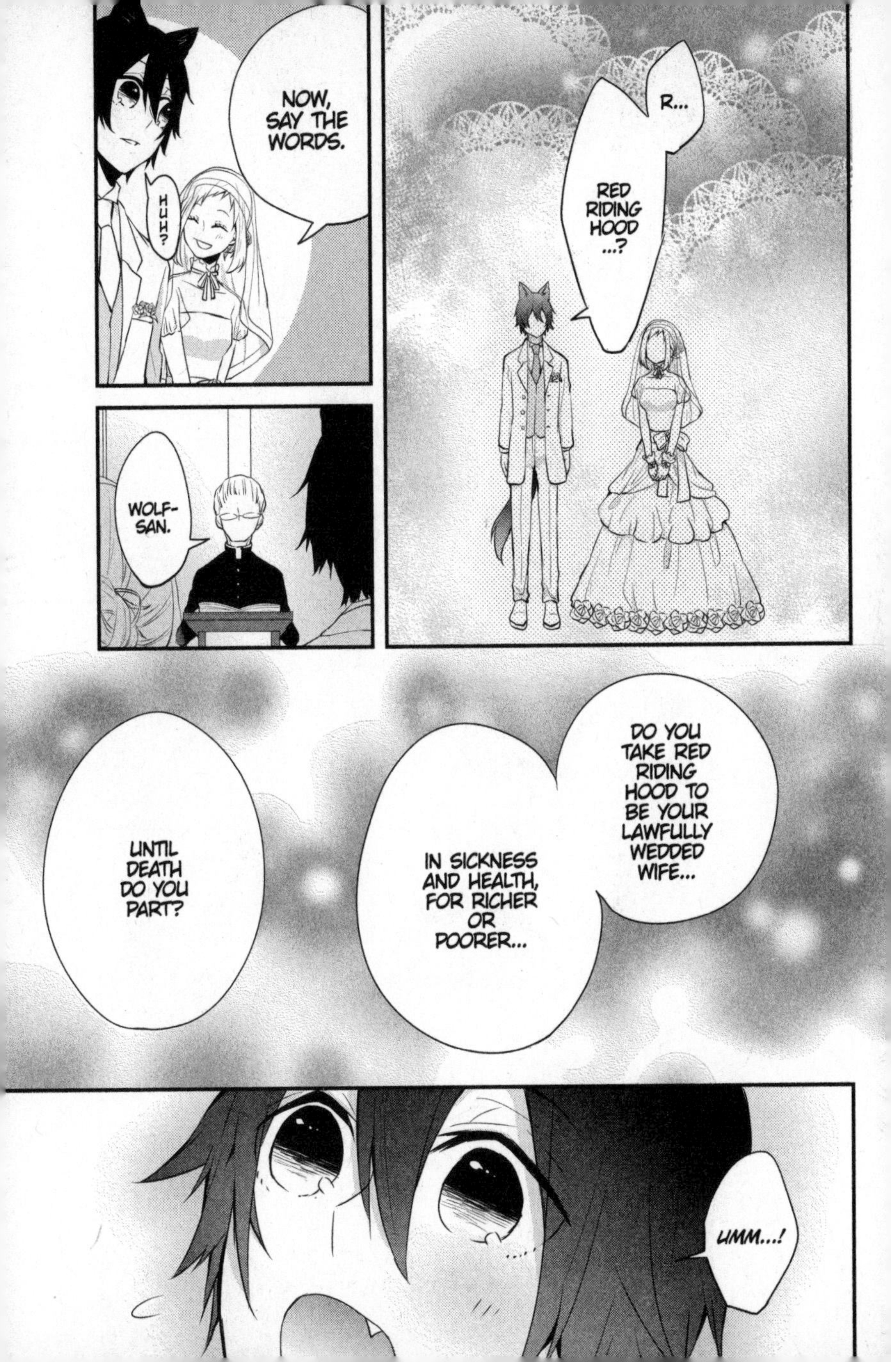
R...
RED RIDING HOOD ...?
NOW, SAY THE WORDS.
HUH?
WOLF-SAN.
DO YOU TAKE RED RIDING HOOD TO BE YOUR LAWFULLY WEDDED WIFE...
IN SICKNESS AND HEALTH, FOR RICHER OR POORER...
UNTIL DEATH DO YOU PART?
UMM...!

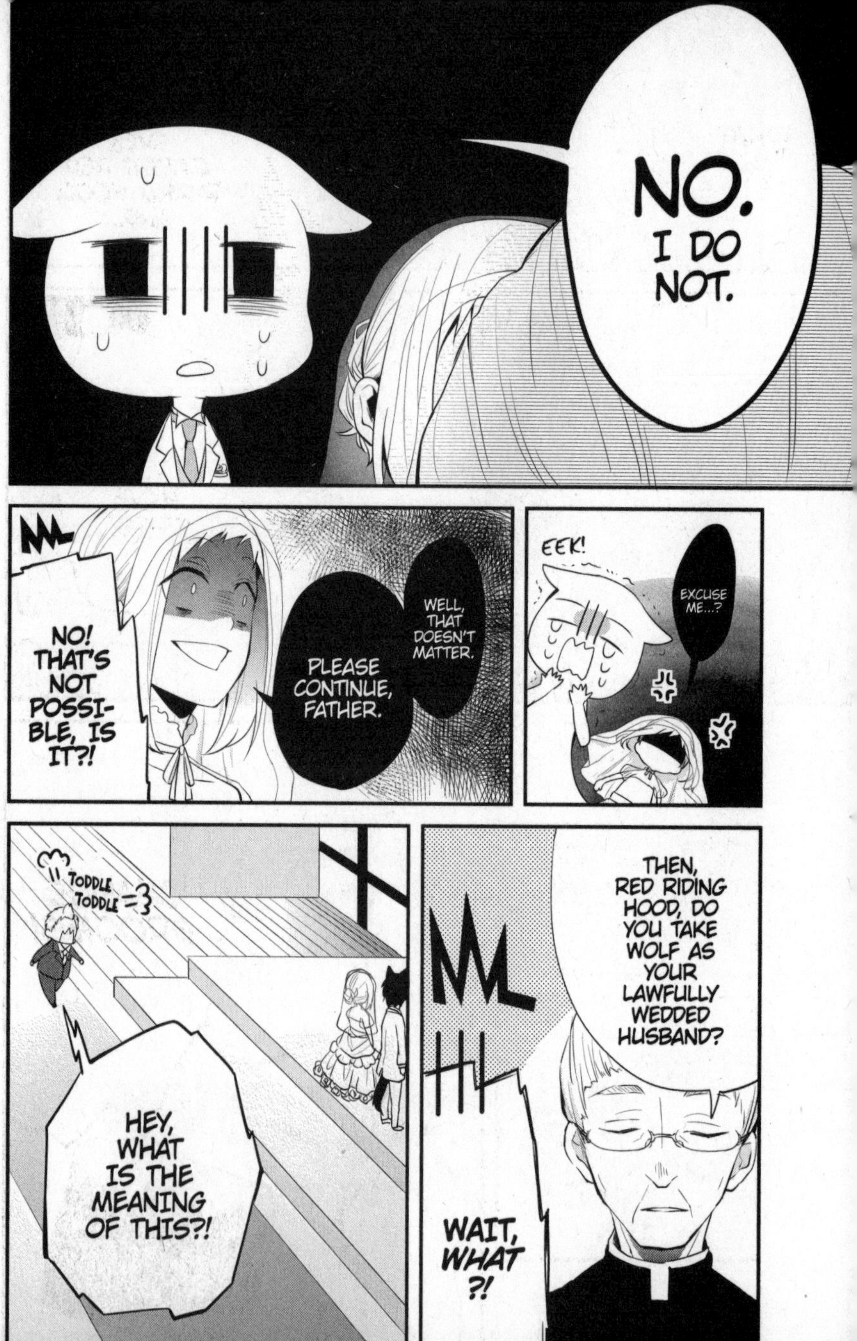
NO. I DO NOT.
EEK!
EXCUSE ME...?
WELL, THAT DOESN'T MATTER.
PLEASE CONTINUE, FATHER.
NO! THAT'S NOT POSSIBLE, IS IT?!
THEN, RED RIDING HOOD, DO YOU TAKE WOLF AS YOUR LAWFULLY WEDDED HUSBAND?
WAIT, WHAT?!
TODDLE TODDLE
HEY, WHAT IS THE MEANING OF THIS?!

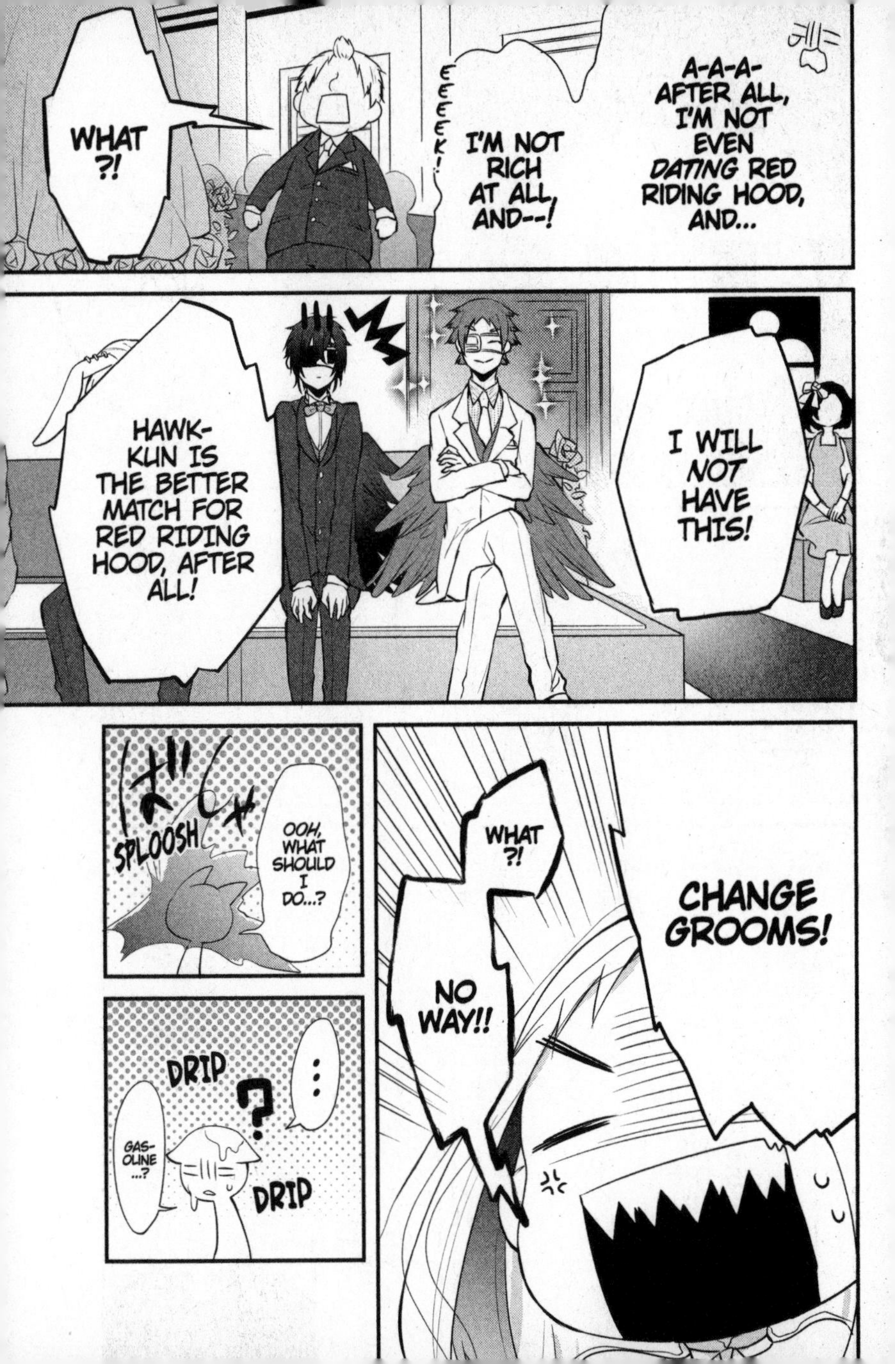
A-A-A-AFTER ALL, I'M NOT EVEN *DATING* RED RIDING HOOD, AND...
EEEEK!
I'M NOT RICH AT ALL, AND--!
WHAT?!
I WILL *NOT* HAVE THIS!
HAWK-KUN IS THE BETTER MATCH FOR RED RIDING HOOD, AFTER ALL!
CHANGE GROOMS!
WHAT?!
NO WAY!!
ばしゃ
SPLOOSH
OOH, WHAT SHOULD I DO...?
...
?
DRIP
DRIP
GAS-OLINE...?

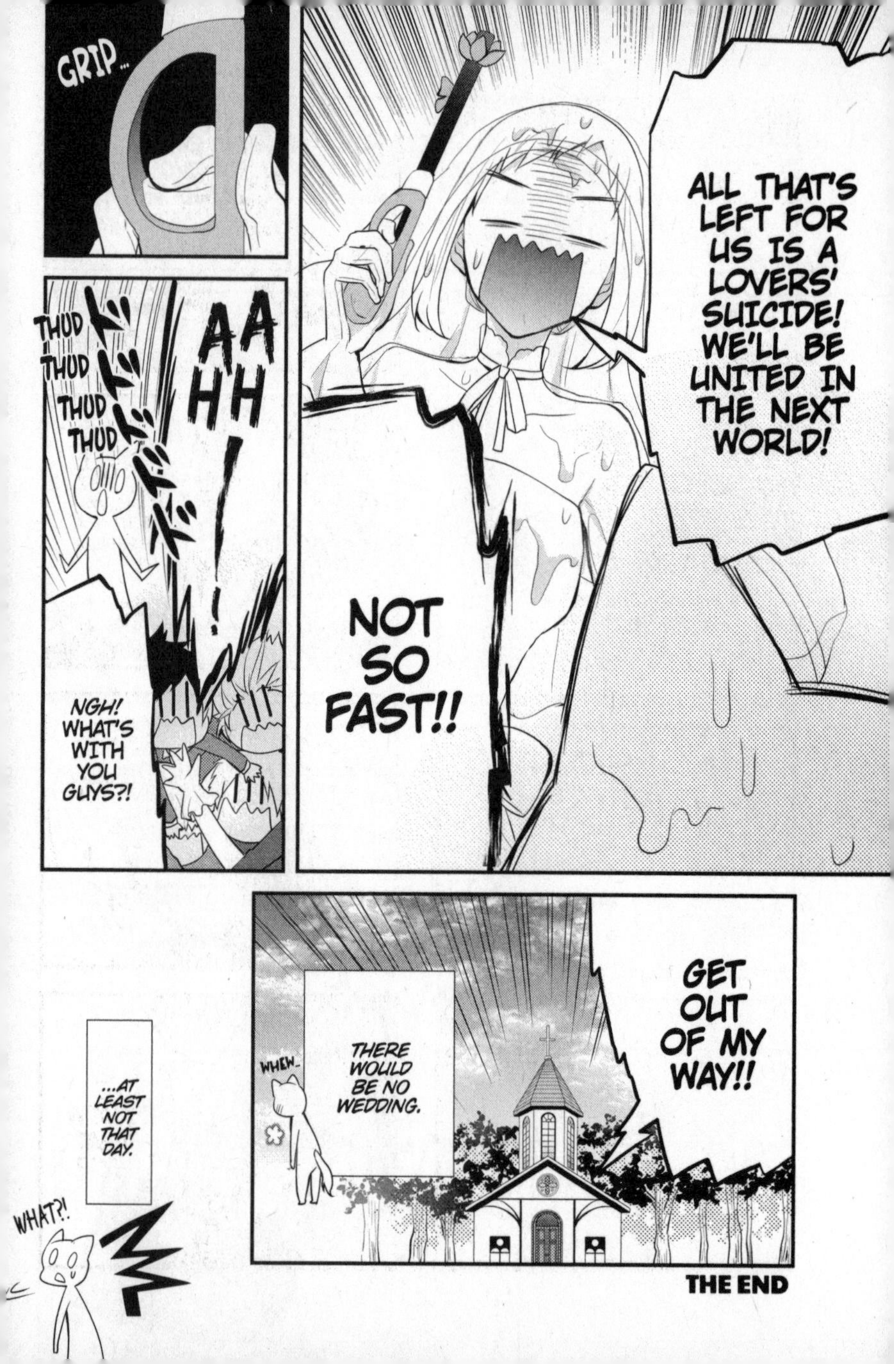
ALL THAT'S LEFT FOR US IS A LOVERS' SUICIDE! WE'LL BE UNITED IN THE NEXT WORLD!
NOT SO FAST!!
GRIP...
AAHH!
THUD THUD THUD THUD
NGH! WHAT'S WITH YOU GUYS?!
GET OUT OF MY WAY!!
THERE WOULD BE NO WEDDING.
WHEW...
...AT LEAST NOT THAT DAY.
WHAT?!
THE END

CROW'S CONFESSION

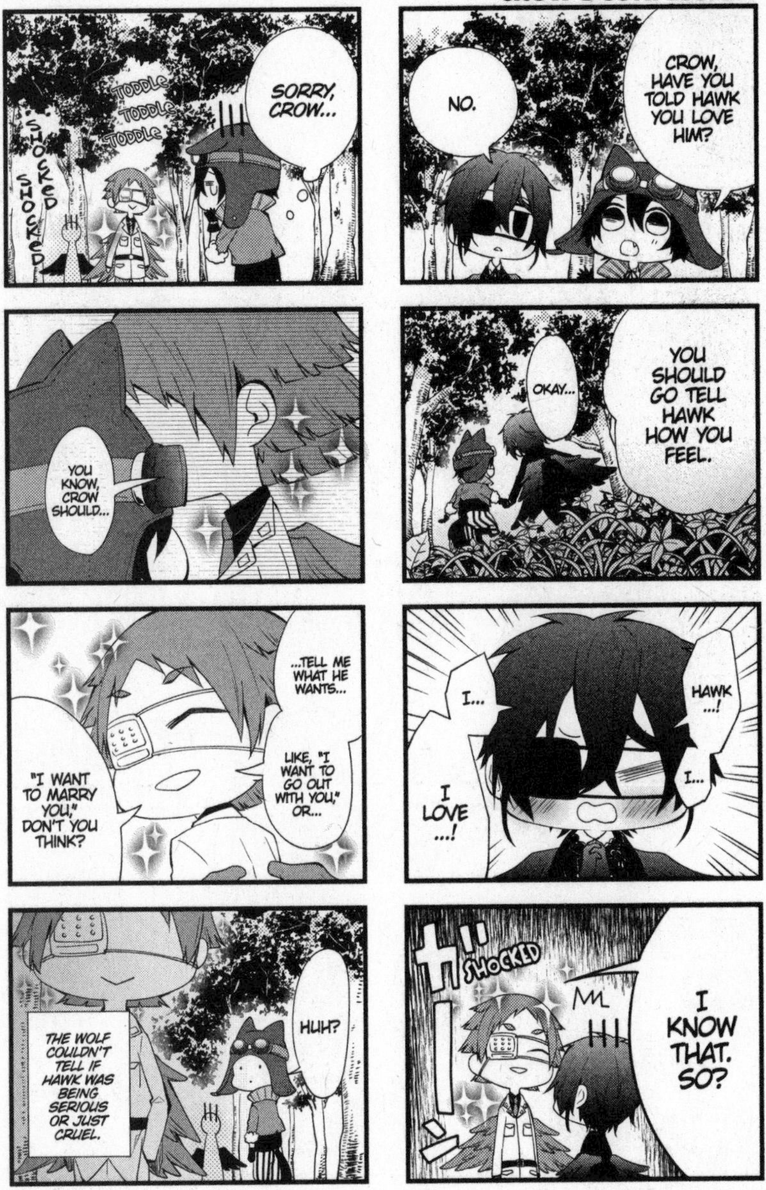
CROW, HAVE YOU TOLD HAWK YOU LOVE HIM?
NO.
YOU SHOULD GO TELL HAWK HOW YOU FEEL.
OKAY...
HAWK ...!
I...
I...
I LOVE ...!
I KNOW THAT. SO?
SHOCKED
SORRY, CROW...
TODDLE TODDLE TODDLE
SHOCKED SHOCKED SHOCKED
YOU KNOW, CROW SHOULD...
...TELL ME WHAT HE WANTS...
LIKE, "I WANT TO GO OUT WITH YOU," OR...
"I WANT TO MARRY YOU," DON'T YOU THINK?
HUH?
THE WOLF COULDN'T TELL IF HAWK WAS BEING SERIOUS OR JUST CRUEL.

REGARDING DRESSES

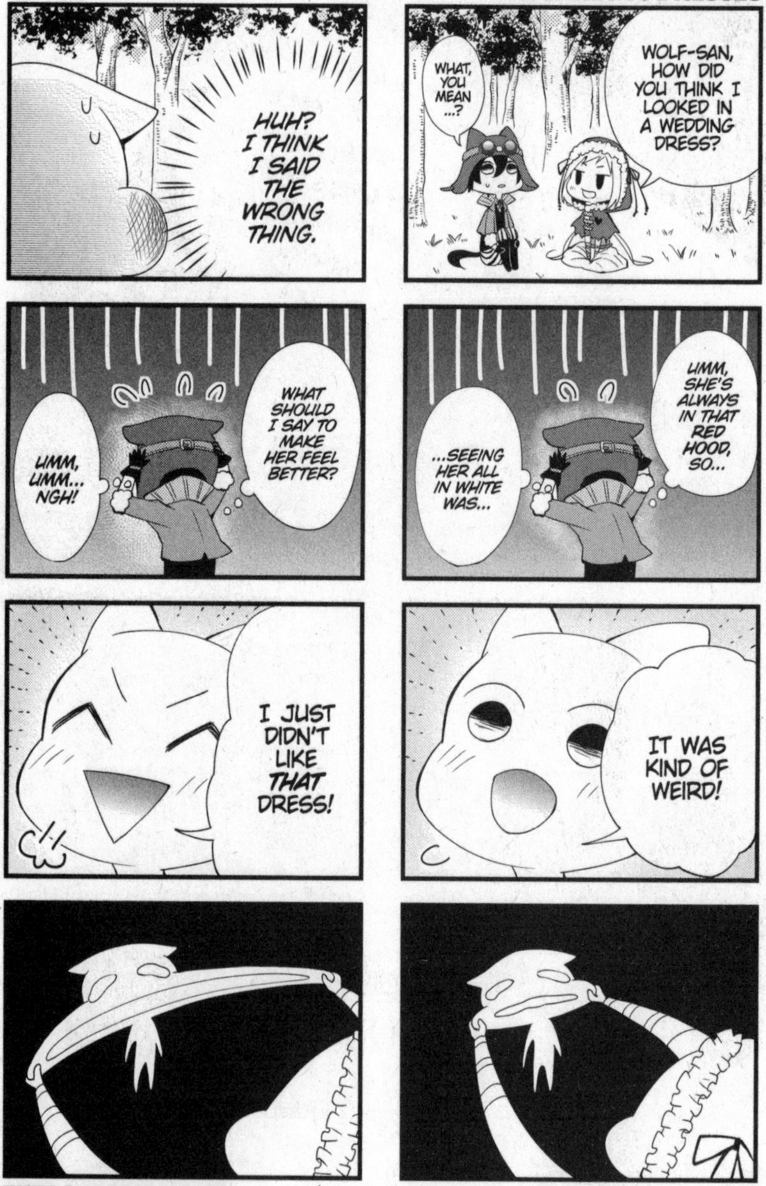
WOLF-SAN, HOW DID YOU THINK I LOOKED IN A WEDDING DRESS?
WHAT, YOU MEAN ...?
HUH? I THINK I SAID THE WRONG THING.
UMM, SHE'S ALWAYS IN THAT RED HOOD, SO...
...SEEING HER ALL IN WHITE WAS...
WHAT SHOULD I SAY TO MAKE HER FEEL BETTER?
UMM, UMM... NGH!
IT WAS KIND OF WEIRD!
I JUST DIDN'T LIKE THAT DRESS!

EXTRA MANGA/END

Afterword

Thank you for picking up Red Riding Hood and the Big Sad Wolf Volume 2! It's my first series, so I stumbled a little at times. But it was a lot of fun to be able to write about Wolf, Red Riding Hood, and everyone else.

Thank you very much for reading!

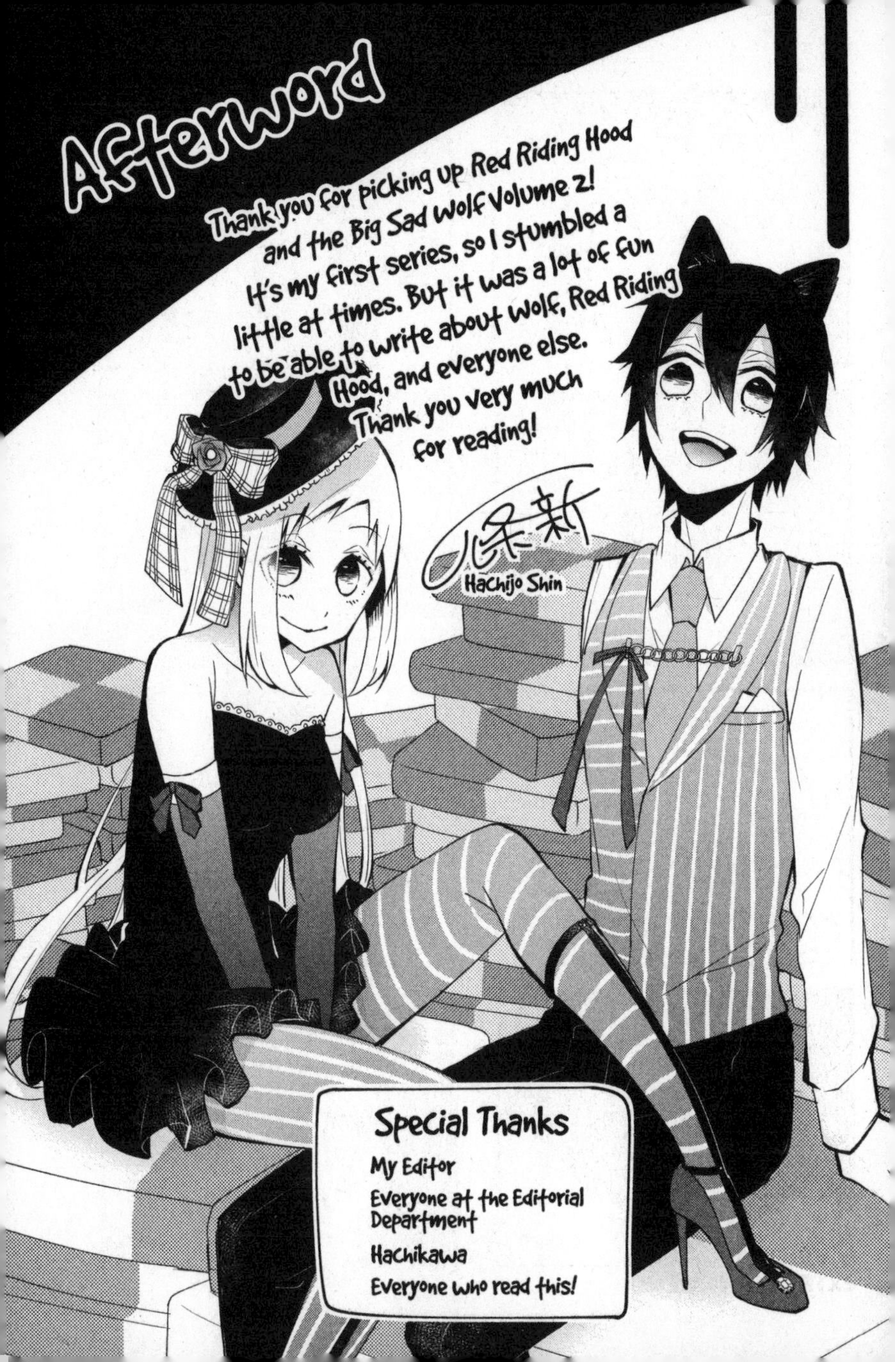
八条新
Hachijo Shin

Special Thanks

My Editor

Everyone at the Editorial Department

Hachikawa

Everyone who read this!

RED RIDING HOOD AND THE BIG SAD WOLF

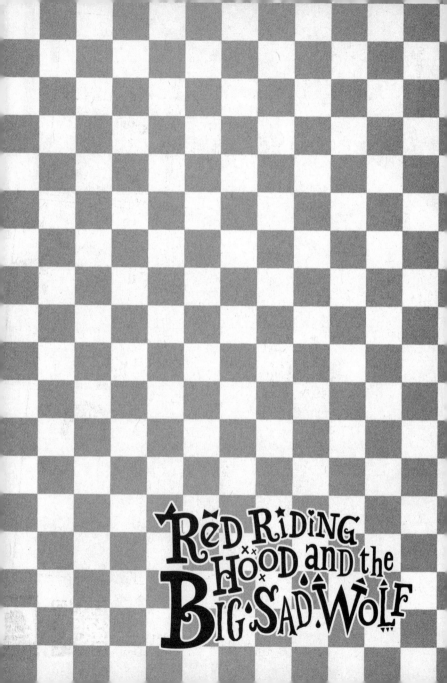

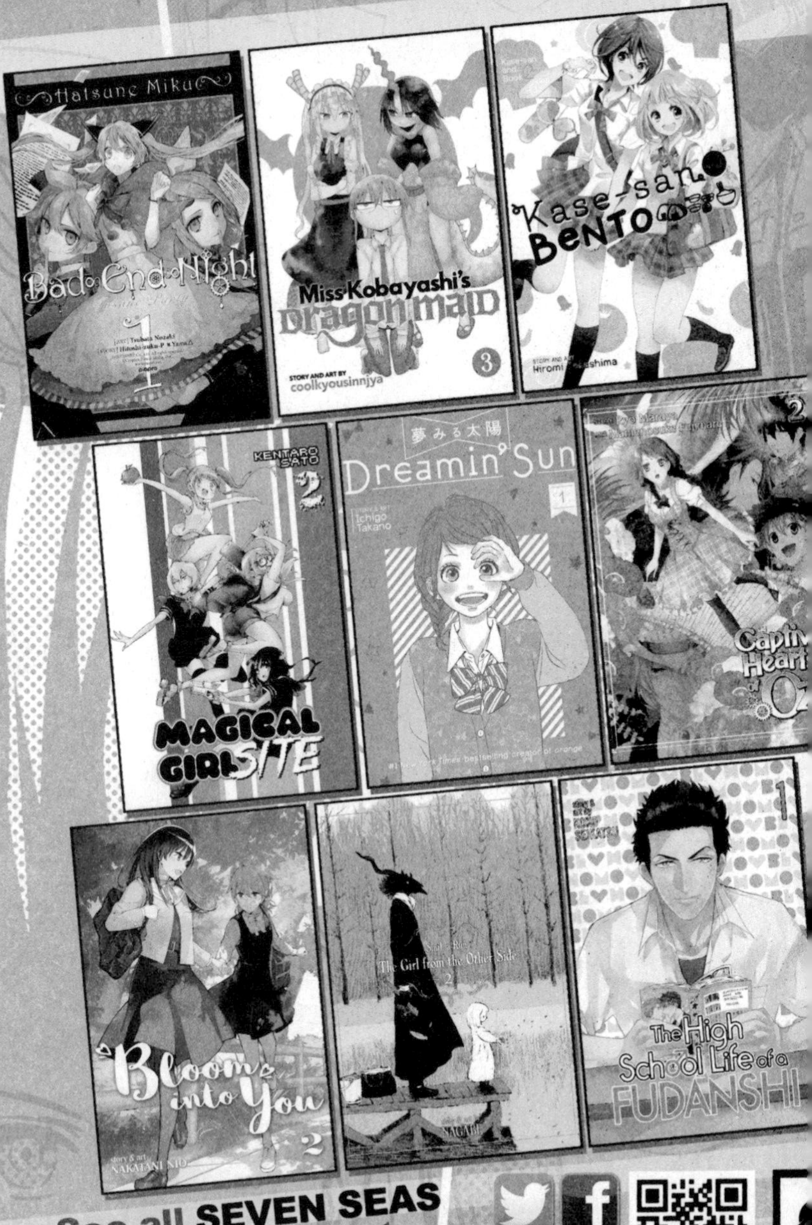

Hatsune Miku
Bad End Night
1
Miss Kobayashi's Dragon Maid
3
STORY AND ART BY
coolkyousinnjya
Kase-san and Bento
KENTARO SATO
2
Magical Girl Site
夢みる太陽
Dreamin' Sun
Ichigo
Takano
1
Bloom into You
2
story & art
NAKATANI NIO
The Girl from the Other Side
2
NAGABE
1
The High School Life of a Fudanshi

SEVEN SEAS ENTERTAINMENT PRESENTS

RED RIDING HOOD AND THE BIG SAD WOLF

story and art by SHIN HACHIJOU

VOLUME 2

TRANSLATION
Beni Axia Conrad

ADAPTATION
Shanti Fader

LETTERING
Kaitlyn Wiley

LOGO DESIGN
KC Fabellon

COVER DESIGN
Nicky Lim

PROOFREADER
Tim Roddy

ASSISTANT EDITOR
Jenn Grunigen

PRODUCTION ASSISTANT
CK Russell

PRODUCTION MANAGER
Lissa Pattillo

EDITOR-IN-CHIEF
Adam Arnold

PUBLISHER
Jason DeAngelis

RED RIDING HOOD AND THE BIG SAD WOLF VOL. 2
© SHIN HACHIJOU 2017
First published in Japan in 2017 by ICHIJINSHA Inc., Tokyo.
English translation rights arranged with ICHIJINSHA Inc., Tokyo, Japan.

No portion of this book may be reproduced or transmitted in any form without written permission from the copyright holders. This is a work of fiction. Names, characters, places, and incidents are the products of the author's imagination or are used fictitiously. Any resemblance to actual events, locales, or persons, living or dead, is entirely coincidental.

Seven Seas books may be purchased in bulk for educational, business, or promotional use. For information on bulk purchases, please contact Macmillan Corporate & Premium Sales Department at 1-800-221-7945 (ext 5442) or write specialmarkets@macmillan.com.

Seven Seas and the Seven Seas logo are trademarks of Seven Seas Entertainment, LLC. All rights reserved.

ISBN: 978-1-626925-66-3

Printed in Canada

First Printing: October 2017

10 9 8 7 6 5 4 3 2 1

FOLLOW US ONLINE: **www.gomanga.com**

READING DIRECTIONS

This book reads from *right to left*, Japanese style. If this is your first time reading manga, you start reading from the top right panel on each page and take it from there. If you get lost, just follow the numbered diagram here. It may seem backwards at first, but you'll get the hang of it! Have fun!!

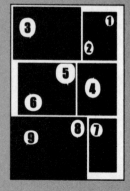